Applying Neural Networks
A Practical Guide

Applying Neural Networks
A Practical Guide

Kevin Swingler
Centre for Cognitive and Computational Neuroscience
University of Stirling
Stirling, Scotland, FK9 4LA.
and
Neural Innovation Limited.
email: kms@cs.stir.ac.uk

ACADEMIC PRESS
Harcourt Brace & Company, Publishers
London   San Diego   New York
Boston   Sydney   Tokyo   Toronto

ACADEMIC PRESS LIMITED
24/28 Oval Road
London NW1 7DX

United States Edition published by
ACADEMIC PRESS INC.
San Diego, CA 92101

This book is printed on acid free paper

A catalogue record for this book
is available from the British Library

ISBN 0–12–679170–8

Printed and bound in Great Britain by Hartnolls Ltd, Bodmin, Cornwall

Preface

The expensive bit is learning the techniques, running them, developing them. It's dangerous to imagine you can just take the data, feed it through the neural network and get a result.
    Inderjit Sundhu, Senior technical consultant, Barclays Bank.
    PC User, December 1994

Aims and objectives

Using neural networks in real world applications

The aim of this book is to present a set of techniques which would allow a business or industrial reader to apply neural network technology to real world applications. With this book and a neural network simulation software package, the reader should be able to confidently run and manage a neural computing based project. The base techniques combine to provide a framework much like that of a software engineering project. When carrying out such a project, a programmer is able to follow a set of procedures to ensure the smooth running of the project and the correct operation of the final product. The book hopes to present a set of procedures to provide a neural program developer with an equally rigorous methodology.

Introducing a set of technical tools

The book concentrates on the most common type of neural network: the multi–layer perceptron. It introduces a core set of neural tools and methods which are useful in a number of different situations, showing how each relates to the others, its advantages and limitations, and the procedures by which it is implemented. The core tools are introduced as they are needed and described in greater detail as the book progresses. In this way I hope to give the reader the confidence that they are using a consistent set of methods rather than a number of ad hoc patches.

Scope of the book

The assumption that the reader is using a commercial neural network simulator is borne strongly in mind when comparing available techniques. Methods for improving results are presented which do not require the writing of new network architectures. In fact, only one type of neural network architecture—the multi layer perceptron— is discussed as it is applicable to such a wide range of problems. The reader is strongly encouraged to obtain a good neural network simulation program on which to implement their project.

Structure of the book

You will find that this book is split into two parts. The first part is a DIY manual for running a neural network based project. Each chapter is split into three sections: the first contains a discussion on the issues covered in the chapter. This section contains no maths or equations and is intended to give the reader an understanding of the reasons behind the methods discussed in the second section. The second section is strictly how-to-do-it, and contains equations and procedures to follow to implement the techniques discussed in the first section. Each chapter ends with one or more worked examples.

Part II of the book reviews a number of common application areas in which neural networks have been used. The chapters cover the use of neural networks in areas such as financial prediction, process control and signal processing, and make constant reference to chapters in part I in order to demonstrate the techniques used. Chapters in part II are by no means detailed manuals for the application areas they cover, rather they aim to illustrate how the techniques introduced in part I may be applied to a wide range of real world problems.

The accompanying disk

A disk containing a number of programs written in C and C++ is provided with this book. A competent programmer would be able to use these routines to implement most of the methods discussed in the book. Those without the knowledge or inclination to write their own neural programs will find a number of neural simulators on the market. The reader is referred to the final page of this book for details of a software package designed to guide a commercial user through every step of a neural network based project.

Acknowledgements

Thanks are due to many people, without whom this book would never have seen the light of day. Everyone in the Centre for Cognitive and Computational Neuroscience at Stirling University has helped with advice and comments. Of those, Leslie Smith and Paul Miller deserve special mention. My girlfriend, Anne-Michelle, has been understanding to the point of even putting up with me taking the proofs to read on our summer holiday this year. Many of the practical issues within the book were clarified for me by my colleagues at Neural Innovation Ltd. George deserves a mention, though I doubt he can read and I'd like to thank the Ford Motor Company for showing an active interest in neural network research. Alan Murray and Jim Austen provided many useful comments on the text and finally thanks to Tig for posing for figure 1.1.

Contents

Part I

Techniques for building neural networks

Part I

Techniques for building trust
networks

Chapter 1

Introduction

Keep it simple:
as simple as possible,
but no simpler.

Albert Einstein

1.1 What are neural networks?

1.1.1 Statistical models

Neural computing is concerned with the theory and application of neural networks. Neural networks are statistical models of real world systems which are built by tuning a set of parameters. These parameters, known as *weights*, describe a model which forms a mapping from a set of given values known as *inputs* to an associated set of values: the *outputs*. The process of tuning the weights to the correct values— *training*—is carried out by passing a set of examples of input-output pairs through the model and adjusting the weights in order to minimise the error between the answer the network gives and the desired output. Once the weights have been set, the model is able to produce answers for input values which were not included in the training data. The models do not refer to the training data after they have been trained; in this sense they are a functional summary of the training data.

1.1.2 Function mapping devices

As the number of inputs to a network need not be equal to the number of outputs, a neural network can be described as performing a mapping from one set of variables onto another set of a different size. The total set of combinations of possible values a set of variables can take is referred to as its *space*; therefore the input variables can take any set of values in input space. Each set of values can be thought of as a point in this space and the neural network can be thought of as a machine which knows the route from each point in the input space to the correct point in output space.

1.1.3   Classifiers or continuous mapping functions

Neural networks are used mainly to learn two types of task:

- **Classification**

  Tasks where the input is a description of an object to be recognised and the
  output is an identification of the class to which the object belongs are referred to
  as classification or recognition tasks. For the purpose of this book, the following
  definition is used:

  > *A classification task is one for which the target outputs cannot be
  > arranged along a meaningful continuum; each possible output of the
  > network is a separate entity, discrete from all others.*

- **Continuous numeric functions**

  These functions describe the relationship between different sets of variables
  from a real physical system. Examples of such systems include stock markets,
  industrial plants, and customer profiles. The following definition will be used:

  > *A continuous function is one for which the target outputs fall along
  > a meaningful continuum; each possible output of the network has its
  > place along that continuum. There may be many such continua for a
  > multi-dimensional output space.*

As we shall see, a large number of industrial and commercial problems turn out
to be concerned with classification or function mapping. Although the distinction
is made between the two cases throughout the book, it is intended that networks
are not thought of as being of one type or the other as the two tasks may easily
be incorporated into a single neural network. Nevertheless, different techniques are
applicable to each and the distinction is a useful one.

Category variables and values

As the word category may be slightly misleading, I will define a set of terms below
which form the basis for the assumptions made throughout the book. These terms
are: *category variable, category value, example* and *feature* and are defined below.

A *category variable* encompasses the entire set of possible *category values* and *examples*; it describes the whole set of objects to be categorised. A *category value* is the
name given to any single category. Each *example* of a member of a category is described by a set of *feature variables* which take specific *feature values*. To illustrate the
point, we might say that *animals* is the category variable. The *category values* might
be *canary, cat, mouse*, the *features* might be *number of legs, has fur?, has wings?* etc.
and an example would be any set of feature values such as *four legs, has fur, no wings*.
A category is usually defined as a set of examples which share or display similarities
in certain features.

The astute reader will notice that the features are similar to category variables, *has
fur?* for example, being the category variable with *yes* and *no* as category values. The

difference is that the categories are outputs from the network and the features are inputs to it. It is consequently safer to refer to inputs using the terms *feature variables* and *feature values*. Note that feature values may be numbers or names, *height*, for example, is a legitimate feature variable which could take numeric values along any range.

1.1.4 Static or temporally dependent functions

Neural networks are also capable of learning temporal dependencies in a system. A system which does not contain such dependencies is referred to as being static.

- **Static systems**
  Static systems are not affected by previous system states. That is to say that they have no memory and are affected solely by their current inputs. This does not rule out systems which change over time or are affected by certain temporal considerations. A model of shop sales would naturally be high on a Saturday for example, but this is not a dependence on the previous day's sales, just on a certain cyclical event. For the purpose of this book, the following definition is used:

  > *Any given input to a static system will always elicit the same system output regardless of any previous inputs to that system or any previous system state.*

- **Temporally dependent tasks**
  Temporally dependent tasks are the opposite of static tasks. One cannot know the effect a given input will have without knowledge of the system's current state or past behaviour. For this reason the system—and likewise a model of that system—requires a memory. Currency exchange prices may be viewed as such a system. A machine for mixing paint is a similar case. The effect of adding a certain colour to the mix will depend on the colours which were previously included.

  > *A system is said to be temporally dependent if a given input to that system elicits a different response depending on previous inputs to that system or the previous system state.*

1.1.5 Smoothing operators

Neural networks can be used to fit arbitrarily smooth functions through noisy data. That is to say that they will take a noisy data set and draw a smooth, curved line which best describes the shape of the data. The more complex the network is, the more of the small bumps in the data it models, and so the finer the scale over which the smoothing takes place becomes. The smoothing carried out by a neural network is, as we have already seen in section 1.1.1, model based. Although a data set may be smoothed simply by using a moving average, such a method leaves one with a

smoothed data set rather than a model describing the data. The degree of smoothing
a neural network achieves is related to the complexity of the neural model. This book
is concerned with optimising that complexity and balancing the trade-off between
accuracy and generality which it determines.

1.1.6   Approximations to theoretically perfect methods

With a modern computer, storing and retrieving large amounts of information should
be a simple task. Unfortunately, as we all soon learn, our computers are dumb. Very
dumb. If all we want to do is store and retrieve data, then we must record every piece
of information we need, and then search for it when required. Given unlimited storage
space and an unfeasibly fast computer, there would be no need for neural networks
in a lot of cases. We could simply calculate the required output for each input and
store every single one in a large look up table from which we would read each required
output.

Such an approach suffers from two practical limitations. Firstly, it requires that the
system to be modelled is measured at every single operating point, and secondly it
requires computer performance beyond the capabilities of current machines. Neural
networks solve both of these problems firstly by generalising over a small sample of
measurements from the system to be modelled, and secondly by removing the need to
search for an answer by implementing what is known as a *content addressable memory*.
A content addressable memory takes a key as input (in the case of a neural network,
the coded input data) and returns, by means of a calculation and not a search, an item
which is associated with that key. As there is no need for a search, such memories are
very fast.

1.1.7   Computer programs and silicon chips

Neural networks are normally implemented in computer programs. The final network
is defined by its set of weights and is normally small enough to be built into VLSI
hardware. Such implementations add to the speed gained from not needing to carry
out a search, as discussed above. The program required to build and train a neural
network, a *neural simulator*, is far more complex than the *neural interpreter* required
to run a trained network. The neural simulator produces a set of weights and network
descriptors which are used by the interpreter. This allows the network to be trained
on a different platform from the one on which it will finally run.

1.1.8   Models of physical systems

Figure 1.1 shows how a neural network can be considered as a model of a physical
system with raw materials or data as input and with a product or answer as output.
Several examples of real systems are also shown.

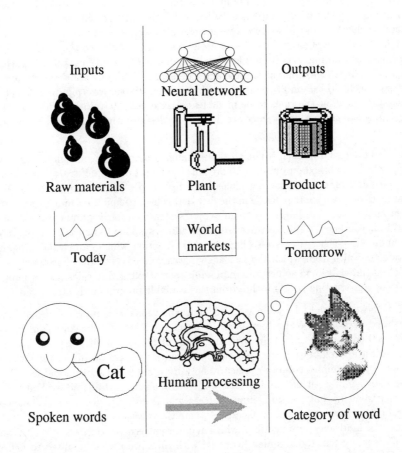

Figure 1.1: Any real world system which has measurable inputs and outputs may be modelled by coding those measurements and training a neural network to predict the outputs from the inputs.

1.2 How does neural computing differ from traditional programming?

Traditional computing solutions are based on the rules or equations which define a system and must be explicitly programmed. Whilst this is perfect in situations where the rules are known, many systems exist for which the rules are either not known or difficult to discover and it is these systems to which we can apply neural computing techniques. Madey et al. [60] present a useful comparison between the techniques of traditional computing, traditional artificial intelligence (AI) and neural computing. Traditional AI is based on rules, facts and inferences. Solutions are programmed in languages such as LISP and PROLOG which are designed to process logical predicates. Fuzzy systems allow the rules to be made less precise, but the values associated with fuzzy concepts such as *hot* or *nice* are derived by design rather than by a statistical process.

The rule based AI approach is not all that different from traditional computing techniques which are based on building algorithms from a set of simple structures such as *if ... then* and *repeat ... until*. The rules are simply expressed on a higher level. The advantages of these approaches lie in the fact that rules and functions may be formally stated and proved. Adding rules to an expert system is a fairly simple process, provided that you know what the rules are. This allows systems to be easily understood and updated. Such systems also have a *why?* function which causes the program to state the rules from which the last answer was derived. The disadvantages lie in the labour intensive and sometimes impossible task of extracting rules from a human expert or constructing an algorithm from the available programming structures.

Neural networks might be seen as good approximations to a perfect rule or function based approach. While they lack the exact precision and formal rigour of the traditional computing approach, they are powerful enough to allow us to construct near perfect approximations to systems about which we have insufficient knowledge to allow a programmed solution. A neural network is a generalisable model, based on the experience of a set of training data and consequently contains no explicit rules. It is consistent in that the same input pattern will always produce the same answer. Neural networks are useful in applications where the precision of the traditional techniques is a hindrance; applications which require pattern recognition or simulation of a physical system too complex to model with rules are perfectly suited to neural computing techniques. Applications for which exact rules are known, for which every case is unique, and for which no generalisations may be made can be implemented with traditional techniques. Figure 1.2 shows how the two approaches are related.

Early criticisms of neural network techniques centred on the fact that, unlike rule based systems, neural systems could not provide explanations for their answers or measures of how accurate any particular answer might be. This book presents a series of methods for overcoming such limitations without the need for redesigning the basic neural network architecture. The resulting consistency is designed to allow the reader to build a neural network based system to which any of the techniques presented may be applied. Each technique presented within this book is compatible with every other; assuming they are combined in a sensible way.

Programming approach	Neural Computing approach

• Follows rules
• Solution formally
  specifiable
• Cannot generalise
• Not error tolerant
	• Learns from data
	• Rules are not
	  visible
	• Able to generalise
	• Copes with noise

Figure 1.2: The main differences between traditional programming based software development and a neural computing based approach.

When would I use a neural network?

As we have seen, neural networks are useful for solving problems for which no rules are known, but for which a set of examples from which a solution could be learned are available. Clearly then, a substantial quantity of training data are required. The exact amount of data needed to train a neural network is discussed in chapter 5. Neural network models possess a number of qualities which make them ideally suited to certain types of problem and these are listed below:

- **Neural networks operate on numeric representations**
  A task must be expressed in terms of a function from one numeric coding to another. If a problem cannot be expressed in such a way, it cannot be solved by a neural network. Chapter 2 describes several methods for representing a problem in a numeric way.

- **Neural networks are non-linear functions**
  A task is non-linear in nature if the effect that a change in any variable has on the output is dependent on the value of that, or any other input variable. Categories are linearly separable if it is possible to use a straight line to split data points which describe objects in different classes. Chapter 7 investigates non-linearity in more depth.

- **Neural networks are differentiable**
  It is possible to differentiate the function which a neural network learns. Many industrial or physical systems need to be expressed in terms of the effect a small change to the inputs would have, rather than the effect of a new input setting altogether. Chapter 7 demonstrates how differentiation may be used to discover the reasons behind an answer given by a neural network.

- **Neural networks are able to generalise**
  As we have seen, a neural network is a generalisable model of a data set. The ability to generalise means that neural networks are able to learn from noisy or incomplete data. Generalisation must be seen as a non-linear averaging over a

set of examples however, so noise and bad data do have an effect. Chapters 2 and 5 investigate the effects of data quality on a neural network model and present methods for ensuring that training data are sufficient in both quantity and quality.

1.3 How are neural networks built?

1.3.1 Feedforward multi-layer perceptrons

The mathematical model a neural network builds is actually made up of a set of simple functions linked together by the weights. The weights describe the effect each simple function (known as a *unit*) will have on the overall model. This book is concerned with a particular type of neural network known as a multi layer perceptron (MLP). An MLP has a set of *input* units whose function it is to take input values from the outside, a set of *output* units which report the final answer, and a set of processing *hidden* units which link the inputs to the outputs. The function of the hidden units is to extract useful features from the input data which are, in turn, used to predict the values on the output units. The network is arranged in layers of units: an input layer, one or more hidden layers, and an output layer. The value displayed by each unit is known as its *activation* and measures the degree to which it affects higher units. The activation of the input units is set by the input values given to the network and the activation of the output units is decoded to provide the final answer.

The MLP is only one example of a neural network. It is however, the most popular type of network and many of the concepts which apply to its use apply equally well to many other neural network types. You will notice that the terms neural network and MLP are used apparently interchangeably throughout the book; however, I have tried to restrict the use of the acronym MLP to situations where the subject under discussion is specific to their use. Where I refer to neural networks, then my comments are of a more general nature.

Figure 1.3 shows a schematic diagram of a basic MLP architecture. Each unit has activation flowing into it from the units below, which is multiplied by the strength of weight along which it flowed. As input flows from many units into each one in the layer above, the vector of resultant inputs must be summed and passed through the unit's function before being passed onto the next layer. This function must squash the summed input into a given range (usually between zero and one) and so is referred to as the *squashing function*. Figure 1.4 shows this process schematically. The squashing function reflects the fact that numbers close to the extremes of the input range are squashed into an ever decreasing small part of the output range.

MLPs also use a *bias unit* which is always set to one and which connects to all units except those in the input layer. Its job is to pull the inputs to the hidden and output units into the correct range for the squashing function. The weights from the bias unit are learned in the same way as all the others.

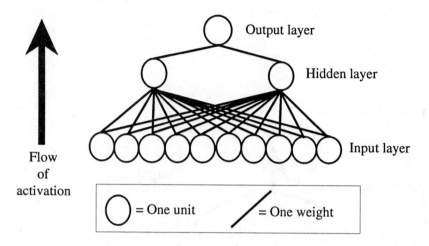

Figure 1.3: The basic architecture of a multi-layer perceptron with a single layer of hidden units.

1.3.2 Recurrent MLPs for time varying data

The only extension to the MLP architecture discussed in this book will be that of the recurrent MLP. Recurrent networks of the type proposed by Elman [33] are used to process time varying data: to predict future values, classify time series, predict system behaviour and so on. The addition to the MLP architecture involves a **copy** of the hidden layer which acts as an extension to the input layer. This copy holds the values of the hidden units from the previous time step and uses them as input for the current time step. In this way, the recurrent layer acts as a short term memory or context store for the network. Figure 1.5 shows the basic architecture. The learning algorithm is shown in section 1.8.1.

Elman's network was limited, however, to prediction of a single sequence and so was not capable of categorising multiple sequences as there is no provision for switching between examples of one sequence and another during training. Swingler [102] proposed an extension to the recurrent architecture which used several context layers: one for each time series to be processed by the network. This allowed a set of time series to be learned in parallel whilst the many context layers kept track of the network state (hidden layer activations) for each.

1.4 How do neural networks learn?

Learning, in a statistical sense, refers to any process requiring the use of data for tuning a set of parameters which describe a statistical model of that data. It does not imply any human qualities such as understanding, consciousness or intelligence associated with our learning abilities. MLPs learn by a process called *back propagation*

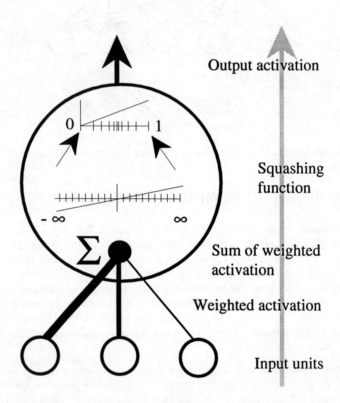

Figure 1.4: Activation from below is multiplied by the value on the weight it travels along. It then enters a unit, is summed and squashed, and passed out to the next layer.

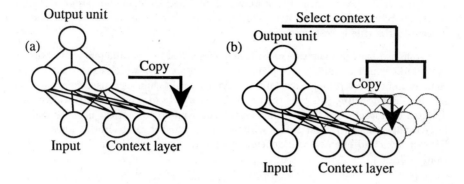

Figure 1.5: (a) The context layer in a recurrent network is a copy of the hidden layer from the previous time step and now forms part of the input layer. (b) A network with multiple recurrent layers as used during learning.

of error [86] which involves calculating the error at each output unit and changing the values of the weights which led to the error. The contribution that each weight makes to the error is calculated from the value of the weight and the error on the unit above. The weight is then changed so that the error would be slightly smaller if the same input-output pair were presented again.

It is important to note here that it is not the absolute errors that are used in changing the weights, but the derivative of the error with respect to the activation values. This means that we multiply the error value by the derivative of the activation function so that the effective change in the input to the unit—caused by changing the incoming weights—has the desired affect on the output. In other words, we change the unit's input with respect to the effect our change will have on its output. The weights affect the unit's output via its activation function, rather than doing so directly. This is a point worth labouring as it is of remarkable use in some instances.

Calculating the errors on the output layer is simple as we know what their values should be, so calculating the weight changes for the top layer of units is straight-forward. We also need to change the weights to the hidden layers—which requires calculating the contribution to the final error which the hidden units are making. The effect each hidden unit has on the final error depends on the activation of that hidden unit and the strength of the weights which connect it to the output units above. Each hidden unit has a single error value associated with it. To calculate this error we first multiply each weight from the hidden unit in question by the error on the unit to which it runs. Adding these values up tells us how much of the total error above is produced by each hidden unit. As before, this error value is multiplied by the derivative of the unit's activation function before being used to update the weights below.

This method of learning is referred to as *gradient descent* as it involves an attempt to find the lowest point in error space by a process of gradual descent along the error surface. An associated problem with gradient descent is that of *local minima* which are dips in error space which are not universal minima. An algorithm designed simply to always reduce error will not be able to climb out of a local dip to continue its descent to the true lowest point.

The standard back propagation algorithm makes use of two parameters which control the rate at which learning takes place. A *momentum term* which causes the weight changes to be affected by the size of the previous weight changes is used to avoid local minima. The *learning rate* tells the network how slowly to progress. The weights are updated by a fraction of the calculated error each time to prevent the network making large swings about the best values without ever getting it right. Both values will be between zero and one and will depend on several factors which will be discussed in chapter 3.

1.5   What do I need to build an MLP?

It is possible, using commercial software, to build an MLP quite easily but while we can think of neural networks as an alternative to algorithm based solutions, we must not forget all we have learned about software engineering. A neural network, like a computer program, must be seen as an object which is designed and built according to a plan. The plan sets out exactly what will be required at each stage along with a method for achieving each requirement.

Clearly, access to, or a method of collecting ample data is required. Neural networks remove some of the need for understanding the internal dynamics which determine how a system works, but it can be a dangerous practice to use them blindly if the system to be modelled is insufficiently understood. It is also important to have a definition of the final goal of the neural system or the exact nature of the problem which neural networks are being applied to overcome.

1.6   The neural project life cycle

The neural network project life cycle is summarised below.

1. Task definition and design: Stating the exact requirements from the final system.

2. Feasibility: is the problem suitable for a neural network solution?

3. Data coding: Coding the data for presentation to the network.

4. Network design: Ensuring an accurate and generalisable model.

5. Data collection: Measuring required data quantity.

6. Data checking: Determining whether the data will allow the problem to be solved.

7. Training and testing: Building the best network from the data.

8. Error analysis: Determining the types and causes of errors and assigning confidence limits to the network output.

9. Network analysis: Deriving explanations and rules from the final network.

10. System implementation: The final use and monitoring of a neural system.

The given ordering is based on the order in which things **happen**, not the order in which design decisions should be made. Data collection, for example, is quite often an expensive and time consuming process which one wouldn't want to carry out until the whole project had been planned from start to finish, and the possibility of one needing to say *"I wish I'd collected this type of data"* has been eliminated. The basis for this book is that such endeavours should be thought of as a complete project, rather than as the task of building a neural network. Software engineers run projects, they don't write programs; and so should it be with those who use neural networks. Chapter 8 describes the neural project life cycle in more detail.

1.7 The generalisation-accuracy trade-off

The underlying goal towards which many of the techniques presented in this book are directed is that of optimising the degree of complexity of the neural model. There is a trade-off between building a model which generalises well and is robust, and one which is more accurate but more brittle. Viewing the decisions to be made at each stage in terms of their effect on model complexity allows us to sew a common thread through an entire project. The more complex, accurate, yet brittle a model becomes, the more of the data points in the training set it fits to. A more general model describes a smoother curve through the training data points, missing some, but resisting the effect of noise or peculiarities which might be present.

At each stage of the project development, it is possible to effect the level of complexity in the model. At some stages it will be far easier than at others to implement a given technique. The underlying goal of this book is to show that a neural network based project may be planned from start to finish so that model complexity may be manipulated at the points where it is most convenient to do so. I also aim to highlight the intrinsic qualities of a data set or network task which constrain the level of complexity it is possible to achieve. Ideally, we would like a model which is both accurate and able to generalise well and in some cases this may even be possible, but it is not usually the case with commercial applications. In such cases the goal facing the neural engineer is to build a model with a complexity which matches the level of information present in the training data.

As a general rule, the simpler a model, the better it is at generalising to data it has not seen. If we can model the training data with a simple model then we should do so. The preference for simpler models is based on the so called Ockham's razor. William Ockham was an old monk who said (and lets face it, how many sayings of old monks hold scientific sway today?) that of two explanations for any natural phenomenon, the simplest should always be chosen. And so should it be with neural networks. If we

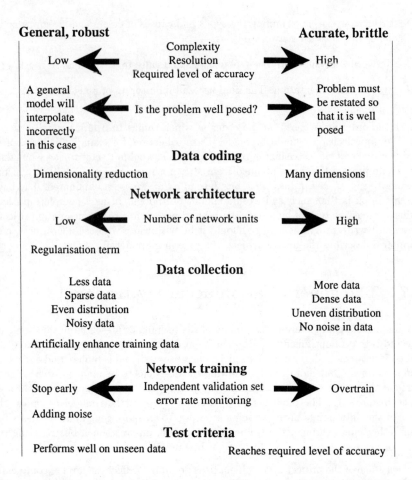

Figure 1.6: There many constraints and techniques which determine the complexity of a neural network model.

have several different neural network models to choose from, we should always choose the simplest which is able to explain the data on which it is trained as it will also possess the best generalisation ability. Our task when building a neural network is consequently to build the simplest model which is able to learn our data. Figure 1.6 shows some of the decisions which enable us to steer a course to the desired level of complexity for a given task.

1.8   Implementation details

1.8.1   The back propagation algorithm

There is one algorithm which is central to the training of multi-layer perceptrons: the back propagation algorithm. The following algorithms and functions are presented to give the reader a better understanding of how a neural network learns; details of activation functions, error measures and learning parameters are excluded as they are discussed in full in chapter 3.

The standard algorithm is presented along with two variations: the first shows how a simple recurrent network is trained, and the second demonstrates the training process for a multiple recurrent network. Chapter 4 describes the training and use of recurrent networks in more detail.

Standard back propagation learning

1. Build a network with the chosen number of input, hidden, and output units.
2. Initialise all the weights to **low random values**.

Repeat

   3. Choose a single training pair at random.
   4. Copy the input pattern onto the input layer.
   5. Cycle the network so that the activation from the inputs generates activation in the hidden and output layers.
   6. Calculate the error derivative between the output activation and the target output.
   7. Back propagate the summed product of the weights and errors in the output layer in order to calculate the error on the hidden units.
   8. Update the weights into each unit according to the error on that unit, the output from the unit below and the learning parameters.

Until the error is sufficiently low or the network settles.

Simple recurrent back propagation learning

1. Build a network with a single recurrent layer equal in size
   to the hidden layer.
2. Set the network weights to **low random values**.
Repeat
   3. Reset all the context layer values to indicate the start of a sequence.
   Repeat
      4. Present the next element in the sequence along with the
      context layer values in the recurrent layer as input.
      5. Cycle the network and adjust the weights using the
         standard back propagation method.
      6. Copy the contents of the hidden layer back into the context
      layer used in step 3.
   Until the end of the sequence is reached
Until the error is sufficiently low or the network settles.

Multiple recurrent back propagation learning

1. Build a network with a context layer equal in size
   to the hidden layer for each sequence to be learned.
2. Set the network weights to **low random values**.
3. Assign a context layer to each sequence.
Repeat
   4. Reset all the context layer values to indicate the start of a sequence.
   5. Choose a single sequence at random from those chosen in step 2.
   6. Present the next element in the chosen sequence along with
      the context layer values associated with that sequence to
      the network as input, along with the target category
      or required value as output.
   7. Cycle the network and adjust the weights using the
      standard back propagation method.
   8. Copy the contents of the hidden layer back into the context
      layer used in step 4.
   9. If the end of a sequence is reached, reset the associated
      context layer and return to the start of the sequence.
Until the error is sufficiently low or the network settles.

1.9 Activation and learning equations

The following equations are based on the notation listed below.

- A single unit will be referred to by the indices i and j attached to the symbols listed below. Unit j may be on any layer in the network but, where both i and j are used, unit j will be closer to the output layer than unit i.

- The values n and m denote the number of units in the current layer.

- w_{ji} denotes the strength of the weight from unit i to unit j on the next layer. The weight change to be made is denoted by Δw_{ji}.

- o_j denotes the output from unit j.

- v_j denotes the input to unit j.

- d_j denotes the desired output from unit j.

- e_j denotes the error derivative on unit j.

- $f(\cdot)$ is the network activation function and $f'(\cdot)$ is the derivative of the network activation function.

- η is the learning parameter.

- α is the momentum term.

1.9.1 Activation functions

Specific activation functions are discussed in chapter 3. The general form of the activation function sums the product of the output from each unit below and the weight with which it is connected to the current unit:

$$o_j = f(\sum_{i=1}^{m} w_{ji}o_i) \tag{1.1}$$

1.9.2 Simple output error measure

The simplest and most common output error measure is the difference between the output from a unit, o_i and the desired value, d_i, for that unit. The error derivative for the output unit is calculated as:

$$e_i = f'(o_i)(d_i - o_i) \tag{1.2}$$

Note that the error is now expressed in terms of the derivative of the activation function.

1.9.3   Back propagating errors to the hidden layer

The error on each hidden unit in layer i is calculated as the summed product of the error derivatives, e_j of the units in row j above and the strengths of the weights connected to them:

$$e_i = f'(o_i) \sum_{j=1}^{n} e_j w_{ji} \qquad (1.3)$$

The new error is expressed in terms of the derivative of the activation function.

1.9.4   Updating weights

The change in the weight from unit i to unit j is calculated as the product of the learning rate, the error derivative for unit j and the output from unit i:

$$\Delta w_{ji} = \eta \, e_j o_i \qquad (1.4)$$

where unit i is in the layer below unit j.

1.10   A simple example: Modelling a pendulum

A simple example of a problem to which either traditional computing or neural networks might be applied in different situations is that of predicting the movement of a pendulum. Two possible situations might exist: that we know the differential equations governing the motion of the pendulum or that we have some data describing the observed path of the pendulum. In the first case, we would write a program which encapsulates the differential equations. Given a particular position and velocity of the pendulum, we would use the program to calculate its next position.

In the second case, we would present the data describing the observed path of the pendulum to the neural network which would learn the relationship between each position, its previous position, its velocity and its successive position. Once the network has correctly learned to predict the pendulum's movement, it can be used in exactly the same way as the programmed solution.

Figure 1.7 shows how the inputs and outputs to the neural network are derived from the physical measurements of the pendulum. The first input is shown as a measurement of the pendulum's velocity and the other two are measurements of the last two positions of the pendulum as single coordinates along its trajectory. The inputs now contain sufficient information to calculate the next position of the pendulum. During training the neural network learns a function relating the two. We may then use the network as a prediction tool with no further training.

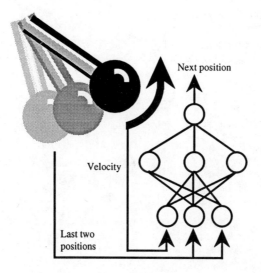

Figure 1.7: Training a neural network to predict the movement of a pendulum. The network is trained by presentation of measurements of pendulum position and speed along with the coordinate of the subsequent position. Once the network has learned, it is able to predict the coordinate of the subsequent position with reference to the input measurements alone.

Chapter 2

Data encoding and re-coding

Politics is perhaps the only profession for which no preparation is thought necessary.

Robert Louis Stevenson

2.1 Introduction

Neural networks are able to process data from a wide variety of sources. They are, however, only able to process that data in a certain format. Furthermore, the way in which the data is represented affects the way in which the network learns. It is consequently important to choose an appropriate data coding scheme for a given network task. Design of a data coding scheme proceeds before data collection as it is important to know what you are going to do with your data *before* you go out and collect it. Data collection and data quality will be dealt with in chapter 5.

In order to teach an MLP a given task, the task must be stated in terms of a set of input vectors and their associated target outputs. In practice this does little to constrain the type of problem an MLP can tackle as it is possible to codify practically anything. In this section we present an overview of the considerations to be made when choosing a coding scheme for a neural network project and subsequent sections discuss each in greater detail. The chapter finishes with a look at coding schemes for time varying data.

There is a difference between data encoding, which refers to the process of converting raw data into a form with which a neural network can be trained, and data re-coding which refers to manipulating either the raw data, or its encoded equivalent. Re-coding may be be used to make certain aspects of the data more explicit, or to select certain elements of importance. It may be used to re-express the data in a smaller dimension, or to transform the type of representation used. Taking the Fourier transform of a time series is one example of such re-coding. Data encoding will follow data re-coding as it is the process which produces the final values which the network will use.

2.1.1   Two principles of neural network data representation

The two main principles with which we are concerned when choosing a data representation for use with a neural network are the number of variables used (which determines data *dimensionality*) and the extent to which the information the network requires is made explicit. For reasons of speed and complexity, there is often pressure to minimise the number of variables (input and output) that a neural network has to deal with. This pressure also has a bearing on the resolution at which data is represented; the finer the data resolution, the greater the complexity of the network and, consequently, the amount of training time and data required. This brings us to the second principle of training data representation: *explicitness*. Given the limit on the number of input variables a network may see, there is pressure to ensure that the variables which are used contain the information required to carry out the task to be learned in a form which is as explicit as possible.

2.1.2   The data preparation process

Generally, the following steps are taken when converting a set of raw data into a neural network training set. They must be applied to each input variable and each output variable independently.

1. **Data type classification**
   Each input and output to a neural network will either vary along a continuous scale, or be made up of a set of discrete events. The type of each variable must be identified as each requires a different coding method.

2. **Global statistics calculation**
   Certain simple statistical properties of each training variable are needed for some of the data preparation stages. For continuous scaled data, the mean, standard deviation, maximum and minimum must be calculated. For discrete data, the number of different events (i.e. values each variable can take, or categories to choose from) must be established.

3. **Outlier removal**
   Ninety-five percent of a normally distributed data set lies within two standard deviations of the mean. Discarding values outside that range is a simple method for removing outliers which, due to their abnormal size, can have an effect on the network out of proportion with their importance. In such cases, removing outliers can produce a network with a smoother learning curve. If outliers are important, then data must be coded an collected in a way which properly reflects that importance.

4. **Quantity checks**
   There are several factors affecting the quantity of data required for training a neural network, and they are discussed in chapter 5. A related consideration is that of data dimensionality. The more variables a model contains, the more training data points are required. Problems caused by these limitations may be solved either by enlarging the data set or by reducing its dimensionality.

5. **Building a sample data set**

For very large data sets, it may not be practical (or feasible) to carry out a complex analysis on every point collected. In such cases, it is acceptable to take a random sample of the whole data set on which to base data pre-processing decisions. Sampling must be unbiased, must span the entire range of each variable of interest and include sufficient data to be representative. Once a sample set has been built, the mean and variance of each variable must be compared with that calculated from the whole data set in order to verify that we have a fair sample. The following techniques may be carried out on the sample, and not on the full data set. The network however, will still be trained on the entire data set.

6. **Quality checks**

In order to build a well balanced model, it is important to have an even distribution of training examples. It is also advisable to carry out statistical tests to verify that the data contains the information required to carry out the chosen task.

7. **Dimensionality reduction**

A neural network with a large number of input units contains a large number of weights. A network with a large number of weights requires a (sometimes exponentially) larger number of training examples. Similarly, sampling theory tells us that there is an exponential relationship between the number of dimensions in which we are sampling, and the number of points which must be sampled in order to correctly describe the data. Reducing the number of inputs to a network allows us to collect less data whilst maintaining a correct level of network complexity.

8. **Data scaling**

Output data must be scaled to the range which the output squashing function can produce. Sigmoidal squashing functions, for example, can only produce values in the range from zero to one. It is often convenient to scale the input data to within the same range. Scaling may be linear or non-linear, depending on the distribution of the data. The most common scaling functions are linear, softmax, and logarithmic. It is also possible to split the data into several ranges, each with different scaling factors.

9. **Data encoding**

Once the data has been re-coded, it may still need to be encoded for input to a neural network. Scaled numeric data may be used as it stands or transformed further. Categorical data must always be encoded.

2.2 Data type classification

In the introductory chapter to this book, we saw how any data may be classified as one of two possible types: numeric or categorical. Numeric data is that which varies along a sensible continuum and consequently yields a concept of distance between different values. Categorical data does not fit to such a continuum and so each value is discrete from all others and no distance metric may be derived.

2.2.1   Coding integers: categories or numbers?

We will see how numbers and categories are coded in different ways and how numbers may be treated as categories by the use of spread encoding. There is a special case where the choice between coding numbers in a distributed (as numerical values) or local (with spread encoding) fashion is a little less clear cut. This is the case of integer (i.e. whole) numbers. Although we have stated that values which lie on a sensible continuum should be treated as numeric rather than categorical, many integer numeric representations which fulfil that criteria would be better coded as categories.

As an example, let us take a measure of *number of children*. This will be an integer value: 0,1,2..., and does appear to fall along a continuum. However, the range is very small and fractional values are meaningless; nobody has 0.3 of a child. Using a spread encoding scheme which only ever takes activation values of 0 or 1 transforms a single numeric variable into a set of category variables. Clearly the range must be known precisely as there will be a unit per value, but several advantages arise from treating the variable in this way.

Firstly, the discrete nature of the difference between each number is made explicit. Changing the value of a number now involves a change to more than one dimension in the model which can make the task of splitting up the input space far easier. Secondly, if the variable in question is a network output, the network will produce values which correspond to the probability that the answer is each of the given possibilities. This tells us how confident we can be in a network's output. Finally, the possibility of producing nonsense outputs such as *number of children* = 0.3 is removed.

The disadvantage of re-coding integers as categories is that the network becomes larger and consequently requires more training time and data. In the battle to keep complexity low, folding a single unit out into several produces a most unwelcome increase in network size.

2.3   Initial statistical calculations

Several of the data manipulations discussed later in this chapter require a few simple statistical measures from the training set. These include the mean, maximum, minimum, and standard deviation of numeric data and the number of different values (i.e. categories) a categorical variable may take.

2.3.1   Outlier removal

Values which are abnormally far from the mean value of a variable can have an effect on the network which is out of proportion with the error they produce. This effect is worsened if the outlying values were produced by noise. For this reason it is advisable to remove such outliers before training. The mean and standard deviation of a variable may be used to remove outliers from the training set. Outliers are values which are abnormally far from the mean and which consequently may have a disproportionally large effect during training. An outlier is defined as a point which lies more than a given number of standard deviations from the mean. Two standard deviations cover 95% of a normally distributed data set and three standard deviations cover 99%. Condition 2.5 (section 2.9.3) is used to check for outliers as discussed above.

Remember, if any of the variables in a given input-output pair are outliers then the entire example has to be discarded. This may seem obvious, but if variables are stored in different files then it is easy to forget and remove data from a variable in one file without finding its corresponding values in other files. The consequences of such a mistake are that the vectors become mis-aligned and your data becomes nonsense.

It is also worth noting that the simple outlier removal technique suggested above is limited by the fact that it only works on single variables independently and that outliers may also manifest themselves as abnormal combinations of values which, in isolation, are acceptable but which combine to fall outside the normal data cloud. Such outliers often show up in a plot of the first two or three principal components of a data set so if you are serious about removing outliers and you suspect that they are present, then it is worth carrying out such an analysis.

If data is scarce and the act of discarding an example simply because one of its elements is an outlier is to be avoided, outlying values may be replaced with some other value: the mean for that variable is a good choice. Extra care must be taken during testing to ensure that the replacements have not biased the network if such a strategy is adopted.

2.4   Dimensionality reduction

Chapter 5 discussed the relationship between the size of the network and that of the required training set. One way of reducing the network size—and consequently reducing the data requirement—is to reduce the number of network inputs or outputs. This is referred to as dimensionality reduction. There are two different ways in which the dimensionality of a data set might be reduced. The first is to simply remove those variables which carry the least predictive power. A less destructive method involves projecting a high dimensional data set onto a lower dimensional space. This involves combining the set of variables into a smaller number of new variables which describe as much of the data as possible. Input data dimensionality reduction may be carried out with reference to one of two entities. It may either be carried out in terms of other input variables, or in terms of the output targets.

2.4.1   Removing less useful variables

It makes sense to discard individual variables if they are dependent on other input variables. Inputs both for occupation and salary, for example could be unnecessary if, once we know one, no additional predictive benefit is gained by knowing the other. The first step in dimensionality reduction involves spotting such cases. It also makes sense to discard variables which have little or no predictive power, independent of the other variables. Knowing the current speed of a pendulum is not sufficient on its own to allow us to predict the next position, but is sufficient and essential if we also know the current angle. Knowing the colour of the pendulum tells us nothing of its position however much else we know. It is important then, to establish whether a variable in isolation seems to have no predictive power because it is spurious, or because its value must be combined with another before it is of use.

Specific knowledge of the problem may be of use when making decisions on which variables to discard. Where no domain knowledge is available, analytic methods must be employed. Hints may be gained from simple statistical tests. For categorisation tasks, for example, a t-test could be used to compare the distribution of each variable in each of the different classes, using only those which differ significantly.

The independence between the different input variables may be measured by calculating the covariance between each pair of variables. Covariance between a pair of variables: x and y is calculated as

$$\sigma_{x,y} = \frac{\sum_{i=1}^{n}(x_i - \overline{x})(y_i - \overline{y})}{n-1}$$

and measures the extent to which one variable varies with another. Carrying out this calculation for each pair of a set of m variables produces $m \times m$ values: the covariance matrix. Any pair of variables with high covariance are dependent, and one may be chosen to be discarded. A less destructive method for using the covariance matrix for reducing dimensionality is presented below.

A final brute force (but effective) method for removing variables from a model is to build a neural model with too many inputs, and a small number hidden units. If the weights in the network are initialised with small, random values, then there will be no pressure for the weights from the less useful input variables to move far from their original position. Consequently, the input units in the trained network which have not moved far from their original values may be most safely discarded. A second network may now be trained on the new data set. The disadvantage of this method is obviously the time it takes to train a large network. The advantage is that the performance of the second network may be compared with that of the first to verify whether the variable reduction was successful. A practical advantage of this method is that it requires no extra mathematical analysis; writing software to calculate principal components or entropy values is inconvenient at best, and impossible[1] at worst.

---

[1] If we assume that a business user has access to a neural network simulator, but no compiler or programmer.

Choosing target output categories

The number of output classes may be reduced using the entropy based analysis discussed in section 5.3.2. As an output denoting each category is a discrete event, a measure of how predictable each category is may be gained from the conditional entropy of each output pattern, given each input pattern. Categories with high entropy values are not well predicted by the data. This only works because although the network output is spread across a number of units, only one category (i.e. a single event in the probability analysis) is present at any given time. Section 11.3.4 describes the use of this technique in a case study example.

Selecting input variables using entropy analysis

Battiti [12] has shown how it is possible to use information theory to select a set of input variables for a neural network. By measuring the mutual information between each input variable, and the set of target outputs in the training set, he was able to select the single feature with the most predictive power over the outputs. Further features may then be selected by two criteria. A new feature must predict something about the outputs, but it must not predict much (or anything if that is possible) about the input variables already selected. That is to say, a new variable must have a high mutual information score with the outputs which the network is required to produce, but share low mutual information with the variables already selected as network inputs. By applying this technique, it is possible to choose a set of variables which are independent and which predict the output data well. The technique is not optimal, but will reach a usable solution in a short time. Carrying out every calculation required to select the optimal set of variables is computationally unfeasible. See section 5.3.2 for an in depth discussion of the use of information theory for data validation.

2.4.2 Projection onto a lower dimensional space

Principal components

A common method for reducing the number of variables used as input to a network involves taking principal components of the original data set. It is clear that once we have calculated the covariance matrix, it would be wiser to combine variable pairs with high covariance in such a way that a new single variable is created which describes as much of the original data as possible. This is equivalent to drawing a regression line through the points described by the original data pairs, and describing a new point as the distance along that line. Repeating this N times for an N dimensional data set produces a new set of points which still describe the original data perfectly, but in a different coordinate system. The advantage of the new coordinate system is that we can order the coordinates with respect to the amount of variance in the data set they account for. We can simply throw away those coordinates which account for the least.

Full principal components reduction takes a covariance matrix and produces a set of vectors called *eigenvectors* which may be used to project a set of variables from the original coordinate system onto the new system. An eigenvector describes an axis in the new system. Each eigenvector has a length, measured by its *eigenvalue*. The percentage of the sum of all eigenvalues which any individual value contributes tells us the percentage of the variation in the data which is accounted for by its associated vector. A good principal components algorithm may be found in the book *Numerical Recipes* [77].

Morris [67] has pointed out that this has the disadvantage that it is a linear reduction and so can destroy any non-linear structure that you are trying to model with the neural network. This is only a problem in cases where the non-linearity occurs within the structure of the input set. In the case where the input patterns are linear but map to the output in a non-linear fashion, it is not a problem.

Auto-associative networks

The self-associative network is a solution to the concern raised by Morris above and an easy-to-use non-linear projection method. This method involves building an MLP in which the target output is the same as the input. Using an MLP with one hidden layer which contains fewer units than the number of inputs will cause those hidden units to act as feature extractors. The values of the hidden units can be used as inputs to the final network. This differs from adding another layer to the MLP to act as the feature extractor as it is easier to train a separate self-associative network and it keeps the number of weights in the final network lower. The inputs to the final network are generated by entering the full input vector into the reduction network and extracting the hidden unit activation scores.

The disadvantages of data projection

In chapter 7, we shall see how it is possible to extract explanations from a network in terms of which inputs were of most importance in arriving at the current output. If the inputs have been combined into a new set of variables, it becomes difficult to understand the network's outputs in terms of the original variables. This becomes more important if we have to use this information to make alterations to the input values.

Many types of data give themselves easily to reduction. Sound and other waveform data may be transformed into the Fourier domain and reduced into frequency bands. Images can be pre-segmented and coded. Textual data about people can be re-coded into smaller bins: by age group, profession, and so on. Most of these methods are discussed in detail in their relevant case studies in Part II. Reduction of textual data is discussed below.

2.5   Scaling a data set

We have mentioned that it is essential that the target outputs for a neural network with sigmoidal output units lie in the range from zero to one. The reason behind this is that the output from the sigmiodal function can only reach values in that range. Some output functions operate over different ranges: the tanh function, for example, covers the range from minus one to plus one. Linear output units are unbounded in the range they can cover.

It is necessary in the former cases and desirable in the latter to scale a data set so that every value falls within a given range. Although input units are usually linear it is still desirable to scale the data before training. One advantage of such an operation is that we are forced to make a few basic statistical considerations concerning the distribution of the training data and the effect of outliers in the training set.

Another reason for scaling each variable to within a fixed range is that there may be situations where one variable covers the range (say) 10,000 to 100,000 and another variable covers the range 0.3 to 0.6. Clearly, the errors due to the higher valued variable will have a greater effect during training than those due to the lower value as their magnitude will be greater. Ensuring that every variable covers the same range also ensures that errors on each variable contribute the same proportion to the change in network weights.

In the case of the input units, it might seem prudent to try and ensure that the activation they pass to the hidden layer falls within the correct operating input range for the hidden unit activation functions. Sigmoidal units, for example, should receive inputs in the range ± 5. In reality we need not worry about the input range on this account as the weights and the bias unit move the incoming values to the correct position for the hidden units' sigmoidal functions. It can, however, make the task facing the bias unit easier if the input values are small and have a mean of zero. For this reason and those discussed in the previous paragraph it can be prudent to normalise each variable to zero mean and a standard deviation of one for input to the network. The input normalisation function used to produce this new distribution is given in equation 2.8 in section 2.9.3. The rest of this section discusses scaling values to within the range from zero to one.

2.5.1   Linear scaling

The simplest method for squashing a set of data into a given range is by subtraction and division. If the desired range falls between zero and one, then each value, V, must have the lowest of all the values subtracted from it and the result divided by the original range to generate the new value S. This has the advantage of preserving the relative positions of each data point along the range. Linear scaling works best when the data is spread evenly over its range. Using linear scaling on a data set which contains outliers, or an uneven spread of values results in a large proportion of the data values being squashed into a small part of the input range, leaving most of the rest unused.

2.5.2   Softmax scaling

A useful method for squashing unevenly distributed data into an appropriate range
uses a function called the softmax. A softmax function has a similar form to the
standard sigmoidal squashing functions of neural network units. In a neural network,
the bias unit ensures that the data is scaled by the correct part of the squashing
function. When using a softmax function however, the degree to which each value is
squashed depends on its distance from the mean (we want to squash values which are
far from the mean more than those which are close) and the standard deviation of the
data set (a larger standard deviation requires a larger degree of scaling).

Values which fall further from the mean are squashed to an exponentially greater
degree. The softmax function will squash any values which fall outside the range
for which it is designed to a value close to one or zero. If the original data is evenly,
linearly distributed, then all of the data points will lie within three standard deviations
of the mean. Softmax can consequently squash the entire range into the linear part of
the squashing function. Thus there is no need to choose whether a linear or softmax
squashing function is used as softmax is equally valid for linearly distributed data.

Care must be taken when using the resultant network on new data as values which
fall outside the training range will be squashed to between zero and one, and produce
an incorrect extrapolation result.

As the measure of mean and variance is only valid for (approximately) normally or
evenly distributed data, this method will not produce useful results for data with very
non-normal distributions. Extreme outliers should still be removed, and the mean and
standard deviation recalculated for use in the softmax function. This ensures a more
accurate fit to the data.

Ad-hoc non-linear scalers

If we have a general idea of how a data set is distributed, then we can make an educated
guess at the type of scaling function to use. Sources such as power spectra produce
data with a logarithmic distribution; the majority of the points are distributed around
a low mean, but there are a number of exponentially higher values. In such cases,
a logarithmic scaling function allows us to avoid wasting a large proportion of the
new scale for coding a few, large values. Data can generally be scaled in this way if
the maximum value in the data set is greater than the exponential of the mean, i.e.
$max(x) > e^{\bar{x}}$.

Clearly, such scaling is only appropriate if the larger values—which become squashed
into a range which is very small relative to their original range—do not carry much
relevant information. If the larger values were actually the important ones, then
linear scaling would produce a better model. Logarithmic scaling may be achieved
using equation 2.9 given in section2.9.3.

Scaling for spread encoding

Spread encoding (which is introduced in section 2.6.6) presents an interesting addition to the task of scaling input values to within a given range as although the values themselves are never presented to the network, they do determine which input units are activated, and to what extent. The need for inputs between zero and one is removed as the units are always activated in proportion the the distance of the value from their centres. Some scaling may be required however, to allow the unit centres to represent an optimal range of the input data. Weigend [95] suggests that unit centres should be chosen in a manner which ensures that each unit accounts for a range which contains an equal number of points. The centre and range of each unit is easy to calculate by arranging the input data in ascending order and counting off N/i elements where N is the total number of points in the data set and i is the number of input units to be used.

The extremes of the data range clearly have to be strictly fixed for use with spread encoding as there simply will not be the neural units to represent data which falls outside the chosen range.

A more accurate scaling method

The same approach as that applied by Weigend [95] to spread encoding may also be applied to scaling data for input into a non-spread-encoded network. Centres are allocated at even steps along the target range between zero and one. Points are then chosen along the original range so that an even number of points are associated with each centre along the target range. The centres are allocated in exactly the same way as those used in spread encoding. The difference lies in the fact that rather than choosing a given input unit to activate, a given point along the range of a single input unit is chosen.

Each centre in the original range has a place on the target range associated with it. Once the centres have been calculated, a new value is scaled by choosing the target centre which is associated with the original centre to which it is closest, calculating its distance (positive or negative) from that centre, and adding a linear scaler of that distance to the target centre value. Clearly this method is time consuming and should only be used when it is not possible to derive any other approximation to the data distribution.

The effect of non-linear scaling on model accuracy

The disadvantage of using a non-linear scaling function is that it introduces a structure to the data which is not naturally present. We have already stressed the importance of an evenly distributed training set for building a correct generalisable model. In such cases a linear scaling term is the obvious choice as the distribution of the training set is flat. A second consequence of using non-linear scaling now becomes clear: it magnifies the effect of the imbalance in the training data by grouping the already sparsely sampled data points into even less accurate groups. On the other hand, it

builds an accurate model of the region about which it knows the most and a general
model of the region where data was sparse. In chapter 6, we see how error bars may
be attached to network output in order to measure how accurate a particular part of
a model is.

Scaling to within a smaller range

As we have seen, the output values of a network with a sigmoidal squashing function
fall within the range from zero to one. So that ever increasing input values still fit
into the range, the gradient of this function at its extremes approaches zero. This can
present a problem if the target output of the network is one or zero as a very large
input value is required to push an output unit to its extremes. A potential method for
avoiding this problem is to set the target range between 0.1 and 0.9 to avoid the ends
of the squashing function. We will soon see that such an approach does not apply
well to categorisation tasks as it does not allow the outputs to sum to one. A second
problem with such an approach is that it becomes possible for the network to produce
an output outside the target range (0.95 for example). In reality, the full range may
not be used due to the stretching effect of outliers. For practical purposes, it is only
important to make reasonable use of the range available.

2.5.3   Re-scaling

Clearly, if the answers produced by a network are to be interpreted sensibly, they must
be scaled back to the original range. Any scaling function must have an inverse with
which the original value may be calculated. The inverse of a logarithmic function, for
example, is an exponential function. The same does not apply to input values if the
network is only being used to generate results. Re-scaling is required, however, if any
analysis is to be carried out based on the inputs. Such analysis might, for example,
be directed at discovering an optimal setting or required change for the inputs to a
real world system.

2.6   Neural encoding methods

In this section we discuss the three basic techniques for encoding data for use with
a neural network. We will first introduce the basic concepts of coding data for any
given use and then examine the way in which these methods may be used for neural
computing.

2.6.1   Three encoding methods

This section investigates data encoding schemes which can be used to represent different types of data in a numeric form. There are three common data coding methods

which underlie most representations. They each have their advantages and drawbacks, and they are considered in turn below.

Local encoding

Local encoding[2] uses a single receptor (or unit) for each value of each dimension to be encoded. Such receptors—so called because they cover a receptive field across a section of the data range—may be either on or off; when a single object is being represented, all but one of the receptors will be off. Multiple objects may be represented simultaneously by turning more than one unit on. Every different entity in a data set is represented by an individual unit. The drawback associated with local encoding is that you require a large number of receptors to code an event. Entities in N dimensional space with k values along each dimension would require k^N units to code every possible value.

Distributed encoding

Distributed encoding[3] assigns a single continuous valued receptor to each *dimension* to be encoded. The value on each receptor will encode the place along that dimension which corresponds to the encoded value. Variable encoding suffers from a phenomenon known as *metamery*, or the *binding problem*: each receptor can only code a single value at a time. Attempting to code several objects in a distributed coding system will lead to the average being taken over all the values required to represent the different objects. This may not be a drawback if you only ever want to represent a single item at a time, but any system which produces probabilities of a variable taking each of a set of values will fail under such a coding scheme. Note that if a system varies over only one dimension, a distributed representation will contain only one unit but will still qualify as being distributed as that unit may be used to code more than one event or entity.

Combining the two

As a compromise, it is possible to combine local and distributed encodings when more than one distinct variable or feature constitutes an entity. Let us imagine a two dimensional space with dimensions X and Y, covering x and y points respectively. If we wanted to represent the position of a dot in that space we could use a purely local representation of $x \times y$ elements. Any number of dots could be encoded by activating the appropriate units. A distributed representation would require two units: one to code the X coordinate, and one to code Y. Here the binding problem is clear. There is no room to encode even a second dot. Combining the two methods by using a local coding for each dimension, but not for each entity, we would need $x + y$ units. The binding problem now manifests itself by the fact that it is possible to code the

---

[2]Local encoding is also known as labelled-line encoding, value encoding or place encoding.

[3]Distributed encoding is also known as intensity encoding, variable encoding or rate encoding.

presence of two or more dots, but it is not possible to know which X coordinate is paired with which Y coordinate.

If I were to say, "There are two dots: the X coordinates are 3 and 6, the Y coordinates are 4 and 9", then it would be impossible to know which of the four possible coordinates: $(3,4),(3,9),(6,4)$ or $(6,9)$ contained the two dots. If we were able to take a sufficient number of small overlapping local codings then the confusion caused by binding could be reduced to an arbitrary level. This method is called *coarse encoding*.

Coarse encoding

The solution to the binding problem is known in the perceptual sciences as channel encoding. The idea is based on the coarse coding scheme from computing science [48] which uses overlapping square receptive fields which cover an area of the space to be coded. Looking at the combination of levels of activation in each of these broad scale receptive fields narrows the uncertainty about a value's location to an area equal in size to the distance between consecutive squares.

Snippe and Koenderink [93] showed how a set of smooth overlapping receptive fields could be used to achieve hyper-acuity, that is, an accuracy greater than the sampling distance.

2.6.2   Encoding for a neural network

The discussion so far has considered coding single entities. The given input or required output for a neural network consists of a vector of one or more coded entities. Let us us again consider the input to the network as a single entity, but one which now comprises of a set of features. Each feature may have its own coding system: some local, some distributed.

Encoding methods to suit the data

Some types of data will be better suited to each encoding system than others. Any set of features which do not naturally form a continuum should not be coded in a range over a single variable. Colour, for example would be coded in a local fashion with an element for red, one for blue, and so on. Continuous variables such as height, temperature or sales revenue are better suited to a distributed representation. A more subtle form of distributed coding involves splitting each dimension into a set of component parts which represent a position along that dimension. Such a method requires extra knowledge about the data in question. The colour of an object, for example would require a local coding of one unit per colour to be represented unless one was able to derive, for example, the component RGB values which make up each colour. Now only three continuous values are required. Note that the binding problem still applies.

2.6.3   Mapping networks

Neural networks designed to learn continuous functions do not present many difficulties at the data coding stage. The mapping from input to output must be continuous
and well posed (see section 5.3.3). Values must be scaled or spread encoded, as discussed later in the chapter.

2.6.4   Categorisation networks

Representing data for categorisation tasks requires more thought and provides far
more possibilities. Training data can represent a far wider range of objects than is
the case with mapping problems. Data representing objects such as text, images, or
categories must be converted into a set of numbers in the range from zero to one.
Categorisation type data which is used as the input to a neural network is often
referred to as a *feature* descriptor. A feature may be the colour, or occupation of
an object to be encoded, or it might indicate the presence or absence of some event.
A consequence of this is that a network may have any combination of continuous or
discrete representations on its input and output layers.

Encoding inputs

Where categorisation tasks are concerned, it is often the case that the input to a
network is a point in input space, i.e. a set of coded features which describe the
current entity, and that the output is a unique identifier of the class to which the
object belongs. On the whole we will only want to present a single input at a time to
the network for classification so the binding problem is not encountered. This allows
us to use a continuous representation where applicable. Where an input entity is made
up of several features, more than one of which may be present, a local representation
would be chosen. For example a system to diagnose car faults may have a binary
input for each of the features: starter motor does not turn over, engine starts and
stalls instantly, engine backfires, and so forth. In this case more than one unit may
be activated to indicate the presence of more than one feature.

Encoding outputs

An encoding for interpreting the outputs from a categorisation network should provide a method for carving output space so that it is linearly separable, capable of
representing a set of continuous valued probabilities concurrently and which does not
require a large number of units. This is possible because, unlike the case of the input
coding, we have total control over the way output space is arranged.

The output from a classification network will quite often be required to represent
membership of more than one category; in other words, class intersection. Moreover,
the representation will not be binary as in the case of the local representations discussed so far, but continuous. For this reason we do not make the common distinction

between local and distributed representations as being binary or continuous. The target codings for such a network *are* however binary in nature. It is only the way in which the neural network learns which causes them to become continuous and, as discussed later, come to represent the posterior probabilities of the input falling into each output set.

An exclusive binary representation, often known as 1-of-n encoding, may be built by assigning a single neural unit to each value to be represented. To represent a given value, you set all the units' activations to zero except for the single unit which represents the value to be encoded. This unit has its activation set to one. Such a representation is equivalent to the local encoding scheme discussed above.

Encoding features which do not sum to one

It may be the case that we need to predict a set of features which may or may not be present in a certain output. Such a representation is discussed here with reference to the input units in section 2.6.4 which uses car fault diagnosis as an example. Let us assume such a system must output a number of checks to be carried out given the faults listed at the input layer. They could be *check there is petrol in the tank* or *check the brake pads aren't worn*. For some faults, more than one check will be necessary, and the outputs will consequently no longer sum to one. In such cases, each feature (checks to be carried out in this case) must be treated as single two class variables. The value of any output will be the probability of that feature being present. The probability of that feature *not* being present is calculated as one minus the output value. These two measures clearly sum to one. Each unit must be analysed in isolation from the others.

A multiple non-exclusive binary representation, often known as m-of-n encoding, may be built in the same way as the 1-of-n scheme presented above. The only difference is that any number of units may have activation values of one. In such cases, care must be taken if the binding problem is to be avoided.

Extending the output representation

We have just seen how more than one set of classes may be represented on a neural network's output layer. It is actually possible to combine any set of different output representations in the same neural network, treating each variable separately. For example we could code an object's colour over a set of binary units which sum to one, its height on a single unit, and the presence or absence of a number of features across another set of binary units which do not sum to one (some objects will have more, or less, features than others). Section 5.2.3 describes a limitation which must be overcome in certain situations when the output of a neural network refers to more than a single category label.

As we know, forcing a network output to one or zero at the far reaches of the squashing function is difficult, so it has been suggested that it is preferable to use targets of 0.1 and 0.9. It has also been suggested [65] that the best encoding method for such categories is to use 0.5 as the target value, as it is in the centre of the range and easiest to get to. It is a little difficult to see however, how the targets for non-membership should be chosen or how probabilities would be represented, as it would seem most appropriate to use targets which always sum to one.

2.6.5 Encoding textual data

Ideally, data would have been collected with training a neural network in mind. In reality however, this is often not the case. Data collected for a completely different purpose must be massaged into a usable form before attempting to build a neural network model. A common example is data which has been collected as text. For example, a questionaire might have been filled in with entries such as **occupation**: *road sweeper*. As neural networks cannot be given text strings directly, encoding must involve transforming occupations into codes. Given the number of possible occupations, and what we now know about data representation, it is necessary to group all the occupations into a few subsets which are considered useful. Let us say we split them into *Professional* or *Blue collar*: we can now have a single input unit for each.

Having a large number of inputs: one for *dustman*, one for *teacher*... will not only give us a large and unwieldy network, and require a huge amount of training data, but limit the effect any one occupation will have due to the small proportion of the input vector it occupies. The network will have to extract the important groupings with no prior knowledge; it is obviously much better if you do so for it.

Let us take, as another example, that of addresses. There is generally little information in an address which, in its raw form, is useful to a neural network. This is because none of the fields vary along a continuum or share qualities with which they can be classified. In reality, the address or postal area of an entry may hold useful information but in order to allow a neural network to learn a useful representation of that information, it must be translated into a form from which generalisations may be made. Let us assume we know that there is a connection between postcode and credit risk score. This is undoubtedly true, but there is nothing inherent in a postcode which holds that information; no common features contained in postcodes which, nationwide, lead to poor credit scores. The only way of forming the association is to form a look-up table.

Alternative ways of coding addresses may be to use an external guide, such as the credit risk tables mentioned above, to code the address along the scale or into the groups in which you are actually interested. Type of area for example may be coded as *inner city, suburb, tower block*, or as an indicator of which political party holds council office, or as height above sea level. Such details must be looked up separately and add significantly to processing time.

2.6.6   Spread encoding

The simplest method for implementing coarse encoding for use with a neural network is to use *spread encoding*. This is implemented by dividing the data range into smaller sub-ranges and assigning each unit to represent the centre of each sub-range. A value which falls exactly on a centre value will cause the appropriate unit to be set to one and the others to be set to zero. When a value falls between two centres, each of the two units involved take a value proportional to the distance of the value from the centre of each unit. The two values must sum to one, a consequence of which is that the lowest centre must be the lowest value in the range and to the largest centre will be the largest value in the range. Scaling the numbers to within the range from zero to one before applying spread encoding not only makes the maths easier, it also ensures that we do not come across numbers outside the scope of the encoding system. Data scaling is described in section 2.5 later in this chapter. In this case, the bottom bin will represent zero and the top bin will represent one.

A set of J bins will place a centre at values from zero to one in divisions of $1/(J-1)$. This is the case regardless of the number of units used to code each value. As a single bin is represented by a single unit, the two words may be used interchangeably in the following text.

Spread encoding in one dimension

Spread encoding along a single dimension proceeds as follows:

1. The two units (or one if the value falls exactly on a centre) to be used are identified as those whose centres fall the smallest distance from the value to be coded.

2. The absolute (non-negative) distance of the value from each centre is calculated as a fraction of their sum.

3. Each unit is given a value between zero and one equal to that fraction.

This method builds overlapping, linearly shrinking receptive fields over the data range as shown in figure 2.1. We shall see later how the representation can spread over more than two units and how the receptive fields can shrink in a non-linear fashion.

Multi-dimensional spread encoding

This method may be extended for use in more than one dimension in one of two ways: the simplest way is to code each dimension separately and concatenate the resultant vectors end on end to form one long input vector. This method suffers from the fact that encodings for a single object no longer sum to one.

The second method, and the one with rather more finesse, requires multi-dimensional receptive fields. Extending the concept is not difficult as the same principles apply:

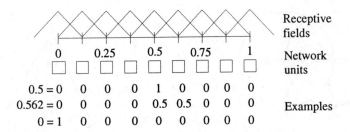

Figure 2.1: The overlapping, linearly decreasing receptive fields of a spread encoding system along a single dimension. Note the overlap at the midpoint between each receptive field centre, relating to an encoding of 0.5 0.5 spread across the two fields involved. The binary representation would require nine units. Example encodings are shown in the figure.

there is a unit for each receptive field, the activation value of each unit diminishes the further from its centre the current point falls, and the total activation sums to one.

In order to code a point, we must measure its distance from the centre of each unit in the representation. In practice, most of the units are not affected by a given point, and only the distances from those units which represent a receptive field into which the point falls need be measured. Having identified the centres to which the point is close, and for the total representation to sum to one, the output of each unit (i.e. the value to which that unit must be activated) is calculated as its proportion of the sum of the distances from the point to be coded to the bin centres which will be used.

Decoding the unit outputs

If we code the output of a unit in this way, we must also be able to decode it in order to discover the true value of a network output. Section 6.3.5 shows how, in a single dimension, the output of a unit can be thought of as the probability of the output being the value represented by the bin centre, and how these values can be used to calculate the expected value of the output. In more than one dimension, a little more care is needed. Each bin centre represents n coordinates, or a single point in n dimensional space. The outputs from the network consequently represent the probabilities of the expected values representing each possible point in output space. These values may be averaged in any number of dimensions to calculate the expected value of any single variable (i.e. dimension).

Figure 2.2 shows how four receptive fields, centred at zero and one along two dimensions can be used to build a very coarse scale coding. By using many smaller receptive fields, the accuracy can be increased at the expense of extra units and consequently, weights.

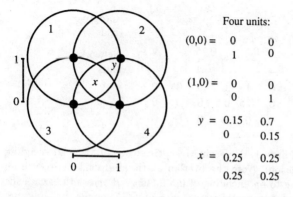

The receptive fields have a diminishing strength further from their centre

Figure 2.2: A view from above of four receptive fields covering a two dimensional space. The shape of the receptive field is coded in the third dimension: height, as shown on the right of the figure. Two example encodings are shown in the figure: the numbered fields correspond to units, the small black circles to their centres and x and y are example points.

Spread encoding with larger receptive fields

It should now be clear that any number of units can be included in the spread encoded representation simply by calculating the distance of the centre of each from the point to be coded. The resulting distances are summed and proportions are calculated in the same way as that shown above.

It may also be useful in some cases to use a weighted or non-linear function when calculating the distances. In this way, centres which are further from the point to be coded can be made to contribute a proportion which is smaller than that dictated by their distance alone.

The advantages and disadvantages of spread encoding

Spread encoding can be very useful. As we will see, it allows us to solve the problem created by ill posed data sets. Later we shall see how it is possible to use spread encoding to derive confidence measures for the predictions made by a neural network with very little extra work.

The technique also has its disadvantages. It requires far more weights than a normal continuously coded system. This has consequences for required training time and data set size. It also introduces the potential for overfitting as the resultant model has greater complexity. Finally it can make the learning task more difficult as it converts a naturally continuous modelling task into an arbitrarily divided categorisation task. The very fact that we are able to derive statistical confidence measures from the results of a spread encoded network requires that a model of greater complexity is built.

2.6.7   Encoding techniques summarised

- **Continuous values** may be coded either with a single continuous unit or spread across several discrete "bin" units.

- **Categories** are mutually exclusive and are coded using a separate unit per category. The target is that only one unit may be active at any time. A properly trained network will spread probabilities of class membership across output units coded in this way with a summed activation of one.

- **Features** are coded in a binary fashion to indicate the presence or otherwise of a set of features. Any number of features may be present at any time so the representation is not mutually exclusive and there is no constraint on the summed activation.

A neural network may use any combination of the above encoding techniques on the input and the output layer. This is referred to as *data fusion*. It is also possible to use one method on the inputs and a different method on the outputs.

2.7   Temporal data

The problem with time is that it doesn't happen all at once; you have to remember things that went before and wait for those yet to happen. One way of achieving this is to develop a memory and a method for encoding that memory so that it interacts with new information as it is received. In effect, this is what a recurrent network does. Such memories are not always the most efficient way of dealing with time varying data. Sound recognition is a good example here: your brain doesn't have to cope with remembering a stream of air pressure values caused by the sound to be recognised, the ear pre-processes the data, re-coding it into, amongst other things, frequency bands.

2.7.1   Time delay neural networks

Finding structure in a time varying signal is not easy and if we can make things simpler for our neural network then we should. The simplest way of converting a time varying signal into a static vector is to store up values as they occur and present the last n values to the network as a single vector. As each new data point becomes available, the data is shifted along to accommodate it. This method can be seen as a moving window which covers the last n values in the sequence. Note that unless we use a recurrent network to provide a memory, the output caused by each window is unaffected by any previous windows. Waibel [112] used this coding system as a method for speech recognition, referring to it as a time delay neural network or TDNN (see Part II for more details—there is more to a TDNN than simple windowing, but for now we will limit our consideration to that aspect of the TDNN). Several authors, such as Waibel [112], Refenes [79] [81], Weigend et al. [116], Mozer [115], and Jang et al. [50] have shown how the temporal dimension can be transposed into a spatial vector by taking a moving window over the last n elements in a series. Chapter 4 describes the use of time delay networks in more detail.

Weighted time windows

An obvious extension to the TDNN idea is to weight the past values so that certain elements in a window have a greater effect than others. Figure 2.3 shows a few possibilities: the plots show the amount each previous value contributes with the current time slice at the right hand side. (a) shows the simple TDNN with a square window. (b) shows a linear decrement which gives less weight to values the further away in time they occur. (c) shows the same idea but with an exponential drop in value as suggested by Mozer [68].

Figure 2.3 (d) will require a couple more lines of explanation. It is derived from what de Vries and Principe [111] called a gamma Mmemory. Gamma memory is an attempt to maximise the trade-off between memory depth (how far back we go) and memory resolution (how much we have to abstract in order to go back that far). A square windowed TDNN has low depth and high resolution as it does not weight distant inputs and cuts off suddenly. The exponential trace on the other hand has high depth but lower resolution. A gamma memory is built using two parameters which control depth and resolution and so can be altered to trade one off against the other for a specific task.

In practice, knowledge of the task must be used in choosing a weighted time window. It is possible to change the parameters which describe the window as an adaptive process during learning (Bodenhausen and Waibel [17]) but not without an overhead of time and complexity.

2.7.2   Re-coding temporal sequences

More sophisticated methods for re-coding time varying data involve extracting information based on the periodicity of the signal. The most common method for such re-coding strategy involves the Fourier transform which takes a vector of lagged values over time and produces a measure of the power present in a set of frequency ranges. The size of each range—the *spectral resolution*—is limited by the original sampling rate, as is the highest frequency which it is possible to measure. This maximum frequency—the *Nyquist limit*—is equal to half the sampling frequency. The Fourier transform is useful for temporal processing not only because it makes certain qualities in the data explicit but also because of the relationship between transformations performed on the data in the Fourier domain and those performed in the temporal domain. Chapter 9 describes a set of Fourier based neural network techniques.

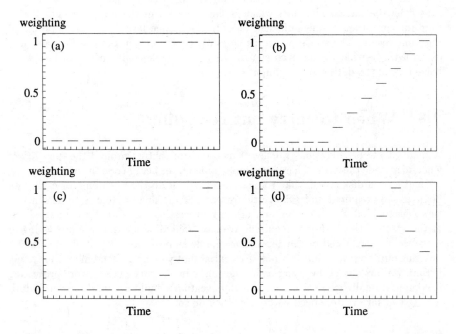

Figure 2.3: (a) The simple TDNN with a square window. (b) A linear decrement which gives less weight to values the further away in time they occur. (c) The same idea but with an exponential decrement in value. (d) A gamma memory.

Temporal spread encoding

Gent et al. [38] used spread encoding in both recurrent and time delay networks as a method for deriving confidence limits[4] for a network prediction. The encoding scheme is identical to that in the static case and requires no further explanation. Gent et al. also demonstrate that spread encoding improves the ability of a neural network to learn complex mappings. They rightly point out that this is due to the increase in the number of units required by a network in order to implement the spread encoding. The claim is that, as different areas of input space are represented by different input units, the network is better able to learn local differences in the function. They fail, however, to investigate whether it is simply the increase in the number of weights caused by the increase in units which is the true root of the improvement. If this were the case, then adding sufficient units to the hidden layer would have produced the same result. The spread encoding certainly contributes in both of the ways just described. To what extent each contribution is made depends on the variability of behaviour of the data across its input range.

2.8   When to carry out re-coding

A final set of considerations worthy of mention are centred around the question of when to re-code the data. There is a simple trade-off: either re-code the whole training set and lose in disk space what you gain in speed, or do the re-coding for each data point as it is required and achieve the reverse. If the final system is to run in real time, ensure that the re-coding and network processing can actually be carried out at the speed with which it is required. We have said all along that pre-processing to make the task required of the network as simple as possible is essential. It is worth pointing out, however, that it is not *so* essential that you must spend more time doing it than you are saving by using neural networks in the first place. If pre-processing is computationally expensive, and you can eventually build a neural network which manages at far greater speed without it, then do so.

---

[4]Confidence intervals are discussed in chapter 6 on error analysis.

2.9 Implementation details

2.9.1 Coding output categories

A simple local representation of one unit per category is coded as

$$o_i = \begin{cases} 1 & \text{if the input vector is in class } i \\ 0 & \text{otherwise} \end{cases}$$

2.9.2 Spread encoding

The following section describes the spread encoding scheme for values which have **already been scaled to values between zero and one.**

Calculating activation values for spread encoding

The Euclidean distance in N dimensional space of the point P from the centre C where $i = 0 \ldots N$ and $P = p_1 \ldots p_N$ and $C = c_1 \ldots c_N$ is calculated as follows:

$$\text{dist}(P, C) = \sqrt{\sum_{i=1}^{N} (p_i - c_i)^2}$$

The output of a unit is calculated as

$$o_j = \frac{1 - \text{dist}(P, C_j)}{\sum_i (1 - \text{dist}(P, C_i))}$$

where o_j is the output of unit j of J units (i.e. J bins), C_j is the centre of bin j, and P is the point to be coded. The sum is taken over all the units which are to be used in the encoding (usually two). All other units take values of zero.

A set of J bins will place a centre at values from 0 to 1 in divisions of

$$\frac{1}{J - 1}$$

Calculating the true output from spread encoding

For a set of n bin centres ζ_i where $i = 1 \ldots n$.

The mean expected output is calculated as the sum of each bin centre multiplied by its output activation.

$$\mu = \sum_{i=1}^{m} o_i \zeta_i \tag{2.1}$$

The variance of the output is calculated as

$$\sigma^2 = \sum_{i=1}^{m}(o_i^2 \zeta_i - \mu^2)$$

The modal expected output is calculated by choosing the set of S adjacent units which have the highest summed activation, and re-scaling their outputs, o to $\hat{o}$ so that they sum to one. S must be equal to the number of bins a value is spread across when initially coded (usually 2). Those bins are in the set $\{w\}$. All other network outputs are then set to zero, and the mean calculated as above.

To rescale the network outputs from o to $\hat{o}$, use

$$\hat{o}_i = \begin{cases} \dfrac{o_i}{\sum_{j \in \{w\}} o_j} & \text{if } i \in \{w\} \\ 0 & \text{otherwise} \end{cases} \tag{2.2}$$

Once the values have been re-coded, the expected value may be calculated using equation 2.1 above.

2.9.3   Scaling functions

For a set of n values, $V = v_1...v_n$ the mean, $\overline{v}$ is calculated as

$$\overline{v} = \frac{\sum_{i=1}^{n} v_i}{n} \tag{2.3}$$

and the standard deviation, σ_v is calculated as

$$\sigma^2 = \sqrt{\frac{\sum_{i=1}^{n}(v_i - \overline{v})^2}{n}} \equiv \sqrt{\frac{\sum_{i=1}^{n} v_i^2 - \frac{\sum_{i=1}^{n} v_i^2}{n}}{n}} \tag{2.4}$$

Linear scaling

If a set of data with a maximum value of $\max(v_{1...n})$, a minimum value of $\min(v_{1...n})$, an average value of $\overline{v}$ and a standard deviation of σ_v falls within the following bounds:

$$\max(v_{1..n}) < \overline{v} + \lambda\sigma_v \text{ and if } \min(v_{1..n}) > \overline{v} - \lambda\sigma_v \tag{2.5}$$

then linear scaling may be applied.

The parameter, λ determines the number of standard deviations from the mean a value must fall before it is labelled as an outlier. The condition simply checks for the presence of outliers. If none are present, then a linear scaling may safely be applied.

To linearly scale a value, v to within the range from zero to one, producing a new value, s:

$$s = \frac{v - \min(v_{1...n})}{\max(v_{1...n}) - \min(v_{1...n})} \qquad (2.6)$$

To rescale from s to v, The inverse of a linearly scaled value is calculated as

$$v = \min + s(\max(v_{1...n}) - \min(v_{1...n})) \qquad (2.7)$$

Linear normalisation

A variable can be normalised to zero mean and unit standard deviation by applying the following function to each point:

$$s = \frac{v - \bar{v}}{\sigma_v} \qquad (2.8)$$

Logarithmic scaling

A logarithmic scaling function may be implemented as follows:

$$s = \frac{\log v - \log \min(v_{1...n})}{\log \max(v_{1...n}) - \log \min(v_{1...n})} \qquad (2.9)$$

For a logarithmically scaled value, the inverse rescaling function is calculated by the following equations which are shown in two steps for ease of expression only.

$$\begin{aligned} x &= \log \min(v_{1...n}) - s(\log \min(v_{1...n})) + s(\log \max(v_{1...n})) \\ v &= e^x \end{aligned} \qquad (2.10)$$

Softmax scaling

If $\bar{v}$ is the mean of the variable to be squashed, σ_v is the standard deviation, λ describes the number of standard deviations from the mean which are to fall in the linear section of the squashing function, and v is the value to be coded, the softmax function has the following form, again expressed in two steps for clarity:

$$x = \frac{(v - \bar{v})}{\lambda \frac{\sigma_v}{2*PI}} \qquad (2.11)$$

$$s = \frac{1}{1 + e^{-x}}$$

The choice of λ is dependent on the importance of data values at the extremes of the range. A value of 2 squashes 95% of the data into the linear portion of the function and a value of 3 squashes 99% of the data into that range. $\lambda = 3$ ensures that linearly distributed data is linearly scaled.

The inverse of the softmax function is

$$v = \overline{v} + \frac{\lambda \sigma_v \log \sqrt{-1 + \frac{1}{1-s}}}{PI} \qquad (2.12)$$

Care must be taken when implementing equation 2.12 on a computer as the limit in accuracy will cause values very close to one to be rounded up. As $1/(1-s)$ is not defined (or becomes infinity) when $s = 1$ we must introduce an extra condition to the equation to set any value of one to be equal to the maximum value in the original data range, i.e. $v = max$.

Due to the square root term, the true inverse of the softmax function has two solutions in theory. The second is calculated by inserting a minus sign before the square root in equation 2.12. However, as logarithms are not defined for negative numbers, we must only use the positive result of the square root term.

Chapter 3

Building a network

The truth is rarely pure, and never simple.

Oscar Wilde

3.1 Introduction

Building a neural network has an inherent quality of experimentation, even—as Hecht-Neilson [45] puts it—alchemy. Although it is certainly true that experimentation is required before the best solution is arrived at, the field is now at a point where we can make reliable predictions about the behaviour of a network under a given set of conditions and so make plans accordingly. The main concern when building a multilayer perceptron is that the network has the correct degree of complexity. Complexity, as we shall see, may be traded in a number of different ways.

3.2 Designing the MLP

3.2.1 Network size

The decisions to be made when building an MLP concern the number of layers and the number of units contained within each. As the number of input and output units a network requires is determined by the data coding system, and this is considered elsewhere in the book, we shall start our investigation of MLP architecture with the choice of hidden layer size.

3.2.2 Hidden layer size

There is a single trade-off between accuracy and generalisation ability which we seek to optimise when choosing the number of hidden units for a given neural network. The number must be sufficient for the correct representation of the task, but sufficiently

51

low to allow generalisations to be made. It can be useful to think of weights as terms, or parameters, in a function. Just as we need to add extra higher order terms to a quadratic model to account for more complicated curves in our data, we must add more weights to a network. Just as you can only model a single turning point with an x^2 term, needing to add an x^3 term to accommodate another, a single hidden unit is only able to model a single turning point in the data. Decision boundaries in classification tasks can be thought of in the same way. The more curves and turns required to split up a data set, the more hidden units are required to build a model.

There is no simple method for determining the number of hidden units a network requires. As we can see above, the choice depends on several factors. Throughout the book, methods for manipulating all of the above factors are presented. Some are pointed out in the discussion below.

There are several conflicting constraints on the number of weights a network requires. First is the fact that one must have sufficient data for the number of weights in the network. The number of weights is constrained partly by the number of input and output units and consequently by the input and output codings used. Secondly, one must have sufficient weights to contain the information present in the training set. The upper bounds on number of required weights depend on the training data being fully loaded with information (i.e. using every available bit pattern to represent a distinct item). Sparser representations will require fewer weights. This fact leads to the problem of overfitting; we cannot simply use the theoretical maximum number of weights because the network will learn to deal only with the training data and so generalise poorly. In this sense, the choice of hidden layer size is problem dependent. Any network which requires data compression, for example, must have a hidden layer smaller than the input layer.

If more data is required to match the required network complexity determined by the number of input parameters, then either more data must be collected or the existing data needs to be expanded, as described in chapter 5. Chapter 5 also presents methods for measuring the degree of accuracy to be expected from a data set.

As we shall see, several researchers have suggested formulae for calculating bounds on hidden layer size. We shall also see how these bounds vary greatly between the different techniques. Each formula is no more than an aid to estimation: a limit to what might even be considered. A certain amount of trial and error cannot be avoided at this stage and a fair amount of room for error is provided by other methods for restricting a network's complexity.

Fan in against fan out

A simpler decision than choosing the number of hidden units is that of choosing whether your network will fan in to the hidden layer (i.e. contain fewer hidden units than input units) or fan out. For any task where the hidden layer is required to extract features from the inputs in order to generalise or reduce the dimensionality of the data set, it is essential to fan in.

A good example of how a fan in network functions can be seen in the work by Cottrell et al. [26] on image compression. They took a set of images and fed them into an MLP with a single hidden layer and an output layer with the same number of units as the input layer. The hidden layer contained fewer units than the input layer. Coded versions of each image were fed into the network and the same coded images given as target outputs. This caused the network to use the fewer hidden units to code the images in a more concise way. The hidden unit values for an image could be extracted and used as compressed versions, to be decoded by a copy of the output weights at a later date. The same method can be used to extract non linear principal components from a data set and is a good way of reducing its dimensionality before training on an MLP. In the example just given, the compressed versions of the images could be used to train a new network to classify each image. The new network would require fewer inputs, and consequently fewer weights, than a network which took the whole images as input. The same method will be discussed later on, in relation to novelty detection networks.

The number of hidden units depends on the number of input units, as shown in equations 3.1 and 3.2, section 3.4.1; both give an upper bound which is greater than the number of input units. This upper bound assumes that each input pattern must be loaded into the hidden units without loss of information. If any feature extraction is required, as discussed above, the number of hidden units will be considerably less. The closer you are to needing a look-up table because similar inputs map to very different outputs, the more of a fan out you will require and the less generalisation you will be able to expect.

When using recurrent networks, it must be remembered that the hidden layer is copied back as part of the input layer: forcing the input layer size to be equal to the number of input units plus the number of hidden units.

3.2.3   Calculating network size analytically

The following sections describe a set of loose guidelines which may help in choosing network size. There is no simple formula and not always a single correct answer. Network size is dictated by many factors, some of which are easy to measure, some of which are not. The following section discusses those which are, but those which are not should still be borne in mind. Chapter 5 discusses the factors which affect the required quantity of data for a neural network; the same considerations should be made when choosing network size.

Relating hidden units to input units

Hecht-Neilson [45] used Kolmogorov's theorem—which states that any function of n variables may be represented by the superposition of a set of $2n + 1$ univariate functions—to derive the upper bound for the required number of hidden units as one greater than twice the number of input units. That is to say that you will never require more than twice the number of hidden units as you have inputs. This bound is stated in equation 3.1.

Girossi and Poggio [39] point out that Kolmogorov's theorem requires that the component functions are chosen to fit each particular case and not, as is the case with neural networks, that the functions are fixed and parameterised. They also point out that a neural network requires a smooth function in order to generalise and that Kolmogorov's theorem does not guarantee this. Kůrková [56] however, states that the fact that a neural network is only an *approximation* eliminates both of these difficulties. Kůrková was able to re-state Kolmogorov's theorem in terms of a set of sigmoidal functions.

Chapter 2 tells us how to reduce the dimensionality of the input space if required. In doing so, we can reduce the complexity of the network model.

Incorporating the number of training patterns

As we know, neural networks are models described by a set of parameters called weights. Upadhyaya and Eryurek [110] have applied the fact that the number of parameters required to code P binary patterns is $\log_2 P$ to derive the upper bound on the required number of weights in a network shown in equation 3.2, section 3.4.1.

A network of this size will encode every pattern in the training set and so is the absolute maximum number of weights to be used. For problems requiring generalisation, the equality must become an inequality describing the upper bound for W. This theory is not necessarily applicable, however, as it assumes that binary representations are used and this is rarely the case. The number of patterns to be coded by a neural network is not necessarily the same as the number of training points or the number of categories. It is most accurately thought of in terms of the number of regions the input space must be split into in order to classify each training data point, and will consequently fall somewhere between the number of categories and the number of training points. The more hidden units there are in a network, the closer we move towards building a look-up table of the training data pairs.

Relating to the number of output units and training patterns

Widrow and Lehr [118] considered the fact that, in a classification network, the number of training patterns to be learned is reflected in the number of output units in the network. Equation 3.3 in section 3.4.1 describes the resultant bounds on the number of weights in a network.

Relating to the training set size and error

Baum and Haussler [13] showed perhaps the easiest estimate to put into practical use. Assuming an error limit of $0 < \epsilon \leq 1/8$, the number of training examples required approximately equals the number of weights in the network multiplied by the inverse of the error limit. An error limit of 0.1 for example, would require a training set of size 10 times the number of weights. Equation 3.4 in section 3.4.1 describes this relationship.

The reason that the error value is important is related to the trade-off between generalisation ability and accuracy. A small training error gained by an overfitted network does not constitute a successful training session. Equation 3.4 tells us that if we wish to use more weights than the data set can fill, we must settle at a higher learning error in order to maintain generalisation ability. This forces us to sacrifice accuracy rather than the generalisation ability of the network.

As the numbers of input and output units are mostly determined by the task, it is a simple process to express equations describing the number of weights in terms of the number of hidden units in a fully connected feedforward network with one hidden layer: $h = w/(i \times o)$.

Relating to the degree of noise in the training set

Weigend [116] points out that the more noise there is in a data set, the larger the risk of fitting that noise with a neural network model will be. If a data set contains no noise, then there is no risk of overfitting as there is nothing to overfit. As the level of noise in a data set increases, the effective size of that data set decreases and the chance of overfitting increases. Both of these consequences dictate that we should use fewer hidden units, the noisier the data set becomes. As we shall see below, adding noise to a data set is one method for avoiding the risk of learning any noise present in the training set and as we shall see in relation to data collection, as the amount of noise present in a data set increases, so does the required data set size.

Conclusion on number of hidden units

When choosing the number of hidden units h:

- Never choose h to be more than twice the number of input units.

- You can load p patterns of i elements into $i \log_2 p$ hidden units. So never use more. If you want good generalisation, use considerably less.

- Ensure you have at least $1/\epsilon$ times as many training examples as you have weights in your network. Chapter 5 discusses training set size in more detail.

- Feature extraction requires fewer hidden units than inputs. If you know that your data is reducible, use fewer hidden units.

- Learning many examples of disjointed inputs requires more hidden units than inputs. If you have a data set which does not have general properties, you need more hidden units.

- The number of hidden units required for a classification task increases with the number of classes in the task. To be more specific, it is the number of separate regions that inputs space must be split into which is the important factor, rather than the number of classes itself.

- There is a trade-off between generalisation (fewer units) and accuracy (more units) which is application specific.

- Larger networks require longer training times.

As we shall see, the reason for limiting the number of hidden units in a network is that we wish to maintain an ability to generalise. A complex model will not generalise as well as a simple, but sufficient one. We can derive, from the guidelines above, a set of limits on hidden layer size and some intuition gained from any specific problem at hand. The model can be simplified in ways which do not concern the number of hidden units, so a final definitive formula which calculates the required network size, as well as being impossible, is unnecessary.

Chapter 11 describes the process of choosing a correct level of network complexity for a particular application—modelling driver alertness—which requires a very general model from a training set of restricted size.

3.2.4   Constructive algorithms

Many successful attempts have been made at building neural networks which add or remove hidden units as they are required. The simplest method is to start with one unit less than your calculated lower bound and train until the error flattens out. When this happens, another unit is added with low weight values and the procedure is repeated until the error on an independent test set starts to rise. There are several problems with such an approach. Mainly, the new weights may disturb the current network to the extent that it would be better to start again rather than be stuck in the part of weight space chosen by the few weights (which may now have grown too large).

Hierarchical constructions

There are several algorithms for building networks hierarchically, such as the upstart algorithm [37], or cascade correlation [35]. The idea behind hierarchical networks is that child nodes are added to correct the errors of their parents. A binary decision tree can be built in this way if two units are added to correct the two types of possible binary error (wrongly on or wrongly off). Such networks are not MLPs and so the other methods presented within this book will not necessarily apply to them.

Adding new weights and freezing old ones

Refenes [79] proposed an algorithm called CLS+ which requires a network to start with a small number of hidden units and adds to them as more are required. The rather convoluted training procedure requires existing weights to be frozen and new weights to be added from the previous hidden unit to the newly added one. Care is also required that new units are only trained on remaining pairs in the training set so that each hidden unit is responsible for a subset of the training patterns. Refenes does not refer to an independent test set when deciding whether to add another unit. This and the non-standard training procedure and architecture make it difficult to confidently apply accepted techniques to the resulting network, making CLS+ an unlikely choice of algorithm.

3.2.5   Dynamic unit allocation and removal ✕

Bartlett [10] uses an information theoretical approach to dynamic unit allocation. His algorithm starts with a small number of units and trains until the error rate flattens out. At this point a new unit with small random connections is added to the hidden layer and the training continued. The process is repeated until adding a unit does not improve the error rate. At any point during this process a unit may be removed if it does not carry sufficient information about the output targets of the network. This information content is calculated using Shannon's [88] measure of mutual entropy between the hidden unit in question and the desired values over the whole output layer minus the redundancy of that unit with respect to the other hidden units. The equations describing this process are presented in section 3.4.2.

If there is not a discrete number of possible output patterns, but a continuous range on the output layer, this range must be split into bins, say 0–0.1, 0.11–0.2 etc. and the probabilities of values falling into each of these bins calculated for use in equation 3.6. An entropy based learning procedure is, of course, very computationally expensive.

Bartlett does not test the network against an independent test set so his original version would not necessarily produce a network with the best generalisation ability. This could be remedied by calculating the units' importances over a test set rather than the training set.

An easier, but less effective approach known as weight pruning can be used to trim off weights whose values or activation are very low. Such a method is at odds with the goal of producing a network with low weights in order to build a generalisable model however. A more effective pruning method is known as Optimal Brain Damage [29]. This method removes weights based on an estimation of the effect on the error that such a change would have. Weights are pruned if their removal would lead to only a small increase in error.

Discussion of constructive networks

Bartlett points out that having been successful with a 2 × 3 × 1 network,

> *A node is then added to yield a 2 × 4 × 1 network and, curiously, this configuration is also unable to learn the desired mapping before a learning plateau is encountered.*

This suggests that the weights are being moved to a position which is inappropriate once a unit has been removed. The opposite, as I have already mentioned, is also possible: that a network with a small number of units will find a solution with weights which are too high, thus making it difficult for the network to settle on a new solution with evenly distributed weight values.

The DTI best practice guidelines [31] point out that a healthy network must have a set of weights with a normal distribution of size around zero. That is to say that a network with more large weights than small weights is not a healthy network. There is a danger that a constructive algorithm, especially one designed to trim away smaller weights, will produce a rather unhealthy network. A possible way around this problem would involve restricting the growth of the early weights and adding new weights when the first ones pass a threshold. This might cause the weights to saturate, however, and would not gain us an awful lot.

It would seem that the only need for removing nodes in the way suggested by Bartlett would be to counter the effects of adding low random weights to a skewed network. The progressions such as 1,2,3,2,3,4,3 hidden units seen during the construction of such a network suggest that when a new unit is added, it creates a lopsided solution which needs to be trimmed and built several times before settling on a good solution. If care were taken to ensure that a network grew in a healthy manner, the pruning stage would not be required.

Conclusion on constructive algorithms

The field of neural computing is still at the stage where many new techniques are being suggested but each one is either only tested on a small range of problems or, worse still, designed to solve a specific problem. It is not clear how such networks generalise in their applicability to the rest of the work discussed in this book.

So, in building a constructive neural network we have to choose:

- Will we build a hierarchical network or a standard MLP?

- Are the old weights fixed or variable once new ones have been added?

- Will we have lateral connections between the hidden units? If so, the model is no longer a standard MLP.

- How will we decide when to remove a hidden unit, and then which one will we remove?

- How will we set the weights to and from the new hidden units? Will they be random or will they be set to counter the existing errors?

- How do we know when to stop, and how do we backtrack when one too many units have been added?

- How can we be sure that the existing small number of weights really have put us in a position which is better than that which a new, low, random set would?

- Can we restrict the growth of the few weights we start with whilst avoiding saturating them?

It would seem then, that the best way of arriving at the correct set of weights con-
structively is to build a network with a hidden layer size which is determined by rules
and knowledge about the data, train it, and test it. If it falls below expectations,
look at the training and test errors in order to revise the choice of hidden layer size,
and **start again** with new low and random weights. That way you will arrive at a
well balanced solution and save yourself the trouble of choosing and implementing the
right constructive algorithm for your problem.

Here is a simple set of heuristics for arriving at the correct neural network model:

- If the training error is low and the test error is high, you have too many weights.

- If both training and test errors are high, you have too few weights.

- If the weights are all very large, you have too few weights.

- Adding weights is not a panacea; if you think you have enough weights, look at
  the other possible causes of error such as insufficient or unlearnable data.

- Don't add so many weights that you contravene any of the limits set out in
  section 3.2.2.

- Finally, and **very importantly**, the initial weights of an untrained network
  must be set at random over a small range (say between ±1).

3.2.6 Generalisation and precision: other techniques

Ripley [83] has suggested that the number of hidden units is less important than people generally believe and that you can achieve good performance with approximately
correct network size by applying other techniques. This is perfectly consistent with
the approach taken in this book which states that model complexity is determined at
each stage of a project and that it is a mistake to assume that choosing the correct
number of hidden units guarantees a correct model. A simple method for ensuring
an acceptable level of generalisation is to periodically test your network on an independent validation set and stop training when the test error starts to rise. This is a
rather brute force method however, which increases both the training time and the
quantity of data required for a solution. A set of methods with a little more finesse
are described below.

3.2.7 Adding a regularisation term

A more technical approach is to use a regularisation term in the error function designed
to limit the complexity of the solution, usually by limiting the size of the weights. A
network with smaller weights values will have better generalisation abilities. The
easiest way of adding a regularisation term is to alter the error measure so that the
use of large weights is considered to be an error of sorts. The larger the weights grow,

the larger the error becomes, thus introducing a force to choose the simpler of a set of possible solutions for a data set and so improve generalisation ability.

When introducing a regularisation term to the error function of a neural network, it is advisable to take account of the number of training patterns being used. This ensures that the effect of the regularisation is diluted in proportion to the size of the training set. We also need to be able to control the degree of regularisation to be used and to increase the error value in proportion to the size of the weights in the network.

These considerations lead us to the new error function shown in equation 3.21 in section 3.4.5. This equation introduces another parameter which must be tuned (or at least set before training begins): the regularisation parameter, λ. The larger the value of λ, the greater the degree of regularisation that will occur. λ should fall within the range between zero and one. Put simply, this method increases the error value in proportion to the sum of the squared size of the network weights. As the weights grow, so does the error.

Adding noise is equivalent to regularisation

One method of simulating regularisation if your software does not support it is to add random noise to your training data. If the noise is different on each training pass, the network will never have a chance to fit any fine details as it will be "blunted" by the noise. The more noise you add, the more general your model becomes. Bishop [16] has shown how adding noise to a training set is equivalent to implementing Tikhonov regularisation. The regularisation term used by Bishop relies on the fact that adding noise to the input units will have an effect on the network output which is determined by the structure of the network itself. The effect a small change in the input (caused by the addition of noise) will have on the output units is determined by the derivative of the network output with respect to its inputs. An obvious way of implementing this effect as a regularisation term is to calculate the sum of the derivatives of the output unit with respect to the inputs and add that value (or a multiple of it, for finer control) to the error term.

The advantage of this method is that it allows the regularisation parameter, λ to be varied. The same effect could be achieved, without the need for differentiating the network by using an activation function on the input units which perturb the input values they receive by an amount proportional to λ before passing the value to the hidden layer. Input units do not usually have an activation function, they simply pass the input values, via the weights, to the hidden layer. In a sense, any scaling function which is applied to the data before it is presented to the network is equivalent to an input unit activation function. The only difference is that the data can be scaled once, creating a new data set, and thus reducing the computation which is carried out during learning. A noisy activation function with a noise control, λ, such as that described in equation 3.16 may be used to introduce noise to a training set.

If the data has already been scaled to within the range between zero and one, then λ will describe the signal to noise ratio which the network experiences. Although λ is an extra parameter to worry about setting, it is relatively simple to control. Start with λ high (0.1 is 10% noise), and reduce λ each time the training error ceases to fall, until the validation error[1] starts to rise. In this way, it is possible to incrementally approach a general solution based on more than early stopping.

Two important points to note are that:

1. A different noise value must be added to each value, each time it is used by the network. It is not sufficient to simply build a new training set to which noise has already been added. Noise must be added dynamically during learning.

2. Adding noise to the training data must preserve the mean value of that data. That is to say that the noise must have zero mean. This may be achieved by ensuring that the random number generating function produces a value between $-n/2$ and $n/2$ where n is the magnitude of the range over which the noise must fall. Remember to turn off the noise during testing!

Chapter 2 discusses how training data may be scaled to within a constant range for input to a neural network using a squashing function. The squashing function may be implemented as an input unit activation function, and so altered to allow for the addition of noise. Noise should be added after the data has been scaled to keep the amplitude constant across all variables.

The process of introducing and gradually decreasing noise to a neural network during training can also be used as a safeguard against the network becoming trapped in a local minimum early on in the training process. Noise effectively smooths out some of the small dips in the error which a gradient descent learning algorithm might not escape from.

As we shall see chapter 5, there are several methods for reducing the complexity of a data set, including regularisation. The methods presented later for adding constraints to an ill posed problem are equally valid for application to simplifying a neural network in order to improve its generalisation ability. Chapter 5 describes methods for adding constraint functions to the output of a neural network in order to restrict the aspects of a problem the network learns; a technique which is equally applicable to model simplification.

This concludes the discussion on the number of hidden units required to solve a task. Section 4.6.1 discusses the number of hidden units required by a recurrent network.

3.2.8   Number of hidden layers

A network which consists simply of an input layer and an output layer, with no hidden layer, is known as a linear perceptron, or often just a perceptron. Perceptrons are only capable of modelling linear functions and are consequently rarely mentioned. This is a pity as they are actually universal linear approximators and often all that is required for a given task. Unless you know that your problem is definitely non-linear, a perceptron should always be tried before moving on to an MLP.

---

[1]The error which the network produces when tested on data which has not been used to alter its weights and to which no noise was added.

The function of a single hidden layer is to re-code the input representation so that there is a linear mapping to the output representation. An MLP with a single layer of hidden units is a perceptron on top of a linearisation function.

Kůrková [56] uses Kolmogorov's theorem to show that any function can be approximated by at most four layers. Hecht-Neilson [45] shows the maximum to be three but states that in reality the use of more layers could greatly reduce the total number of hidden units required in the hidden layers. Looking at published results, however, reveals that most problems require (or at least, are solved using) only one, and sometimes two, layers. The reason behind this is likely to be based on the difference in complexity between current applications and the theoretic limits discussed above.

3.2.9   Activation functions

The activation function of a unit sums the weighted inputs from all connected units and squashes it into a set range. That range will normally be either 0 to 1 or minus 1 to 1. It is consequently useful for higher values to be squashed into an ever decreasing part of the extremes of the function. For this reason, and for a network to build non-linear models, the activation function must be non-linear.

The most used activation function is the logistic function, which has two main qualities. Firstly, it squashes the input, x into the range from zero to one and secondly, the derivative makes very small changes at either end of the range and larger changes in the middle. Both the logistic and the tanh functions, which are presented at the end of the chapter, are called *sigmoidal* functions due to their S-like shape.

Morris [67] has suggested that one of the hidden units should always be linear. This is because most problems may well have linear components and it is very hard to model a straight line by adding together a number of weighted non-linear functions. A linear activation function simply sums the incoming weighted values and divides the result by some constant.

Note that it is also possible to alter the slope of the functions, and so alter the speed at which they move towards their extremes by introducing a constant term. This slope term determines the sharpness of decision boundaries in a classification network. Whereas a function with a steep slope might learn a task and report two membership probabilities of 0.9 and 0.1, the same network trained on the same task, but with a shallower activation slope might report membership probabilities of 0.7 and 0.3 to the same input.

The linear, logistic and tanh activation functions are shown in figure 3.1. The vertical axis represents the unit's output and the horizontal axis represents its input. Notice that the tanh function has the same form as the logistic except that it covers the range between ±1. It is usually the case that modern computers can calculate a tanh function faster than an exponential (i.e. the sigmoid) and as the derivatives of each are similar in nature, the tanh function should be faster. Another advantage of the tanh function is related to its ±1 range. It can often be desirable to normalise a training set so that it has zero mean and unit standard deviation. Such normalisation is clearly only possible with an activation function which is able to output negative

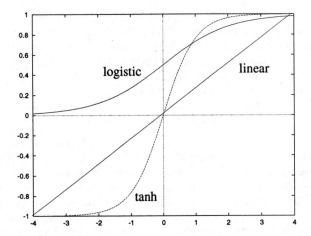

Figure 3.1: The linear, logistic and tanh activation functions.

values. Finally, we shall see later that an asymmetric function such as tanh leads to faster learning (in terms of less required pattern presentations) than a non-symmetric function such as the logistic.

Hardware considerations

Neural networks have a particular advantage of being easy to implement in hardware. Some activation functions are, however, easier to implement than others. The logistic function, for example, is particularly well suited to hardware implementation. The tanh function may either be calculated or derived from a look-up table. The latter method is faster, but there is a cost of storage space. Certain commercially available neural network chips only support certain types of activation function so it is important to establish this and any other constraints on network design (typically number of units) at the outset of a project.

3.2.10   Error measures

The goal of training a neural network is to minimise the error which the network makes at each output unit over the entire training data set. As errors may be positive or negative, it is obviously the size of the error in which we are interested when gauging the average accuracy of the network as a whole. The direction of the error (whether it is positive or negative) is important when an individual error between a given output and a target is calculated. The weights must be changed to move the error value closer to zero.

There are consequently three types of error measure in which we are interested. The first is the error of a single output unit given a single input, and is the form in which the back propagation algorithm presented in chapter 1 requires the errors. The second is the error which the network as a whole makes given a single input, which tells us how far from the correct answer the network is at any given time. The third is the average (or total) error made over the entire training (or test) set, which gives us an idea of how well the network has accommodated the entire data set. The final error type is simply the average, over the data set, of the magnitude of the second type of error. As the second type is often calculated as a distance, it will naturally be positive and can simply be averaged without the need for calculating the absolute magnitudes.

In addition to the two levels of error measure described above, there are several different individual error measures which can be used. Each is designed to produce a network with certain qualities, as discussed below. The most often used error measure is the simple difference. That is $target_i - actual_i$ where the subscript i denotes output unit i. In order to calculate the error of the output of the entire network output layer, we must treat the target and actual outputs as points in multi-dimensional space and calculate the distance between them. As we know from Pythagoros, the distance between two points in the square root of the sum of their squared differences. The error on the output of a network with n output units is consequently the square root of the sum of the squared errors.

This is referred to as the root squared error (RSE). An extension to the RSE is the weighted RSE (the term weight here does not refer to connection strengths, but to the importance attached to each training example). Each training example will have an associated weight which tells the network how good an example the current training pair is. Weights should be between zero and one.

For categorisation tasks, it is possible to set a threshold so that the output of a unit is either one (belongs to this class) or zero (doesn't). This must be done **after the error measure is taken** in order to prevent the error measures all being either zero or one. It is not enough then to say "right" or "wrong", you must calculate the size of the error.

Specifically, it may be possible to define the error in terms of the task the network is designed to carry out. For example, a network designed to trade stocks and shares could be set to make a trade on a given input and the error could be set to represent the inverse of the profit made on the transaction. A small profit (or a large loss) would correspond to a large error. The weights would then be set to output a trading strategy which has been trained directly to optimise profit.

3.2.11   Setting the learning rate and momentum terms

The learning rate, η (eta) and the momentum term, α (alpha) determine the nature of the weight updates. Both are used in the weight update rule seen in equation 1.4 in chapter 1. For simplicity, equation 1.4 shows η—which dictates the proportion of the calculated error that contributes to the weight change—but not α—which will be introduced below. The momentum term, α, relates to the size of the previous update for each weight. Each weight update must consequently be stored for use in the subsequent cycle. The weight update rule with momentum, shown in equation 3.23

in section 3.4.6, includes a term which is a proportion (dictated by α) of the previous weight change.

A high η value will produce faster learning but increase the risk of the network overshooting the solution and then oscillating around it as it flips back and forth using too large a step. A low η value avoids such problems but slows the process down. A high α value will reduce the risk of the network becoming trapped in a local minima but increase the risk of overshoot just as a high η value will.

Starting with a large value for η (say 0.75) and reducing it to (say) 0.25 and then to 0.1 as the network starts to oscillate is a good heuristic. Hertz et al. [46] suggest a value of 0.9 for α pointing out that the oscillations from a high η will be damped and that the new effective learning rate will be $\eta/(1 - \alpha)$. Most of the examples in this book were carried out with $\alpha = 0.9$ and $\eta = 0.25$. Only if it was obvious that different values were needed or if no success was found with the original values were new values tried.

The trade-off between overshooting a solution and skipping out of local minima is obvious, but the following heuristics may help:

1. If the error rate is falling slowly but steadily, you could increase η and α.

2. If the error rate is oscillating about a point, reducing η will help the network converge on the point, increasing η or α may cause the network to shoot out of the oscillation to continue its descent, but it may not.

3. If the error rate is not changing, you have probably converged on a solution. Always save a copy of the weights at this point before trying larger parameters in an attempt to jump the network out of the plateau in case you destroy the solution.

3.3 Training neural networks

Once the neural network has been designed, and the training data has been collected and encoded, the network may be trained. In reality, as we shall see, it may be necessary to build and train several networks on the same data set before a satisfactory solution is found.

3.3.1 Where to start

Although I've stated all along that there is a rule governing every decision to be made, there is one part of a neural network project which requires a little trial and error. We have reached that part. Building a neural network for any but the most trivial application requires that several networks are built, each of different complexity, or stopped at different points during training, or simply started from different random weight configurations. Each network should be saved, tested and analysed, and the most appropriate finally chosen. We have just seen how it is possible to jump out of local minima by setting the momentum term high; and how a copy of the weights should be saved before doing so. Every such trial should spawn a new network, and careful management is required if the resultant weights files are not to get out of hand.

A single final solution may be chosen from the population of networks produced during training, or a selection may be used as a "panel of experts". Results from several networks in the panel can be compared as an aid to determining the accuracy of the answer. Network outputs may be combined in several different ways: the average of all panel members can be calculated, or the output of the network with the most confidence may be used. Networks can be weighted with respect to their test error scores so that better networks contribute to the answer with greater strength. "Better" might mean a different thing in each case; it could mean more accurate, but it could also make reference to other costs associated with choosing an answer.

Another advantage of using a panel of neural networks is that the variation in output values from each may be used as an indication of the reliability of the final answer. The obvious disadvantage of using a panel of more than a few networks is the time taken to train each one.

3.3.2   Training modes: pattern or batch

The act of presenting the entire training set to the network once is known as an *epoch*. Due to the fact that the task for a neural network is to reduce the average error over the entire training set, it might seem a good idea to keep a running total of the errors produced by each output unit given each pattern in an epoch. Once the epoch has been completed, a single average error can be calculated and the network updated once according to that average error. This is indeed a valid mode of operation. It is referred to as *batch mode* learning. The alternative to batch mode learning, known as *pattern mode*, requires that the weights are updated after each single pattern presentation.

Choosing between the two modes is not easy, in fact the differences are often application specific. The following points should be borne in mind when choosing a training mode however:

- Batch mode requires less weight updates and is consequently faster.

- Batch mode provides a more accurate measurement of the required weight changes.

- Batch mode refers only to the weight adjustments; the errors must be back propagated for every pattern. Each unit must consequently store its running total; adding to network storage requirement.

- Batch mode is more likely than pattern mode to become trapped in a local minimum in error space.

- A network project often requires that several networks are trained on the same data before the most satisfactory solution is found. Training in different modes provides a good method for varying the type of solution a network might find.

3.3.3 Speeding up the training process

We have already mentioned how the learning parameter η may be set before the network is trained. It is also possible to dynamically tune this parameter during training in order to speed the process up a little. It is often desirable, although never absolutely necessary, to associate a dedicated learning parameter with every weight in the network. This can add to computation time, difficulty for the programmer and network instability and so should only be used if other such costs are not incurred. The following observations should help us speed up network training:

- If a given weight consistently changes in the same direction for several consecutive patterns, then we may increase the learning rate for that weight. This clearly requires an independent learning parameter for each weight.

- Conversely, if a weight changes in alternating directions on consecutive training patterns then its learning parameter should be decreased.

- If the error surface is very flat, then the learning rate may be increased to skim over that area. This simpler heuristic may be applied when only a single learning rate parameter is being used.

- When the error is large, we can afford to make larger changes to the weights.

- As the error rate becomes smaller, we want to make finer adjustments.

Note that inclusion of a momentum term automatically implements the effect required by the first two observations in the list above without the need for dedicated learning parameters.

The observations made above must be applied by small increments. That is to say that the learning parameters may be changed on a pattern by pattern basis, but any single pattern should only have a small effect on the learning rate. Such control is implemented by the introduction of yet another parameter, which dictates the learning parameter step size. It can also be wise to apply limits to the learning parameters. They clearly mustn't be allowed to reach zero as no learning may occur at that point.

Many software simulation packages contain an option for dynamic learning rate adaption. It should be borne in mind that the same mechanism which allows the algorithm to converge at high speed towards a solution also allows it to reach, and maintain, a local minimum at equally high speed. All of the above heuristics will prevent a network from climbing out of a local minimum. As we have already mentioned, one escape tactic is to save the weights, increase the learning parameters to very high values and then slowly bring them back down again. The hope is that the network will jump from the local minimum and continue its descent. If the tactic destroys the local solution completely, then it has been saved and so may be recovered.

Other hints to speed things up a little

Networks with asymmetric activation functions have been found to require fewer training epochs than networks with non-symmetric activation functions. A function is asymmetric if $f(-x) = -f(x)$. Section 3.4.3 describes a number of different activation functions and indicates their nature of symmetry.

Pre-coding and scaling the training data into a new file rather than doing so from the original data on-line obviously results in faster training times, as does using as small a network as possible. This second point means that time may be saved by starting with an oversimple model and increasing the complexity until the required trade off between accuracy and generalisation is reached.

Finally, it is worth considering the processor demands you may be placing on a computer which runs several windows at a time. Even personal computers running windows will allow you to set the network training in the background while you use another application. This often increases training time and slows the progress of the other programs running on the computer. A neural network is very processor dependent and does not leave many free cycles for other programs. Even having the screen saver running on your PC will eat up processor cycles that the neural network could have used. It is consequently desirable to have the use of a dedicated machine for the network training sessions.

Use can often be made of nights or weekends for training runs and it is advisable to plan a set of processes the computer can run, each with stopping criteria. In this way it is possible to generate several possible solutions over a weekend. Neural networks do take a long time to learn; leaving the computer running overnight is standard practice. It also gives you something to look forward to when you arrive at work the next morning!

3.3.4   When to stop training

There are several reasons for the lack of a simple rule for knowing when to stop a network learning. The first is that the back propagation algorithm cannot be guaranteed to converge. That is to say that it could well fail to find the weights configuration which returns the absolute error minimum. Secondly, the lowest possible error for a noisy data set is not zero, but we may not know what it actually is. The entropy measures presented in chapter 5 provide a good clue, but there is often no way of knowing just how good is good. The final important reason for a lack of stopping criteria is that back propagation is designed to reduce training error whereas our true goal is to reduce generalisation error.

Given the above riders, we can state that a neural network may be deemed to have settled (i.e. reached a point from which no improvement may be made) when one or more of the following criteria have been satisfied:

- The average training error has reached a predetermined target value.

- The average training error no longer falls, or falls by an insignificant amount.

- The average independent test error starts to rise, indicating the onset of overfitting.

3.3.5 Network health measures

Rather than looking at the error performance of a neural network, it is possible to gain an insight into the health of a network from the distribution of its weights values.

Weights histograms

We have seen that a network should have small weights if it is to be able to generalise well. This fact allows us to construct a very simple picture of the health of a network using what is known as a *weights histogram*. A weights histogram shows a count of the number of weights in a network which fall within each of a range of sizes.

Building a weights histogram

The counts may be plotted as a standard bar chart for ease of analysis. To construct a weights histogram, simply calculate the range over which the weights in a network vary. Split this range into a number (10 is a good size) of small sub-ranges and count the number of weights which fall into each sub-range. Plot a histogram with weight size along the bottom axis, starting a the most negative value at the left hand side and finishing with the highest value at the right hand side. The vertical axis shows the frequency of weights of each size.

Analysing a weights histogram

A healthy weights histogram will show a hump around the values with low magnitude (those near zero) indicating that most of the weights are low. Clearly, it is unlikely that any weights will actually carry a value of zero, so that may be excluded from the count. A histogram with peaks at the extremes of the horizontal axis has probably overfitted the data. Typical weight sizes will depend on the activation function used; a look at figure 3.1 reveals that the sigmoid output becomes very close to one or zero with an input of magnitude greater than five. Clearly, summed inputs to such units should rarely be in double figures.

The variance of the weights histogram

The astute reader (or one with a histogram option in their software package) will notice that an untrained network with low random weights will produce a healthy, though rather narrow looking, weights histogram. For this reason it is also a good idea to monitor the variance in the size of the weights as the network learns. Weights which do not move far from their initial random start points may not be contributing much to the solution (unless they happened to carry the correct value when initialised). If none of the weights in a network moves very far from their initial points, then the network has not learned.

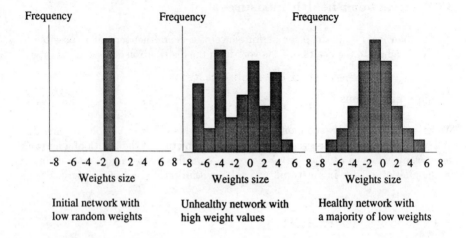

Figure 3.2: Three weights histograms: low random weights; high weights due to overfitting; a healthy network.

Initial weights should be set with random values between ±1; a healthy network might have weights with maximum magnitudes of around 10. Figure 3.2 shows some examples of good and bad weights histograms.

3.4   Implementation details

3.4.1   Network size approximation

The following formulae are really only a guide. There is no single formula for deriving network size as that depends on the structure and quality of the training data. These formulae may help however. The following notation is used:

n = Size of training set
p = Number of training patterns to be learned[2]
i = Number of input units
o = Number of output units
w = Number of weights
u = Total number of units
c = Capacity of a network
ϵ = Low error limit

---

[2]This is distinct from training set size in that a training set may have many examples of each pattern to be learned. The distinction is clear when we have a network which must perfectly remember P patterns but less so when we have N examples of a general nature.

With respect to inputs

$$h \leq 2i + 1 \tag{3.1}$$

With respect to the number of training patterns

$$w = i\log_2 p \tag{3.2}$$

Incorporating the number of output units

$$\frac{w}{o} \leq p \leq \frac{w}{o}\log_2\frac{w}{o} \tag{3.3}$$

With respect to target error

Assume an error limit such that $0 < \epsilon \leq 1/8$. A network which learns to classify the training set to an error of at most $\epsilon/2$ from a data set which satisfies the size constraint

$$n \geq \left(\frac{w}{\epsilon}\right) \tag{3.4}$$

will reach the error limit of ϵ for the test set.

If we can establish that our data set is large enough, then remembering that $0 < \epsilon \leq 1/8$ we can state that

$$w \approx \epsilon n \tag{3.5}$$

3.4.2 Entropy based constructive networks

The information carried by any network node, x, depends on the probabilities $P(g)$ of each of the n possible output pattern g occurring and is defined as

$$H(x) = -\sum_{g=0}^{n} P(g)(\log_2(P(g))) \tag{3.6}$$

The joint information between two units, x and y is defined as

$$H(x,y) = -\sum_{g=0}^{n}\sum_{h=0}^{m} P(g,h)(\log_2(P(g,h))) \tag{3.7}$$

where there are m possible patterns h for unit y to take and $P(g,h)$ is the probability that unit x will hold pattern g and unit y will hold pattern h.

We now need to be able to calculate the interdependency between two units, $U(x, y)$:

$$U(x, y) = 2\left(\frac{H(x) + H(y) - H(x, y)}{H(x) + H(y)}\right) \qquad (3.8)$$

If we calculate the interdependency between a hidden unit x and an output unit y as $HO(x, y)$ and the interdependency between two hidden units as $HH(x, y)$, then the importance of a node, $I(x)$ can be calculated as

$$I(x) = \sum_y HO(x, y) - \sum_{y, y \neq x} HH(x, y) \qquad (3.9)$$

I.e. the sum of the interdependencies between the hidden unit and the output layer minus the sum of the interdependencies between the hidden unit and the other hidden units. The hidden unit with the lowest importance will be dropped from the network.

3.4.3   Activation functions

Any activation function multiplies each incoming activation, $a_{1...n}$ with the weight, $w_{1...n}$ along which it travelled and sums the results. This summed value, x is passed through a transfer function, $f(x)$ to produce the output value, o, for the unit. The standard form of the activation function is consequently

$$o = f(\sum_{i=1}^{n} a_i w_i) \qquad (3.10)$$

Some of the different forms which the function f may take are shown below. They are expressed in terms of an input, x which is the weighted sum given in equation 3.10 above, and an output, y which becomes o in equation 3.10. Each function includes a term, γ which controls the slope of the function so that $\gamma < 1$ reduces the slope and $\gamma > 1$ increases it. The slope of the curve has an effect on factors such as the degree of sharpness with which categories may be separated.

Linear functions

A linear function simply outputs a value proportional to the summed inputs. The proportion is determined by the slope, γ. The activation function is simply

$$f(x) = \gamma x \qquad (3.11)$$

The derivative of such a function is simply the constant $f'(y) = 1/\gamma$, i.e. in order to make a change of δy on the output, you should make a change of $\gamma \delta y$.

Logistic functions

The most used activation function is the logistic function. This has the form:

$$f(x) = \frac{1}{1 + e^{-x}} \tag{3.12}$$

The logistic function is non-symmetric and so may lead to slightly longer training times.

The derivative of this activation function is $1/(e^x(1 + e^{-x})^2)$. By substitution, we can express the function in terms of the output of the unit as

$$f'(y) = \gamma y(1 - y) \tag{3.13}$$

This allows us to translate an error on the output of a unit to one on its input in order to change the incoming weights.

Tanh functions

$$f(x) = \tanh(\gamma x) \equiv \frac{e^{\gamma x} - x^{-\gamma x}}{e^{\gamma x} + e^{-\gamma x}} \tag{3.14}$$

Tanh is an asymmetric function and so may improve learning speed.

The derivative in terms of the output, y is

$$f'(y) = \gamma(1 - y^2) \tag{3.15}$$

A noisy input activation function

Here is a very simple activation function which takes the raw input value, I, and produces a new, noisy value, $\hat{I}$, where the amplitude of the noise is controlled by λ:

$$\hat{I} = I + \lambda \text{rand}() \tag{3.16}$$

where rand() returns a value between minus 1 and 1 and λ falls between 0 and 1 (its normal range, however, will be closer to that of 0 to 0.2 where 0.2 is 20% noise). The noise is added as an aid to generalisation and a method for avoiding local sub-optimal solutions.

3.4.4   Error measures

For clarity, the following notation will be used:

$target_i$ = the desired output from unit i.
$output_i$ = the actual output from unit i.
$error_i$ = the error on unit i.
$\overline{error}$ = the average error over a set of outputs.

Simple difference error

Used to calculate the error on a single output unit, the simple difference error may be positive or negative:

$$error_i = target_i - actual_i \tag{3.17}$$

Root mean squared error

To calculate the error across the entire output for evaluation purposes:

$$\overline{error} = \sqrt{\sum_{i=1}^{n}(target_i - actual_i)^2} \tag{3.18}$$

Simple weighted difference error

The simple weighted error is calculated as

$$error_i = W_p(target_i - actual_i) \tag{3.19}$$

where W_p is the weight associated with training pattern p and falls in the range from 0 to 1.

Weighted root mean squared error

The weighted RSE is calculated as

$$error_i = W_p\sqrt{\sum_{i=1}^{n}(target_i - actual_i)^2} \tag{3.20}$$

where W_p is the weight associated with pattern p. The weight can be seen as a discount term so that errors made on unreliable data appear to be smaller.

3.4.5   Adding a regularisation term to the cost function

A new parameter, λ is introduced which controls the degree of regularisation to be added. The quadratic term is used to penalise larger weights more than smaller weights and to compensate for negative valued weights.

$$reg\_error_i = \frac{\lambda}{p} \sum_l w_l^2 \qquad (3.21)$$

where:

λ = Regularisation parameter
p = Number of patterns in the training set
w_l = Weight l
l = Weight index

The error value to be used for weight update is simply

$$error_i = error_i + reg\_error_i \qquad (3.22)$$

where $error_i$ was calculated by any of the above means.

3.4.6   Use of a momentum term

The weight update rule with momentum includes a term which is a proportion (dictated by α) of the previous weight change. The addition of the (t) term indicates the given value at time t:

$$\Delta w_{ji}(t) = \alpha \Delta w_{ji}(t-1) + \eta \, e_j(t) o_i(t) \qquad (3.23)$$

Note that the recorded value of the previous weight change, $\Delta w_{ji}(t-1)$, will include the momentum term from the step before, i.e. it will simply be the value produced by equation 3.23 at time $t-1$.

Chapter 4

Time varying systems

The future ain't what it used to be

Jim Steinman

Throughout the book we are making two main distinctions amongst neural network applications: they are either prediction tasks or classification tasks, and they are either temporal tasks or static tasks. This chapter investigates the difference between temporal and static neural networks. It presents the standard time delay neural network and simple recurrent network architectures along with a new method which overcomes the limitations of the existing systems.

4.1 Time varying data sets

This section views the task of modelling a time series as being equivalent to that of modelling the system which produced the series of data in question. In chapter 1 a temporally dependent system was defined as follows:

> A system is said to be temporally dependent if a given input to that system elicits a different response depending on previous inputs to that system or the previous system state.

This chapter discusses a set of methods for modelling and understanding such systems.

4.1.1 An introduction to time series analysis

Before investigating the neural network based techniques available for time series analysis, it is worth taking a moment to look at the type of time series based problems we will be addressing. Broadly speaking there are two types of analysis we might like to carry out on a set of time varying data: prediction which involves calculating future values of the time series, and classification which involves describing some fundamental aspects of a set of different classes of sequence. For the main body of this chapter, where we talk about prediction, we are referring to one step ahead prediction. Going further into the future is considered at the end of the section.

Terms of definition for a time series

There are two types of variable to which we can refer when defining a time series: we can define the series in terms of the elapsed time since the start of the series, or in terms of a number of the previous values in the series. In theory it is often easier to define a series by elapsed time, t as the function is often simpler. In practice however, and this applies especially to neural network models, it is unrealistic to use t as an input. This is partly because t may not be important, and partly because t might grow too large.

Let us take the task of learning a sine wave as an example. If we tried to learn the function with respect to time, t, we would be solving $x_t = \sin(t)$. Learning the sequence with reference only to previous values is equivalent to solving the second order difference equation $x_t = f(x_{t-1}, x_{t-2})$ which seems far harder. However, if we try to learn the function with respect to t we would have to deal with a range of input values for t which is unbounded, thus making reduction to the range from zero to one for input to the network difficult. Secondly, it would be less obvious how much training data to use: at which value of t should we stop? If instead, we attempt to learn to predict subsequent values from the two previous values in a series, the inputs are naturally bounded between plus and minus one, and we need only see 2π examples to cover the entire equation space. Clearly in this case, the apparently easier function is in fact the harder one to learn.

Choosing between explicit or implicit temporal representation

When choosing whether to represent time as a distinct explicit variable or allowing the neural network to implicitly learn temporal associations for itself, we must consider whether such temporal associations exist. In chapter 1 we defined a temporally dependent system as one in which the current output is determined by both the current inputs and the previous system state. For such cases, it is not necessary (and often, for the reasons described above, not wise) to code time as an extra variable for models of such systems. However, there are many examples where temporal variables should be coded explicitly.

Considering the example of daily demand forecasting for a baker's, we know that time will be a factor, but we also know that the demand for any particular day will depend less on the demand for the previous day and more on temporal factors such as weekends and bank holidays. Such factors should be coded explicitly. In this case, the fact that today is a holiday or weekend is more important than any temporal dependency. In such cases it is wiser to use a single input unit to flag that a day is a weekend and forget that time is involved at all.

A final point worth making is that a variable does not have to vary in a predictable way before it may be classed as temporally dependent. There are two main reasons why we might be interested in a time series. The first is that we might want to predict the future based on the past, in which case we should choose a variable with predictive power. The second is the case where we need to know about the past in order to make a calculation based on the state of things in the present. The position of a power control on an oven, for example, is not predictable in its self and tells us little about the oven's current temperature. A history of control settings since the oven was turned on, or an abstraction of the oven state based on such a history however, may help us to calculate the current oven temperature. It still cannot help us predict the next oven setting.

Embedding dimensions

When trying to build a prediction model for a time series, it is important to be able to characterise the *embedding dimension* of the series. The embedding dimension defines the number of previous values from the series which go in to determining the next. In other words, it is equivalent to the order of a differential equation which would define the series with respect to previous values. It does not necessarily tell us which values are important, just how many. In the simple case, we assume that the most recent values determine the next one. A time series in which the previous two values suffice to determine the current one (using the sine wave example: we need the last value to know where in the wave we are, and the value before it to know whether we are travelling up or down the wave) has an embedding dimension of two.

The embedding dimension is important when choosing neural network architecture as it affects the number of inputs in a time delay neural network and the number of hidden units in a recurrent network. It also tells us how much data we need to collect in order to build a reliable neural network model.

The state space of a time series

Takens [103] proved that if you take a sufficiently long vector made up of past values in a time series, you can reconstruct the full underlying structure of the system dynamics which produced the sequence. Of course, taking a large number of past values leaves you with an awfully large number of degrees of freedom in your system. Fortunately, it is not often that a system will move fully through the whole space made available by a long series of continuous numbers. Defining the sub-space through which it does move is an important aspect of system characterisation.

Weigend and Gershenfeld [115] define four spaces over which a time series may be considered:

1. The *configuration manifold* of a system is the whole space over which it could move unrestricted by any defining constraints. This space has a number of dimensions equal to the number of time steps you choose to take backwards from t. Taking our sine wave example, to plot the past two values against the

value which follows, we would need a three dimensional space spanning minus
one to one in each dimension.

2. Smaller (most often) than the configuration space, is the *solution manifold* which
   is the space which the system really travels along as it unfolds. By plotting our
   set of three consecutive sine wave values, each one against the others, we would
   see that an elliptical path is described through the configuration manifold. Had
   we chosen a window of more than three steps, we would see that only three of the
   dimensions are actually needed: that only two of the dimensions are required to
   fully determine the value of the third. Thus we have an embedding dimension
   of two.

3. In a different space altogether, we have the *observable*. This is the actual time
   series; in our example the sine wave plotted along a single axis, t. The observables for a single time series move through a single dimensional space, but are
   usually plotted against a second: that of time.

4. It is possible to build a *reconstructed state space* of the observed system by
   taking a time lagged vector as described above or by use of a recurrent neural
   network in which the hidden units represent the solution manifold. Takens [103]
   theorem, which is referred to throughout the book, tells us that it is possible to
   reconstruct state space from the observables alone, and it is this reconstruction
   to which Ruelle refers in the discussion on embedding dimensions below.

Figure 4.1 shows (in three dimensions) how the solution manifold compares to the
observable. Remember that in three dimensions, the configuration manifold would be
a solid cube.

A more tangible example is provided by considering somebody planning a driving holiday in the Scottish Highlands. Our task is to predict where our holiday maker might
go, based on the behaviour of drivers we have observed before him. The configuration
manifold of our task is the entire Scottish Highlands: every hill, glen and loch. As
we have no insight into the internal structure of the country, we cannot see the roads,
but they are there, and they define the solution manifold of our problem; they define,
out of the entire country, the parts along which the solution will lie.

In a slightly tenuous extension to our story, let us say we can look down over the
country at night and watch the headlights describe a set of paths through the darkness.
These are the observables, and if we plot their progress we will end up with a map,
or a reconstructed state space. The hidden states, such as the angle of the steering
wheel, do not need to be measured because they can be inferred from the observables.
This example has one other quality worthy of a mention: it has areas of very high
predictability such as the road which curls through Glencoe, and other areas which
provide no predictive information such as Inverness city centre. This is also true of
many dynamic systems which we may want to model with a neural network.

A final point that needs to be made is that in the example above, it is the environment
in which the system (the car) is acting which defines its solution manifold. There
are also restrictions within the system itself which dictate the limited set of future
positions given the current position. Even if we were following the car across the

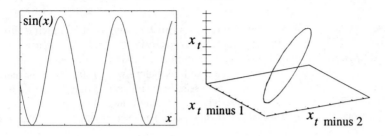

Figure 4.1: The observable sine wave and its three dimensional solution manifold.

Arizona desert, the physics which govern a speeding car would restrict each new position it took to a narrow angular window to the front of the car.

4.1.2 Chaos and non-linearity in time series

If we are planning to model a time varying system using a neural network, then it follows that we know, or at least suspect, that non-linearities are present in the system. A system is said to exhibit non-linear behaviour if it will diverge from two proximal points at a speed which does not remain constant. A system may be non-linear without being chaotic but becomes chaotic when the non-linearaties are such that the system will diverge from two proximal states at an exponential rate. The rate at which the system diverges from two such points is expressed as 2^λ where λ is the Lyaponov exponent of the system. If $\lambda=1$ then the distance between trajectories doubles every step. A system is called chaotic if it has at least one positive Lyaponov exponent. Clearly, no linear system can be chaotic as it can never diverge at a greater than linear rate.

Yao and Tong [122] have claimed that the more information carried in a time series, the greater the divergence rate. Yao and Tong state that an accumulation of noise in the time series reduces the potential for chaos as there is more overlap in the trajectories. They showed how a system could have a different divergence rate at different points in its state space. Such systems would not simply diverge, but would, at places, come back together again. In practical terms this means that we have more predictive power at some points in a time series than we do at others. Yao and Tong showed that for an example data set, divergence rate was smallest at steep sections in the time series, i.e. where $f'(x_n)$ was large. This fact has implications for deriving confidence limits from predictions made by a neural network which has been trained on noisy chaotic data.

4.1.3   Summary of time series analysis concepts

We have seen how a single valued time series can be thought of as moving through
a number of different spaces and that the trajectories through each space may be
modelled from the observables alone. It is important that we know how many steps
back in the series of observables we need to look before we can fully reconstruct the
state space of a time series. We have also seen how time series may be considered as
linear, non-linear or chaotic systems. The task facing a neural engineer is to train a
neural network to reconstruct the state space of a time series and thus either predict
future values or classify previous ones.

4.2   Neural networks for predicting or classifying time series

Neural network architectures and data coding strategies are discussed elsewhere in the
book, but here is a quick re-cap on the two types of temporal neural networks most
often used. Following that is a discussion on the use of these two network types on
the range of problem types discussed above. The pros and cons of each are considered
and, where applicable, recommendations made.

4.2.1   Time delay neural networks

Another look at figure 4.1 tells us that if we wish to predict future values of our sine
wave we may do one of two things: one method is to build a network whose input
consists of the previous two values (two of the three dimensions in the figure) and
whose output equals the current value (the third dimension). As there is a one to one
mapping between the two inputs and the output, this is a good solution. Combining
past values into a static vector is known as time lagging or temporal windowing as you
are using a lagged window which moves over the whole series as the network input.
Networks which use data in this way are called Time delay neural networks (TDNNs)
and are discussed at length in chapter 2 on data pre-processing and chapter 9 on
signal processing.

Waibel [112] extended the concept of a time delay on the input layer to include the
hidden layers. A window is moved over a set of previous hidden unit values to form
the inputs to the next layer. It is not clear how such a practice improves the ability
of the network. It is clear, however, that it increases the number of weights required
by the network and consequently affects the quantity of data required and the choice
of hidden layer size. More advanced TDNNs, as discussed in chapter 9, are made up
of a series of copies of the same set of weights. This reduces the number of degrees of
freedom of the weight space and consequently reduces the complexity of the model.
They are also more difficult to implement.

4.2.2   Recurrent networks

Another method for representing time is to give a recurrent network single values in a sequence in turn and allow it to build its own short term memory to code the trajectory along the solution manifold. Testing this on the sine wave example showed that the hidden unit actually took on the previous value in the series, thus building its own time lag. This is not always the case however. Elman [33], for example, showed how a recurrent network which learned to predict words in sentences structured the hidden layer to arrange words into groups with similar meaning. Pearlmutter [72] has demonstrated how a recurrent network builds a representation of the state space of the system to be modelled. Based on this, Pearlmutter was able to train a neural network to follow circular and figure-of-eight shaped limit cycles which were robust enough to attract the system back onto the cycle after a perturbation.

Elman [33] showed how a recurrent network was able to learn temporal dependencies in grammatical sentences. Williams and Zipser [119] showed how a fully recurrent neural network was capable of simulating a Turing machine and so of reproducing any deterministic sequence and Cleeremans [24] showed how a recurrent network was able to reproduce a finite state automata.

Lin [57] found that recurrent networks, used for reinforcement learning, had the advantage of being able to use the features in the system's history which are relevant to the task to be learned. Here lies the fundamental difference between time delay networks and recurrent networks: the former reconstruct the state space of a system from past system outputs alone whereas the latter build an internal state representation which extracts features from the original sequence. Psarrou and Buxton [78] state that the feature extraction carried out by a recurrent neural network removes the need for a temporal buffer and removes the problem associated with an element having an exact temporal position.

By building a recurrent network with one input unit representing the value of the time series at time t, one output unit representing the value of the time series at time $t + 1$ and a recurrent layer to store and re-apply the state of the hidden layer from time t, we can forecast one step ahead along a time series. By taking the network output and feeding it back as input, this method can be extended to multiple steps forward.

Deriving a target error

When predicting one step ahead along a time series, the target for the training error must be set to a level less than the smallest difference between successive elements in the series. As we will see with reference to financial prediction, there is a locally optimal solution in predicting that the next value will equal the current value if the values change little from step to step. If the sine waves were given in the range zero to one, the network squashed the peaks and troughs so that they did not reach the poles of the range. Such errors are due to the fact that the sigmoidal squashing function outputs values of one and zero only as their inputs tend to infinity. Training with a sine wave which cycles between 0.1 and 0.9 produced better results.

Examining the error rates produced by such networks as they learn revealed an interesting phenomenon. The error would decrease as expected but, as it slowly became smaller, would suddenly leap to a value of anything up to 80%. From this point, the network would sometimes recover and sometimes continue to fluctuate wildly, never settling to a state near that from which it jumped. I was unable to predict or control such instabilities, only to recognise that if a network displayed such behaviour, that the weights which were saved before should be used as the final solution if their performance is acceptable and, if it is not, that the training must start again from a new random point.

Note that when teaching a network more than one example sequence, it is important to mix the presentations from each example at random. When using a multiple recurrent network, the multiple context layers ensure that the series do not become confused with each other when they are mixed. When using a TDNN, each new input window is not related to the last, so ordering is less of a worry, and a window should be picked from a random example sequence on each presentation.

4.3   Choosing the best method for the task

Before we can consider modelling a time varying system, we must consider the type of data series we have. This section discusses the different types of data set which require a temporal network along with a comparison of each type of available modelling technique. Distinctions are made between single and multiple sequences, and between systems which do, or do not require extra non-temporal inputs.

4.3.1   Single or multiple time series

A single time series may occur over several channels and in that sense it is proper to consider a series of vectors rather than of single values. Multiple time series, on the other hand, are produced when there are several example sequences over the same set of variables. Measurement of a sequence of temperature and pressure values as they unfold over time is consequently a single time series based task. Repeating that measure for several different runs of a machine produces multiple sequences. If we have multiple series, we might either want to categorise each sequence, or to build a general predictive model based on all of the example sequences.

There are many examples of problems based on a single time series, for example financial prediction. The network task is to look at recent values in the series and predict values of either the same series or a related one. For example we might look at a history of temperature data and predict either future temperatures or an estimate of the present, or future pressure measurement. A sequential learning task, as we have seen, becomes multiple in nature when a set of example sequences are taken from the same variables. The examples may be passed one by one through a simple recurrent network or, to ensure a more even spread of examples, a multiple recurrent network may be used. Where the number of examples is high, a trade-off must be made between adding extra context layers, which slow down the processing, or concatenating examples at the risk of unbalancing the training process. Training speed is the only cost of adding extra context layers as they are not used in the final model and so do not add to the number of weights the network contains. The process is simply an algorithmic extension to aid the learning process.

Where data is spread over many channels, time delay networks suffer from the need to build a window over each. A recurrent network has the advantage that non-independent input channels may be combined and features extracted at the hidden layer without the need for a specific window over each channel. In the temperature/pressure example introduced above, the hidden layer will be able to build an abstract representation based on the fact that the two input measures are co-dependent. A time delay network will not be able to make use of this fact as the history of each variable, rather than the features from the hidden layer, have to be added to the current input vector at each time slice. The ability of the hidden layer to extract features over more than one channel is related to the intrinsic dimensionality between the inputs, as discussed in chapter 2.

The most obvious type of problem requiring the modelling of many sequences is that of time series classification. The network requires a set of examples from each class of series along with target outputs denoting membership. Speech recognition problems are of this type. Section 2.6.1 discusses coding methods for output categories. Time delay networks are useful for such tasks as they do not have memories and so do not become confused as example time slices from different data sets are presented one after another. They do, however, suffer the same explosion in required input units as discussed above. Simple recurrent networks fail such a task as it is not possible to mix a set of example sequences without disrupting the network's memory. Multiple recurrent networks overcome this problem.

4.3.2 Other variables which affect system behaviour

We have seen that a single time series may actually be a sequence of vectors. The next question concerns the case where not all of the vector components are temporally dependent.

Predictable and unpredictable inputs

Returning to the example of the car in the desert, but assuming that we can measure the steering wheel and throttle control, rather than relying on a map, we see that there are two types of variable which affect the car's next position. The first set of variables are temporally dependent and predictable; given the current speed and direction, and no external inputs, you can predict the next value of each. This is an example of multi-channelled inputs as mentioned above. However, the second set have neither of those properties; the steering and throttle angle are unpredictable from one step to the next and should not be treated as temporal variables. Trying to predict the control movements will meet with no success, but predicting the speed and car angle given their history and the current control movements is perfectly possible.

It is important to identify which values from a set of inputs and observables in a system are temporally dependent. As we shall see in the chapter on process control, there is an important distinction between inputs to the network which are control signals, and those which describe the system state. Throttle movement is a control signal, current speed describes a system state. Both affect the state of the car at the next time slice.

Recurrent networks are unsuitable for tasks which include a non-temporal element. As the entire input layer is referred to when the context layer is built, it is difficult to include static variables without them being treated as part of a time series. Including everything as part of the system history introduces extra complexity which we not only do not need, but which actually makes the task harder as it contains no structure. An obvious way around this limitation is to split the hidden layer in two: one part for temporally dependent variables and another for independent variables. Only the values in the temporal portion of the hidden layer would be fed back into the recurrent context buffer, thus ensuring that the effect of non-temporal inputs is limited to the time step at which they are received. All the hidden units would be connected to the output layer in the normal manner.

It is easy to separate off the non-temporal variables using a TDNN: simply do not use a window over them. The input vector would consist of a window over the time varying data and single input units for the others. In the case where none of the variables is temporally dependent, the network becomes a standard MLP. In the case of our car example, a window would be required over the previous few values of speed and angle, but only a single input each for steering and throttle angle.

There is also the possibility of coding temporal events as static variables. Hours may be coded as a counter, 0 to 23, for example or certain events such as holidays flagged in a binary fashion. This last type of variable seems temporally dependent as it may follow a cycle or be determined by time, but it is not necessarily the case that any predictive information is contained therein. The aspect of a variable which is most salient to the task in hand should govern the method in which it is coded.

Initial conditions

A somewhat confusing issue concerns the initial state of a system before it produces a time series. There are two main cases worth noting. The first is when a system always follows the same path through state space but can start in any state (i.e. any place along that path). The second involves a system with control settings which determine how it acts, which are set at the start and which remain constant throughout a single system run. In many cases these two conditions are more similar than one would expect.

Let us take a very simple time series as an example, where $x_{t+1} = x_t^2$. By setting t_0 to an arbitrary value, we choose the first state of the system. By noting the first output of the system as it runs, we can define the start state of the network. If x_{t+1} depends on more than one previous value, we would need to supply sufficient values to represent the system state. Once a sufficient number of output values have been seen, the system state is defined, so putting the network in the correct initial state is simply a process of showing it a sufficient number of values produced by the real system. This can be seen as a process of matching the model to the real system so that the two run in parallel.

If we now introduce a constant, Ω into the function so that $x_{t+1} = \Omega x_t^2$, we see that a different value of Ω produces a different trajectory through state space. As long as the first few values of the series are available, it is not necessary to explicitly account for Ω in a network as the path the system takes still wholly describes its state. The example below shows how a network trained on such a task is able to generalise to new values of Ω from a limited example set.

A multi-recurrent network was trained on four examples of the time series $x_t = \Omega x_{t-1}^2$ with Ω values of $1, 0.5, 0.3$, and 0.25. The network was not shown the values of Ω, just the data values. Having reached an average error of 0.003, the network was tested on data sets with new Ω values and generalised perfectly. Note that whilst Ω affects the behaviour of the system, it does so in a way which is made explicit by the system's behaviour and therefore does not have to be included as a control variable.

Modelling state space

A TDNN makes the relationship between the time delayed input vector and the predicted output explicit. State space is reconstructed directly from the time lagged vector. Recurrent networks, however, build a representation of state space in the hidden layer. It can be argued that this more abstract representation of state space makes learning easier. Certain systems may have a simple set of internal variables which determine their behaviour more directly than past observables. The immediately obvious problem with such variables is that they are not observable; they must be derived from the observables. Recurrent networks use their context units to do just that and can therefore build simpler models than a TDNN given the same data. Lin [57] found that recurrent networks, used for reinforcement learning, had the advantage of only using the features in the system history which are relevant to the task to be learned. He also found that some problems from which features may be extracted, such as route finding, were better solved by recurrent networks; however, others which do not contain such features, such as pole balancing, were more easily solved with TDNNs.

4.3.3 Problems associated with recurrent networks

Calculating entropy values for data analysis

As a recurrent network uses its own internal states as part of the input vector, it is impossible to know, before the network is trained, what the full network input will be. This means that we cannot use the same information theory based techniques that we can for static data. Given that a time lagged window does hold all the information which the hidden layer could later represent, it is possible to carry out the entropy analysis on such a window. As we saw from Ruelle's theorem, the data requirement for such an analysis grows exponentially with window size. Yao and Tong [122] have shown it is possible to reduce that growth to less than exponential by incrementally building a model of the system which underlies the data. Entropy analysis on a lagged window consequently requires far more data than a recurrent network does and so cannot necessarily be used as a method for calculating the potential applicability of the latter to a given data set. I am not aware of any method for solving this problem which is less complex than the task of building a recurrent network.

Understanding the context layer

The fact that recurrent networks have a short term memory can either help or hinder the user depending on the nature of the problem at hand. The recurrent network might build a more concise model, with all the advantages in generalisation associated with such a model, but it removes some of the ease with which the model may be used and introduces the added mystery of the context layer. What values should it take before any context is known? With a TDNN, there is no mystery: it associates a lagged time vector with a target output. Take any slice of a series and you have all you need to generate an answer. We have seen that a recurrent network is able to move into phase with a simple signal but it is not clear how many steps the network must take before it reaches that phase.

Deriving explanations

Chapter 7 shows how it is possible to derive explanations of network outputs with respect the input values they receive. The context layer is part of the input vector to a neural network and it can be difficult to understand the explanations given in terms of those context units. A TDNN has no such inputs and so it is possible to derive explanations based on the lagged window. Even for a TDNN however, such explanations are not always very useful, so this limitation should not be viewed as a serious one unless explanations in terms of network derivatives are specifically required.

Measuring window size

If the embedding dimension of the system to be modelled is not known, then it can be difficult to choose a good window size for a TDNN. Bodenhausen and Waibel [17] have proposed an algorithm called Tempo2 which automatically adjusts the time delays and the window size in a TDNN. In this way the embedding dimension of the series may be estimated. They also use a Gaussian weighted window rather than a square one which means that a steeply dropping curve is imposed on the vector of past values making more recent values more important than those further away. The peak of the curve may be moved so that a different value is deemed most important. Such a method is described in detail in section 2.7.1.

The memory built by a recurrent network removes the need for worrying about window size, but introduces the difficulty of not knowing how far back the network looks.

Elman [34] warns us, however, that elements which occur over seven time steps previous to the current one have little chance of affecting the current output. The related fact that a recurrent network dictates the size of the input layer is of little consequence as the size of the window has the same effect on a TDNN. The difference in size between the time windowed inputs and the recurrent context layer depends on the degree of abstraction which can be gained by extracting features over the series of input vectors. One would expect the recurrent hidden layer to be smaller than the delay window of an equivalent TDNN however, as it holds one more level of abstraction than the TDNN input.

4.3.4 Summary of choices when selecting a recurrent or time delay network

- The coding of states in a recurrent network requires reference to the previous states of the time series. If you need to operate the network with a small window as input, without reference to previous values in the series, use a TDNN.

- If you suspect that the contents of the chosen window have a simpler underlying structure, a recurrent network will be better at extracting that structure. Structure may also be present across several channels of input data.

- If you do not know how many time steps are needed, use a recurrent network. If you suspect that you would need more than seven however, you may need to use a TDNN.

- If the network needs to use extra, non-temporal inputs, a TDNN is more appropriate.

- If you choose one method and it fails, you have two options: one is to widen the window or increase the size of the hidden layer. The other is to use the method you haven't already tried.

- If you have chosen a recurrent network, use one context layer for each category in your data set. If your software package does not support this option, and you have multiple categories, use a TDNN.

Hybrid solutions

As always, a compromise is possible. For time series in which temporal dependency is deep, or on several levels, it can be a good idea to use a recurrent network with time delayed input. This sentence, for example, might be coded as an input window which recognised each word, and which fed into a recurrent network which was responsible for extracting sentence structure.

4.4   Predicting more than one step into the future

Predicting more than one step ahead in noisy, non-linear, or chaotic time series can be dangerous. The simplest method involves taking the last output and feeding it back in as input on the next time slice. Errors, of course, are magnified and it is easy for the network to wander quickly off track. Refenes [79] presents a model for mapping a lagged window on the input to a lagged output window containing more than one prediction. His paper only ever uses an output window size of one however, probably due to the fact that increasing the window size would require exponentially more training data.

A good solution to the problem of multiplicative errors is to add noise to the training set. In this way the network learns to map a noisier band of inputs to the correct output and so is able to correct small errors. The noise can be random or, when network error is low enough, new training data can be built bont the network's slightly erroneous outputs from the previous pass through the data. In this way a network can learn to correct its own prediction errors.

If the output prediction is a category or a feature which is also available on the input layer, as in the grammar based examples given below, errors can be removed completely by applying a threshold to force the output to zero or one before it is fed back to the input as a binary representation.

4.4.1   Calculating the embedding dimension of a time series

Ruelle [85] has stated that with a data set of size N, the effective embedding dimension is restrained to being less than $2\log N$ which means that the required data set size grows exponentially according to the embedding dimension: the so called curse of dimensionality. Cheng and Tong [23] state that the embedding dimension need only be bounded by

$$d < \frac{\sqrt{N(error)^2}}{\sigma^2} \qquad (4.1)$$

where $error$ is a measure of data not accounted for by a d dimensional model and σ^2 is a measure of the amount of noise present in the system.

Hence the curse of dimensionality may be lifted slightly as this is not an exponential function. To apply this theory for practical use, it is necessary to build several models, each with a different embedding dimension, and calculate the error for each. One must then balance the error with the size of the training set, N, to ensure that inequality 4.1 is satisfied. The theory is of use because it tells us that it is possible to build a predictive model with a training set which is smaller than the exponential of the embedding dimension. It also allows us to manage the trade-off between error (i.e. accuracy) and training set size. Inequality 4.1 allows us to calculate how much more data would be required in order to reduce the error by increasing the embedding dimension.

It should now become clear how this theory relates to the architecture of a temporal neural network. Increasing the embedding dimension increases the size of the input layer in a TDNN and the hidden layer in a recurrent MLP. A larger network requires a larger training set and inequality 4.1 tells us how much larger the training set must be.

That concludes the discussion on time varying systems. The remainder of the chapter demonstrates some of the principles introduced above through a series of experiments.

4.5   Learning separate paths through state space

This section discusses a series of experiments in which we trained multiple recurrent networks on a number of periodic prediction tasks to discover more about their ability. A number of different studies were carried out, each based around the following set of methods:

- A set of training sine waves was built, each with the same amplitude, but each with different frequencies. The waves were fully rectified to fall within the range from zero to one.

- A multiple recurrent network with a number of context buffers equal to the number of sine waves to be learned was trained to perform one step ahead prediction of each of the sine waves.

- Each network was tested on its ability to predict one step ahead and many steps ahead for simple sine waves taken from the training set. One step ahead prediction was done by training the network to output the sine wave value which immeadiatly follows its current input. Multiple step predictions were done by feeding back each single step prediction to be used as input at the next step.

- Networks were also tested on their ability to predict future values of complex waves which were build by adding a number of the simple training waves.

- Networks were also tested on their ability to switch from one sine wave to another within a single time series.

4.5.1   Predicting simple sine waves

Learning sine waves with similar and distant frequencies

Figure 4.2 shows the results of training a multiple recurrent network to predict two sine waves of different frequencies. In one case, the ratio between the frequencies was 4:3, and in the other case it was 4:1. Note that the higher frequency waves were more smoothly predicted in both cases, but in the case where the frequencies are far apart, the low frequency wave is poorly learned.

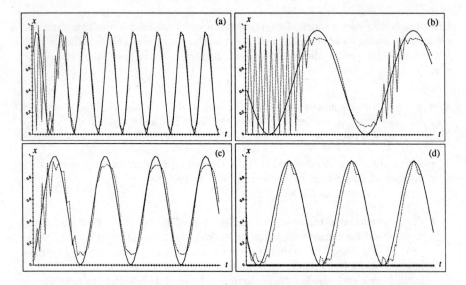

Figure 4.2: Learning two sine waves with varying distances between the frequencies. (a) and (b) show predictions from a network trained on two different sine waves with distant frequencies, (c) and (d) show the same results for sine waves with closer frequencies. The smooth line describes the target values and the other describes the network output.

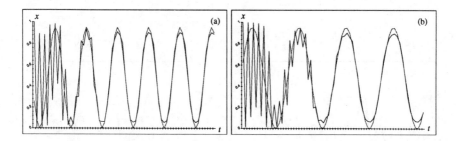

Figure 4.3: Predicting sine waves from a learned population of six different frequencies. Note that high frequency errors are made until the network recurrent layer settles into the correct part of state space.The smooth line describes the target values and the other describes the network output.

Learning more than two sine waves

A second network was trained on six sine waves of different frequencies with ratios of 1:2:3:4:6:8. The network was able to complete the task, and predict values of each sine wave in isolation. Figure 4.3 shows an example of the network making predictions over two simple sine waves taken from the set of six. Note that the initial conditions are identical for every sine wave in that the recurrent layer is reset to zero at the start of the presentation of each. For this reason, the network is not able to instantly follow the given curve, but must wait until the inputs have pulled the recurrent layer into the right area of state space. Again, the errors which the network makes cause it to predict high frequency components when none is present.

Predicting complex waves

The network which had been trained on the six pure sine waves was tested on its ability to predict future values of a complex wave. The complex wave was formed by adding a number of the pure sine waves together, but the network was not re-trained on the data so produced. Figure 4.4 shows two examples of the results of such a task. The only difference between the two conditions is that in (a) the learning process was stopped earlier than that of (b).

Jumping from one frequency to another

The final test of the investigation into the networks' ability to predict one step ahead involved jumping from one frequency to another within a signal. Figure 4.5 shows an example of the network jumping from a low frequency wave to one of a higher frequency. The network is only being asked to perform one step ahead prediction and is consequently pulled from one trajectory to the other.

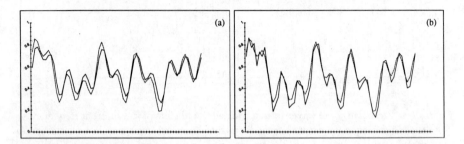

Figure 4.4: Predicting single steps ahead of a time series, x_t on which a network was not trained, but which has component frequencies of pure sine waves on which the network was trained. (a) Shows an undertrained network, (b) shows a network which was overtrained.

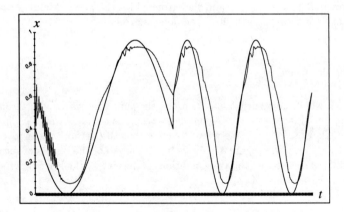

Figure 4.5: Predicting single steps ahead of a time series which jumps from a sine wave at one frequency to one at another. The smooth line describes the target values and the other describes the network output.

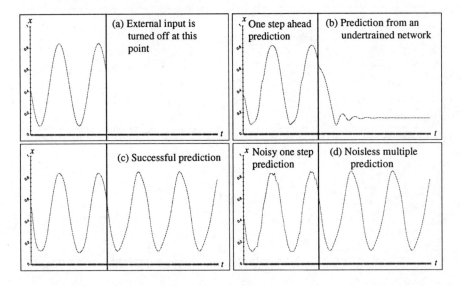

Figure 4.6: Predicting many single steps ahead of a single time series trained with noisy input and tested both on clean ((b) and (c)) and noisy (d) inputs. The vertical lines mark the point from which the neural network is receiving no external input.

4.5.2 Predicting many steps ahead

Figure 4.6 shows the results of attempting to predict a single sine wave multiple steps into the future. The network was trained on noisy input versions of the pure sine wave to improve its robustness. Graph (a) shows the original sine wave and the cut off point, before which the network is required to predict one step ahead, and after which, it is required to predict another 100 steps by taking the previous output as the new input. Graph (b) shows the results of an undertrained network failing to maintain a cycle. Graph (c) shows the same network, trained to a smaller maximum error of 0.001. Graph (d) shows how, when given noisy input, the network produces noisy output, but is able to continue to predict a smoothed version of the wave.

The effect of training set distribution

In order to test whether the high frequency errors are due to the fact that the network is presented with more examples of the high frequency wave at turning points (due to the higher number of such points in a high frequency wave), a new training set was built which contained sufficient examples of the lower frequency wave to cause the network to see a higher number of low frequency turning points. Graphs (c) and (d) show how the network now followed the lower frequency curve.

Figure 4.7 shows how the frequency of the waves affects network behaviour. A network was trained to predict two different sine waves, each of different frequency. Graphs (a) and (b) show the output of a network trained on a data set containing an equal

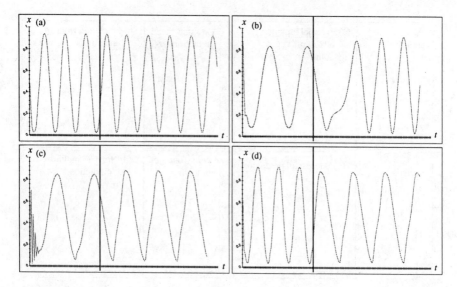

Figure 4.7: (a) The network is able to predict many steps of the high frequency wave, but fails (b) on the lower frequency. When trained on a data set which contains sufficient data points from the low frequency wave to present the network with more examples of low frequency turning points ((c) and (d)), the network now prefers to follow the low frequency curve. The curve to the right hand side of the vertical line is multi step prediction.

number of points from waves at each frequency. The network is able to predict the waves at the correct frequency for one step ahead, but where the network is asked to predict more than one step ahead, it only succeeds on the high frequency wave. Output given the lower frequency wave follows the correct path until a turning point is reached. At this point, the trajectories of the two waves become too close for the accuracy of the network to allow them to be distinguished, and the network resorts to the higher frequency trajectory. Graphs (c) and (d) show the same results from a network trained explicitly to see more examples of the low frequency wave. As you can see, the network now follows that low frequency wave in multiple step prediction.

Predicting complex waves

The network predicts future values of the sine waves by tracing a path through recurrent layer state space. The paths through this space are proximal, but discrete. It should be obvious then, that such a network would not be able to carry out more than one step ahead prediction of complex waves as it would continue along the attractor to which it was closest, resorting back to a pure sine wave once more.

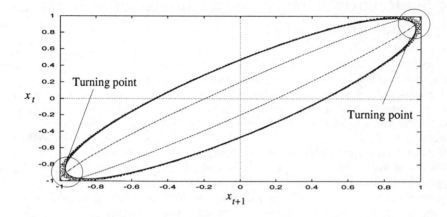

Figure 4.8: Plotting target output at time t against that of time $t + 1$ shows how a network is able to follow different trajectories through state space until reaching a turning point, where the trajectories cross.

4.5.3   Initial conditions

The appropriate recurrent layer of the network had its elements reset to zero at the start of each sine wave. This introduced a discontinuity in the limit cycle which the network learned. Using a training series in which the first element followed directly in series from the last, and no longer resetting the recurrent layer improved the ability of the network to learn each series. The disadvantage of such a system is that it is difficult to seed the recurrent layer with the right values for a given sine wave's state space cycle.

4.5.4   Conclusions from work with sine waves

The single step ahead predictions show that the network is able to follow one of several trajectories through state space as long as it is placed back on the right track at each step. The multiple step predictions show that the networks are predicting future values, and are able to learn turning points. These predictions also show that the network can follow the wrong route from points in state space where trajectories are close. In the case of the sine waves, this happens at the turning points. Figure 4.8 demonstrates how the turning points intersect by plotting each point in a sine wave against the point which immediatly follows it. We have also shown how it is possible to pull the network from one trajectory to another and to force the network to follow more complex trajectories during one step ahead prediction.

4.6   Recurrent networks as models of finite state automata

Any system, be it physical or logical, which passes through a number of states as its behaviour unfolds over time can be described as a finite state automaton (FSA). The rules which govern the system fully describe the set of possible subsequent states to which the system may move from each current state. These rules combine to determine the solution manifold of the system. An FSA can be viewed as a grammar which either generates or parses sequences of observables drawn from a finite alphabet. If the grammar is generative, a transition from one state to another will have an output associated with it; these values are the observables. If the grammar is to be used for parsing (checking that an input sequence is valid for the given grammar), subsequent states are determined by each input during parsing. Where there is more than one possible subsequent state to choose from in the generative mode, a choice is made at random. In practice, the choice may be made by deterministic factors outside the confines of the grammar, but as far as the grammar is concerned, the choice is random. For a full introduction to grammars and FSAs, I can recommend *Languages and Machines* by T. Sudkamp [97].

As many time varying real world applications may be considered to be FSAs, it is useful to understand the process by which a recurrent network is able to learn to act in the same way as the FSA from which its training data is taken. It is of further analytical use to be able to derive a state diagram describing the system from the recurrent network once it has learned. As we must build the model only on measurements we can take from the real world system, we must trust in Takens', [103] theorem, which states that the state space of a system may be constructed from the system observables alone.

Figure 4.9 shows the FSA of the grammar which Elman [33] used to show how a recurrent network could learn the required state transitions from a set of data generated by an FSA. The grammar allows a consonant from {b,d,g} at random and follows each **b** with an **a**, each **d** with **ii** and each **g** with **uuu**. Elman used a recurrent network with local representation of the inputs and outputs and 20 hidden units to learn the grammar in figure 4.9. The network predicted the vowels correctly and, as one would expect, failed to predict the random consonants.

Cleeremans [24] used a recurrent network to parse a grammar in order to accept or reject an input string. A network, trained to predict the next element in a series, was used to verify whether subsequent observables in a string were or were not valid. As choices are made at random within the constraints of the grammar, the network output is required to signal more than one possible answer. A local representation was consequently used. The network was able to model the grammar perfectly. The hidden units form a representation of the system states which is used to predict subsequent observables. Using a cluster analysis technique, Cleeremans found that the hidden units formed similar representations for observables from the same state, but also stated that

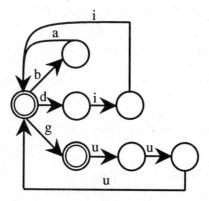

Figure 4.9: Elman's grammar: strings are generated by choosing a random path from each current state and noting the letter (observable) given on that path. Strings are parsed taking each observable in turn and following the path which carries its name.

> The tendency to approximate the behaviour but not the representation of the grammar is exhibited when there are more hidden units than are absolutely necessary to perform the task.

The extra capacity of the oversize hidden layers was used in building a representation of the path which led the system to the current state. The authors did not, however, furnish the reader with any clues as to how many hidden units might be necessary to perform a given task. This question is addressed below.

4.6.1 Choosing a hidden layer size for neural models of FSA

The task of learning an FSA involves two mappings: the first transforms a representation of the current state, along with the current input to a representation of the hidden layer state. The second translates this hidden layer representation into a representation of the output of the system. This fact should affect the way we build and code a network model.

Replicating Elman's results

A recurrent network with six inputs (for a local representation of the six letters in the alphabet of the grammar) and six output units was built. Elman used 20 hidden units, but on reasoning that the grammar had only five states which could be represented in a binary pattern by three hidden units, three hidden units were used. The network learned the task perfectly. Vowels were predicted correctly, and when a consonant was expected, the three output units representing consonants became equally activated whilst the vowel output units remained off. In other words, the network output represented the probabilities associated with each of the possible outputs occurring next.

Secondly, a network with two hidden units was built to test whether the task was possible with less than three. The network learned the task except for one type of error: where a consonant would be expected after a triple of us, a forth u was predicted, though with far less certainty.

Close examination of the hidden units using a Kohonen [55] clustering technique revealed that although the prediction that three hidden units would be required was correct, the reasons behind the prediction were not valid. The hidden units are not free to take a binary representation for each different system state as these states have to be mapped back onto a forced representation on the output layer. The local representation is essential because the network needs to be able to indicate a set of probabilities for more than one possible outcome for any subsequent step. In Elman's example, the network must be able to represent the fact that, when a consonant is expected, it may be one of three possibilities at random.

With two hidden units, the network was unable to find a suitable representation on the hidden layer which could not only represent all the system states, but which could also be mapped onto the output layer. In fact, if we look at the representation on which the network finally settles, we see that its mapping onto the output representations is non-linear. Taking the hidden layer and the output layer in isolation, we are left with a network with a single layer of weights, i.e. a perceptron which is unable to learn non-linear mappings. This problem may be alleviated by adding another hidden layer or, more simply, adding an extra hidden unit.

A first conclusion from this study is that the number of hidden units required by a recurrent network to learn a finite state grammar must be sufficient for a non-linear mapping between the hidden units representing the possible network states, and the output units representing the output values to be possible. It should also be remembered that although the inputs and outputs were both represented in binary, the hidden units did not use a binary coding scheme. It is consequently not correct to choose the number of hidden units in a network based on the fact that N states could be represented by $\log_2 N$ binary hidden units. This is due firstly to the fact that the units do not adopt such a coding scheme and secondly to the fact that such a scheme would not permit a linear mapping from the hidden to the output layer.

Manolios and Fanelli [61] have followed a similar line of reasoning in training recurrent neural networks on a particular type of grammar known as Tomita [107] grammar. Their study focussed on the acceptance or rejection of sequences for binary grammars only. Using a clustering technique to analyse the hidden units in the recurrent network, they were able to reconstruct the finite state automaton from the trained network operating on a set of example sequences. As one would expect, the number of clusters derived from the network was equal to the number of states in the FSA.

By carrying out a similar process during the learning process, they were able to identify two phases through which the network passed as it learned. In the first, the network builds and alters a set of representations for the different states required by the grammar. In the second phase, having settled upon a representation, the network tunes the weights to achieve the lowest error possible.

4.6.2 Extending Elman's grammar

We have concluded that a recurrent neural network is able to follow one of several trajectories in state space until it reaches a point where they coincide. At this point, the network follows the path which it has seen most often in the training data. In order to test our hypotheses more carefully, a set of experiments were carried out, designed to teach a recurrent network to traverse a pair of grammars. The grammars were designed to share two points in common from which the system could follow a path through either. Once such a point had been left however, the system could not swap from one grammar to the other until it reached a common point once more.

A set of experiments were designed to test the network's ability to learn the pair of finite state grammars shown in figure 4.10. The first is the example we have just seen in section 4.6.1 taken from Elman [33] and the second is a similar grammar with different state transition rules. The two grammars differ both in the number of times a vowel is repeated, and in which vowel follows which consonant. They also have points of similarity. The states denoted by a double circle show the points at which it is possible to step from one grammar to the other.

The two grammars were used to build two data sets which were used to train a recurrent MLP with two context buffers. A binary representation was used on both input and output using six units: one for each possible character. A character is represented by activating the appropriate unit with a value of one, and setting all other units to zero. Target outputs are represented in the same way. Each training sequence was 1000 elements long. It is clear that training the network on 1000 examples of one grammar would move the weights a long way from a representation of the other grammar. The multiple recurrent layers allow the two sequences to be learned in parallel.

4.6.3 Testing the new network

Testing revealed that the network was able to follow a route around the correct grammar for each input received. When a consonant (**b,d,g**) is expected, the network predicts each with an equal probability of one third. When the identity of the consonant is known, the network predicts the correct probability of each of the vowels following that consonant. Once the identity of the first vowel is known, the identity of the following characters is fully determined and the network is able to predict the correct characters for the given grammar. The network is able to output the correct number of vowels, as dictated by the initial consonant, and move back to a state where a consonant is expected.

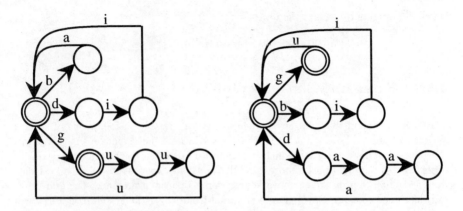

Figure 4.10: Two grammars with similar structure but different generated strings, points of convergence are highlighted with double circles.

4.6.4   Allowing the network to generate strings

The network was programmed to generate strings from the current grammar by stochastically choosing the next input from the current output representation. This allows the network to choose a path when more than one is available, but forces it to follow the correct path when only one remains. The chosen output is converted to a binary pattern for input at the next time step, which ensures that the output does not degrade due to noise. The network successfully traversed each grammar without error. It was found, however, that once the network was producing strings from one grammar, there was not an equal chance of it producing a string from the opposite grammar at the next possible occasion. The network showed a preference for remaining within the current grammar at any given time.

Whether the network skips from one grammar to the other is affected by the length of time it has spent in the current grammar. A long string (e.g **guuu**) is more likely to produce a subsequent string from the same grammar than a short string (e.g. **ba**). The network does not remain solely in a single grammar as there are points common to the two which allow crossover. However, the network never makes an incorrect prediction. Once the required output has been determined, the network always produces the correct answer based on the current grammar. Where two grammars have no points of intersection, the network has no opportunity to cross from one to the other and so is able to cycle in one or the other independently.

4.6.5   Conclusions from work with grammars

The experiments with finite state grammars reinforced the conclusions drawn from the sine wave based experiments. A single recurrent network, trained using multiple recurrent layers, was able to learn two different grammars and follow a correct path around either. It was able to switch from one to the other, only when it was in a certain state which was common to both. From the experiments described above, we can conclude that it is possible to define several distinct paths through the state space of a recurrent neural network. These paths are kept separate during training by the use of multiple recurrent layer buffers, and they remain separate during recall unless the network enters a state common to more than one path.

4.7   Summary of temporal neural networks

We have seen how it is possible to model the dynamics of a time varying system based solely on the observables which it generates. Neural networks can account for temporal dependencies directly via a delay window or indirectly using a recurrent copy of the hidden layer. Such recurrent networks have been shown to be capable of modelling abstract system states from system output alone. Neural networks can learn to predict or classify sequences of real numbers or binary coded entities and can be trained with standard back propagation techniques. This allows us to apply the techniques presented throughout this book to temporally dependent tasks.

Chapter 5

Data collection and validation

It is a capital mistake to theorize before one has data.
Sir Arthur Conan Doyle

5.1 Data collection

Now that we know how we will build our network and code our data, we can go out and collect some. This chapter discusses issues relating to the size and scope of the training set and then moves on to a discussion of available techniques for checking the quality of the collected data. Data quality is defined in terms of its suitability for training a neural network on a given task and data validation is the process of ensuring training data suitability.

5.1.1 How much data to collect

The factors which determine how much data needs to be collected are related to the reasons why we need to optimise network size or expand the data set to improve a network's generalisation abilities. Throughout this book runs the idea that trade-offs may be made between collecting more data, expanding existing data, and altering the network architecture and training procedure. Which methods are finally employed will depend on the cost and availability of data, the time constraints on training a network, and the levels of noise, required generalisation ability, and network simplicity of each particular application.

In relation to network size

As we saw in chapter 3, the size of the network being trained is somewhat constrained by the size of the training set [110] and [118]. The simplest rule [13] was to ensure that the training set was at least equal to $(1/minimum\ target\ error) \times number\ of\ weights$. A minimum error of 0.1 requires a training set ten times as large as the number of weights in the neural network. The following considerations are also affected by the size of the network and the two may be traded-off against one another to a certain extent. The trade-off becomes important when data collection is expensive or existing data is sparse. Where appropriate, such a tradeoff is discussed in the final paragraph of each of the following sections.

Mulhall [70] states that training set size is determined by the intrinsic dimensionality, the required resolution, the probability distribution, the "complexity"—which is determined by how well suited the system is to being modelled by interpolating between examples—and the level of noise of the system to be modelled.

Intrinsic dimensionality

The intrinsic dimensionality of a system is determined by the number of constraints which exist between the input variables. Constraints between inputs limit the number of combinations of input patterns which are possible. Although the size of the input space grows exponentially with the addition of new variables, constraints between these variables reduce that explosion in size. Continuous variables may be constrained by one another by natural laws, the DTI Best Practice Guide Lines [31] cite Ohm's law as an example: $V = IR$. Although there are three variables, any one may be determined by the other two so the intrinsic dimensionality is only two. Constraints may exist in feature and category codings as the presence of certain features in the description of an input entity will limit the range of other features. Let us say we are coding a system to diagnose car faults. The presence of certain faults will limit the number of likely symptoms, thus reducing the possible number of combinations which will ever be entered. For example the fault *third gear not available* is not likely to coincide with the symptom *battery is flat* for any practical example.

If the number of constraints in a system is known, then the intrinsic dimensionality is calculated simply as the number of input units minus the number of constraints. Rigorous analysis based on co-variance or mutual entropy scores between the different input units will yield an accurate measure of the number, and degree, of the constraints but requires a fair amount of work which may not provide a sufficient benefit over that which would be gained from a reasonable understanding of the task in hand. If the intrinsic dimensionality is not known, or if the inputs are independent, then the maximum dimensionality is equal to the number of input units.

Re-coding the input layer so that it contains fewer variables (see this chapter on dimensionality reduction) should leave the intrinsic dimensionality of the data constant, but will reduce the number of weights in the network and so reduce the required number of training examples in relation to network size. If it is possible to identify a smaller intrinsic dimensionality in a set of variables, then it should be possible to reduce the number of variables used to train the network. This is desirable as it reduces the complexity of the model and so benefits its generalisation ability. Ruelle [85] has indicated a requirement of around 2^n data points to build a model in n dimensional space. It is often possible to succeed with considerably less, however, as the solution often lies on a sub-space or manifold within the entire system space.

The intrinsic dimensionality of a time series is determined by its embedding dimension, as discussed in section 3.2.2.

Data resolution

The resolution of the data to be modelled is defined by the number of divisions made along each dimension. For binary codings, the matter is trivial as each unit may only take one of two values. For continuous values, and probability values calculated in place of binary classifications, the measure may be limited only by the accuracy of the computer on which the network is implemented. Certain scales may naturally fall into a number of discrete steps: rainfall in centimetres, for example. If we are not interested in any greater accuracy, then we can save ourselves the need for larger amounts of data by limiting the scale appropriately. Later in this chapter we discuss the need for matching the resolution between the input variables and the outputs so that we do not expect a greater resolution from the output than that which exists in the input.

System complexity

A complex system is one which displays great variation between nearby points. As the generalisation ability of a neural network is based on building a smooth function through a set of training points, any behaviour which falls between data points and which is sufficiently different from a smooth interpolation of those points will not be correctly modelled. In such cases, the data set must be sampled at a scale which is sufficiently fine that smooth interpolation is valid. This is analogous to the need, in signal processing, for sampling a signal at sufficiently high frequency to capture the required bandwidth. Complexity is obviously related to resolution as fewer discrete points along a scale provide less chance for complex behaviour between points.

The greater the system complexity, the larger the number of weights required to model that system. Having matched network architecture to data complexity, the data set size may be derived from network size alone. The converse is also true.

The probability distribution of the data set

We have already discussed the need for an evenly distributed training set. The consequences of this requirement for the data collection stage are twofold. In the first case, we may be able to control the number of examples we collect relating to the system in each of a number of states. In this case, we must take care to collect a balanced set of examples spread across the system's operating range. This may be as simple as choosing the examples with care, or as complex as steering a plant through every aspect of its normal set of operations.

Secondly, if we are not able to control the distribution of the examples we collect, but we are able to measure that distribution, we must collect sufficient data to ensure complete coverage of the system's operating range. If we know that the probability of a system entering a given state is P_s, then we must collect at least $1/P_s$ data points to be reasonably sure of collecting a single example of s. The latter point, whilst workable in one dimension, becomes considerably confused for any practical purposes when more than two or three input variables are used. With a large number of variables, each with uneven distributions, it is best to follow the heuristic which states that:

As the variance in the distribution of the training set grows, so does the number of training examples required to be sure of covering the system's operating range.

Noise and data quality

We have already seen that adding noise to a training set increases the ability of the network to generalise by "blunting" the noise present in the training data. Collecting extra data has a similar watering down effect on the noise as added examples will reinforce any structure in the data and introduce noise which will confound the effect of any noise in the smaller training set. Noise, in this case, is defined as perturbations of the recorded data points from their true values due to inaccuracies in the measuring or collecting process.

Noise may also be present in the form of erroneous values, mis-classifications or outliers. In this case, it can be seen that if 20% of the collected data points are noise, and have no effect on the final network solution, then our training set is effectively 20% smaller than originally thought. In such cases, extra data must be collected to allow for the noise and, where possible, the erroneous examples discarded.

The number of weights in a neural network may be kept low to minimise the effects of noise. In such cases, it might appear that less training data is required as less weights have been used. As we have just seen, this is not the case. Given the uncertainty which surrounds the choice of network size, it is often prudent to choose a network with slightly more hidden units (and consequently weights) than necessary and to increase the size of the training set accordingly. In such cases the trade-off may be decided by the ease and cost of data collection. If data is sparse and expensive then network based methods must obviously be preferred.

The above considerations are summarised by saying that if a system output varies on a fine scale over a large range, we need to sample it at a large number of points. Adding dimensions increases the space from which we sample the points exponentially but constraints between dimensions reduce this explosion. If the points we sample are not spread evenly across that space, we need to collect more points to compensate and if the points contain noise, our effective number of collected points will fall.

5.2   Building the training and test sets

Hecht-Neilson [45] rightfully suggests that the first thing to be done once the training set has been collected is to build a test set. The results of employing the test set should define whether the project has been a success or not and so it should be as exhaustive and potentially destructive as possible. All aspects of normal functioning should be accounted for along with tests of network response to inputs outside the normal range.

However, the goals defined in the project plan should be embodied by the test set and should persist throughout the project development. It would seem prudent then to construct a full training set covering all aspects of the system's behaviour from which a test set may be derived.

Maren et al. [62] suggest a method they call shaping which involves taking a subset of the full training set and quickly training a network to the general shape of this subset. When the network is close to a solution, the rest of the training data is used to refine the model. This method applies a small training set to a network designed for a large one and so, rather than building a quick simple model, it could easily build a quick overfitted model which will need to be undone by the full training set. As most of the general learning occurs in the first few training cycles anyway, this method would benefit us little.

5.2.1 Expanding insufficient data

Section 3.2.2 shows how the size of a neural network is restricted by the amount of data in the training set but there are other limitations introduced by a lack of data. They are presented below along with possible solutions to the problems created.

Setting aside an independent validation set

It is important when training a neural network to set aside an independent validation set; i.e. a percentage (at least 20%) of the training set to be used to ensure that the network is able to deal with new data. When training data is scarce, reducing its volume further is the last thing we want. Hecht-Neilson [45] suggests a method which involves using L minus 1 points in a data set of L points to train a network which is then tested on the final remaining point. This process is repeated L minus 1 times with a different point left out each time. The obvious problem with such a method is that it takes L minus 1 times as long. Less obvious perhaps is the fact that the method provides you with L minus 1 networks to choose from; none of which has been validated properly. Combining the networks is equivalent to using the whole data set to train with as you are still left with no way of validating the final model.

A better approach is to build four training sets, each with a different 25% of the data set removed, and train four networks. If each network works equivalently on its training and test data then you can be confident that they are equally valid and choose any one. There is an argument that says that once a validation set has affected the network being trained, it is no longer independent and should be replaced. However the argument is too academic and circular to be of practical concern; it is more important to choose suitable training data than to worry about the independence of the validation set which, after all, is only there to allow one to detect overfitting.

Many authors suggest a three way split in the data set which includes a training set, a cross-validation set to be used to optimise the generalisation ability of the network, and a final test set to be used as an ultimate test. It is not clear what, having used the test set once, the user is to do with regard to continued training. Strictly speaking, another unseen test set must be collected if further changes are to be made to the network. In this way, the only purpose of the test set is to provide a measure of the final reliability of the network.

In a method called bootstrapping, LeBaron and Weigend [9] build a series of networks, each trained, validated and tested on a different, random combination of data points. In addition to different samples being taken, different network architectures were tried. Across the set of networks, they found that most of the variation in performance was due to changes in data sample and not to changes in network architecture. This is, however, a consequence of the large noise content of the financial data with which they were working rather than a general rule.

Artificially extending the data set

The reason for setting aside a test set is to ensure that the model you have built generalises well. Another way of addressing the difficulty in building a general model with insufficient data is to manipulate the existing training set to artificially extend it. This serves two purposes: not only does it provide a larger training set, but it can also allow us to build a model with more robust generalisation properties. By taking existing training examples and perturbing them, adding noise or transforming the data in some way, it is possible to allow for novel situations not covered by the training data. An obvious example is that of character recognition; letters can be stretched and distorted to simulate different unseen styles.

In the extreme case, a software simulator of the system may be written to produce data. This is of use in cases where the other benefits of using a neural network are required, such as the ability to calculate the derivatives of the function the network builds (see chapter 7 on network analysis). Cressy [27], for example, used a software simulator of a batch distillation process in order to build a neural controller for the actual process.

Synthetic data can be created not only to fill out a sparse training set but also to define network behaviour in regions of input space where no sensible response is possible. Chapter 6 deals in detail with the task of reducing errors by creating new data sets and with detecting data from outside the range covered in the training set.

5.2.2   Balancing the training set

It is important that a training set contains a similar number of examples from each class that you wish the network to learn, especially if one of the classes has, in reality, a relatively tiny number of examples compared to the others. As classification outputs are best coded with one binary output unit per class, it would be nice if we could use the output values we see when using the network (which will rarely be one or zero, but some intermediate value) as *a posteriori* probabilities of the input vector belonging to each class. The problem is that unless the training set is large enough and the distribution of the training example is even, the output values will not be probabilities.

It is not desirable to have the distribution of training examples match the distribution of real world examples, as you want the network to recognise each example as a member of the correct class irrespective of the prior probability which it has of belonging to that class. It is even more important if the real world distribution is very uneven, as the class with numerous training examples will swamp out the smaller examples. This is made clearer by the observation that a network trained to classify data in which the input contains no information about the output (i.e. a random mapping) will learn predict the prior probabilities of data belonging to each class.

For example, we might be trying to predict the Scottish weather from gold prices. Clearly there is no relationship to learn, so the network will learn the only piece of information available from the data: that it rains a lot in Scotland regardless of the current gold price. It will consequently predict rain with, say, 80% confidence regardless of the input and so be correct 80% of the time. This is not the result (nor the weather, to be honest) we would like, as it might suggest that there is predictive power in the inputs. We are stuck with the weather, but we can improve the network. If the training set was balanced so that there were an even number of examples of each weather type, then the network would be seen to score no better than chance, thus reflecting the true lack of predictive power in the data set.

Section 6.3.2 describes a method for deriving true *aposteriori* probabilities from a network trained on artificially balanced data.

5.2.3   A simple method for improving network training

A simple way of improving the chance a network has of learning the correct representation for categorisation tasks is to split the data set into a number of different files, one for each category. The neural network simulator, when choosing the next training pair, must be told to pick a random file from which the next example is taken. When the bottom of a file is reached, the program reads from the top once more. This ensures that the network sees an equal number of examples from each category in a random order.

Such a method is fine when the network output is a choice from a single set of categories. A problem arises however when a more complex output representation, such as that discussed in section 2.6.4, is used. The simplest case concerns an output which refers to a single mutually exclusive feature set and a number of continuous valued measures. For example a neural network for describing insects might have output variables telling us about *colour*, *height*, and *weight* to expect from certain other measures given as input. In this case, the examples would be split into files determined by colour. Now let us assume we add *species* to our output representation. We must either split the data with respect to colour or species, or a combination of the two. Splitting with reference to either individual variable will cause the network to receive an even distributions of examples in that class, but not guarantee that examples within the other are presented to the network in equal proportions. If the data is split into a number of files sufficient to represent the combinations of both features, the network will be presented with an even number of each combination—blue beetles for example—but an uneven number of examples of individual features. It might see more red insects than blue, or more beetles than flies.

We have a choice when training a neural network on such tasks. We can either choose the single most important set of categories to be balanced or decide to balance over all combinations. Of course, we might not need to treat any of the outputs as probabilities and consequently not care whether the outputs sum to one or not. That is fine, but it is always important to ensure that the network is presented with the examples from different classes mixed together, rather than presenting all of the examples of each class in turn. The latter method will cause a great bias in the network towards the class from which the last set of examples were drawn. A network which is presented with a large number of uninterrupted examples from any single class is said to *forget* about previous classes it has seen. It is for this reason that multiple context layers are used when training a recurrent network on more than one sequence.

5.2.4   Unbalanced data from mapping functions

So far, the discussion has been confined to classification tasks. When learning a continuous function, it is also desirable to collect an even distribution of data covering all aspects of the system to be modelled. The main problem is that you need a model which covers the entire operation of a system which may rarely, if ever, display certain modes of operation. The simplest such case involves a system which safely covers its entire functionality, but not with even frequency. It is important, but easy, to ensure that the training set covers the whole range evenly by duplicating examples of rare behaviour or explicitly collecting more examples of such cases. We saw above how such a situation affects the amount of data which needs to be collected.

The harder case involves a system which only enters certain states of interest when things have gone wrong. This problem is particularly severe in system monitoring networks which need to detect failures which would be dangerous or impossible to induce for data collection purposes. Such cases require the novelty detection methods discussed in chapter 6.

Using information theory to spot unbalanced training sets

Section 5.3.2 below demonstrates how information theory may be used to measure how well balanced a data set is. It also presents methods for measuring the amount of predictive power which is due to an imbalance (as in the case of the Scottish weather example above) and how much is due to a relationship between the inputs and the outputs (which is the type of information that we are really interested in).

5.2.5 Summary on required training data volume

The points relating to determining training data volume are summarised below.

- Collect a number of training examples greater than
  $(1/minimum\ target\ error) \times number\ of\ weights.$

- Increase the training set size in multiples equal to the intrinsic dimensionality of the data: a factor of 10 per dimension is a good estimate.

- Collect data which covers the entire operating range of the system, at a sampling rate sufficient to capture its generalisable behaviour.

- If it is not possible to control the distribution of examples in the collected data, and that distribution is not even, then sufficient data must be collected to ensure the recording of the events with the smallest probabilities.

- Increase the training set size in proportion with the amount of noise present in the data or the proportion of collected examples expected to be discarded.

- Allow for a validation set of at least 20% of the training set, and ideally a separate test set too.

- If data collection is expensive, the above constraints may be loosened by applying methods for expanding the data set artificially, reducing the dimensionality of the data, reducing the size of the network, and improving the generalisation ability of the network by algorithmic means.

5.3 Data quality

Building a neural network is a lot like cooking a lasagne. Once you have the dish prepared, you can put it in the oven without too many worries about the temperature, or the amount of time it is in; you just take it out when it looks cooked, or the error looks acceptable. The real skill is in the preparation. Too much cheese or not enough sauce and all the oven related knowhow in the world won't help you. The following sections discuss some methods for ensuring that the data set to be used to train a neural network is properly prepared. I present methods for ensuring that the ingredients which go into a neural solution are present in the correct amounts and proportions, carry the information we require, and are prepared and processed properly.

5.3.1 Choosing the task

Choosing the task for your neural network may seem like a foregone conclusion: *obviously, I know what I want it to do...* but the end result and the task given to the neural network are not necessarily the same thing. The task must be expressed in terms of the types of solution a neural network can offer. That is, in some kind of mapping from one data space to another.

Matching input and output space resolution

It is important to remember that it is impossible to create information. We can derive information, but we cannot create it. As humans, we rely on implicit knowledge about the world when deriving information from a data source. The implicit information is effectively an extra input to our mental processing system. Artificial neural networks do not have access to such implicit knowledge; they must derive all the information required for the answers they give from the input data. All a neural network does is take the information contained in a certain input vector and express it as an output which we can more easily understand. For these reasons, it is important that we are not asking, or expecting, the neural network to create information.

The simplest example of a statistical model which gives the false impression of creating information is the arithmetic mean, often referred to as the average. The mean of a set of numbers is calculated by summing each value and dividing the result by the number of values used. The mean of 3,5,6 and 7 is consequently $21/4 = 5.25$. The apparent information gain can be seen in the increased accuracy of the answer which is expressed to two decimal places. We've all heard the standard mis-uses of this measure: that the average family size is 2.3 children, or that people have, on average, 1.98 legs. While these examples are easy to spot, the same type of mistake can easily go un-noticed in a complex neural network model. For this reason, it is important to consider the amount of information contained in the input data, and that required from the outputs. Section 5.3.2 below discusses a mathematical measure of such information content.

Let's take as an example the task of predicting driver alertness discussed in chapter 10, the basic idea of which is to map the driver's steering behaviour onto a measure of alertness. The alertness measure for the training data is taken using highly accurate medical equipment and coded into a seven point scale. The steering wheel movement however, provides a far less sensitive measure of the driver's mental state. Simply mapping the seven point medical scale onto a forced seven categories of steering behaviour would be doomed to failure as the accuracy does not exist in the latter measurement. In reducing the number of possible output categories, we can re-code the output space so that it has a similar resolution to that of the input space.

5.3.2   Statistical considerations

There is a strange argument concerning whether statistical methods are better or worse than neural networks. It originates from a misunderstanding of what neural networks are, and has somehow survived to this day. The simple answer would seem to be that neural networks *are* statistics. Nobody wonders whether regression pursuit is better than statistics, so why...

Still, there is a lot to be said for understanding the similarities and the differences between neural networks and the host of other statistical techniques. It has been shown that a perceptron is equivalent to a regression model, and that an MLP with one hidden unit carries out logistical regression. Neural network classifiers have also been shown to be equivalent to Bayesian models [43]. Hardly surprising, one might say, given their properties of universal function approximators.

The following discussions assume that a neural network is being built for use as a generalisable model. It is possible, with sufficient weights, to use a neural network to simply build a system which behaves like a look-up table but does not generalise. This is only safe if every data point is covered by the training set and no generalisation is required. The advantage of such a system is that it would operate faster than many conventional search techniques. Such systems are known as content addressable memories but are not considered further within this book.

Using statistics to establish data quality

Let us take an easy example: that of k nearest neighbours. Here we have a simple but effective method for categorising novel objects with reference to a historical data set. One simply takes the new point, finds the set of k closest points, and counts to see which category the majority of those points fall into. Obviously, this is not a model building exercise, unless you count your entire data set as a model, and it is hardly an efficient one either as every point must be looked at k times in order to make the calculation. It is, however, a very reliable method of checking whether the classification task you are about to teach your network is possible. If the k nearest neighbours to each point tell you nothing about the class membership of the point itself, then there is no scope for generalisation and a neural network will fail to learn the task.

Several studies have compared neural networks with k nearest neighbour classifiers and found that the latter often produces the most accurate results. In chapter 1 we described how a neural network could be viewed as a fast approximation to many more complex algorithms or techniques. Clearly, k nearest neighbour is one such technique. Certainly, given a sufficiently fast computer with sufficient storage capacity for each data set required for k nearest neighbour classification, one could accomplish reliable accurate classification. However, in reality speed is an important consideration, and neural networks are fast and compact. Comparing neural networks with other statistical techniques is only sensible within the framework of a particular application, for which the most appropriate technique should be chosen. The reason for this is that a neural network codes the features which describe an object so that the object becomes represented as a point in some multi-dimensional space. Areas in this space are mapped onto areas in a new space—the output space—which has been organised in a way the user understands; in a way which allows a human to look at the output representation and know the identification of the input which caused it. Objects in input space must occupy regions common to their own sort in order to become mapped to common output regions. This means that they must have self similar neighbours which means a k nearest neighbours test would be able to classify them.

How else might we establish whether a data set is a valid representation of the task

we wish to train a neural network to perform? Well, you might be tempted to see
how well the inputs and outputs are correlated. However, the correlation between the
input and output of a function tells us how well the data would be described by the
best straight line you could draw through the data, and not how well you might be
able to fit a curve. Neural networks build non-linear models and so linear statistics
of any sort will not help us in determining whether our data is learnable.

Information theory

A good method of determining how well a neural network might be able to learn
from a given set of data is to measure the *information* which is shared between the
proposed input to the network and its target output. On an intuitive level, it's a good
idea to ask yourself, "*Would it actually be possible to perform the chosen task given
only the training data?*". This is discussed above, but there is a more concise method
for measuring the information contained in a data set.

Shannon [88] introduced information theory in 1948 as a method for measuring information content in communicated signals. The amount of information associated with
an event relates to the probability of that event happening; if a rare event occurs,
we gain more information than we would if a common event occurred. In fact, the
information associated with an event is defined as $\log(1/P)$ where P is the probability
of the event occurring. If we want to know how much information is contained in a
whole system, we must add up the information contained in every possible event and
take the weighted average.

This measure is called *entropy* and measures *uncertainty* in the system. A large
entropy measure (very uncertain) is produced by a system where the probabilities of
different events occurring are similar and so we have little hope of guessing anything
about its behaviour.

Information theory calculations involve logarithms for several reasons. The theory
is based on coding information for transmission, and was developed as a method
for compressing data based on its statistical properties. Data can be compressed by
recoding entities onto a smaller alphabet of variable length codes. Entities which are
transmitted frequently can consequently have very short codes. This is paid for by
longer codes for fewer frequent entities, but as such entities do not occur as often,
we end up transmitting more codes which are shorter than average and less which
are longer. On average we send fewer signals. If we have n entities, all of which are
equi-probable then we must send $\log(n)$ codes to transmit a description of a single
entity (think of the number of binary digits required to represent a single number in a
given range). The base of the logarithm should be equal to the number of characters
in the code alphabet. Any entities which occurs with higher probability can be used
to reduce the number of codes (or bits in a binary representation) required.

When building a neural network however, we are not interested in the probabilities
with which different events might occur. Indeed, a good training set is one in which
all the possible events are covered with equal frequency. The entropy measure is of
use here as it should be as close to its theoretic maximum as possible. The entropy
of the input layer and the output layer, independent of one another, therefore should

be as close to their maximum value as possible. Low entropy at the input or output causes a bias in the network's learning and so should be avoided.

We are really interested in the information which exists between the input data and the output data: referred to as *mutual information*. To do this we must calculate the amount of information we gain about the output by seeing the input.

Mutual information between two data sets is defined as the entropy of one variable minus the conditional entropy of the second, given the first. In other words, our input variables will occur with a given probability, so we know something about what the next input might be (although they should be equi-probable). We want the network to take the input and remove all uncertainty about what the corresponding output should be. The amount of the original uncertainty we can remove depends on the mutual information present in the data. With an ideal training set, once we know the input value, there should be no doubt as to the correct output value: it should be the one value with a conditional probability, given the current input, of one. All other output values should have a probability of zero. As this is rarely the case, we need a measure of the average spread of conditional probabilities over the whole training set.

This tells us the entropy on the output if we know what the input is. To find the entropy associated with the entire training set, we need to take an average, weighted by the probability of each event occurring, over every training example. Figure 5.1 summarises some of the uses of entropy for manipulating before training a neural network. The equations for calculating entropy values are given at the end of the chapter.

The next section discusses ill posed problems and is concluded with an example of how information theory can be used to spot a certain variety of this type of problem.

5.3.3 One to many mappings

The most important check to perform on a training set is that you are not attempting to model a function which consistently maps the same input onto two or more different outputs. If it does, you will find that the average of the possibilities will be learned, yielding a nonsense result. Such cases are examples of *ill posed* problems. The inverse kinematics of a robot arm provide a good example of such a data set: Figure 5.2 shows how an arm with two joints is able to reach the same position with its hand from two different combinations of joint angles. Training a network to calculate joint angles from hand positions will produce a system which averages the two possibilities and produces a gross, but universally minimised, error.

5.3.4 Solutions to ill posed problems

In order to teach a network to solve an ill posed problem, we must either change the nature of the data or the nature of the problem. Figure 5.3 uses a single example to demonstrate each of the following solutions. The forward model in the figure is described by the function

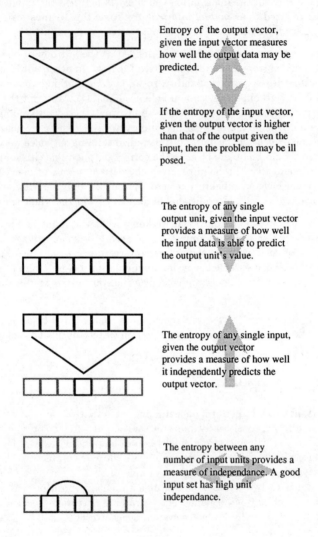

Entropy of the output vector, given the input vector measures how well the output data may be predicted.

If the entropy of the input vector, given the output vector is higher than that of the output given the input, then the problem may be ill posed.

The entropy of any single output unit, given the input vector provides a measure of how well the input data is able to predict the output unit's value.

The entropy of any single input, given the output vector provides a measure of how well it independently predicts the output vector.

The entropy between any number of input units provides a measure of independance. A good input set has high unit independance.

Figure 5.1: Entropy measures may be taken from the layer vectors as a whole or from individual units. Any combination of the two is possible, and most prove useful. Entropy measures can help not only in determining the quality of a data set as a whole, but also of individual variables.

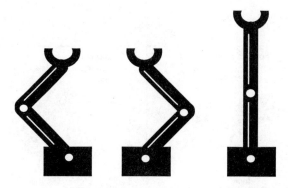

Figure 5.2: The first two arms show different possible angle combinations for the same reach position. The final arm shows the average of the two, as learned by a neural network trained evenly on examples of each.

$$y = x + 0.3\sin(2\pi x) + \rho \qquad (5.1)$$

where ρ is a random term in the range minus 0.1 to 0.1.

Figure 5.3(a) shows the forward model of this function. The neural network has easily fitted a curve through the data cloud. Frame (b) of the same figure shows the result of blindly trying to model the function in the inverse direction.

When the many possible outputs are available together

Let us start with the trivial case. Assume we have a 1:m mapping with small m and a method of collecting all m possible output values for a single given input. Then we simply need a network with m output units, one for each possible output value. It is not always the case, however, that all of the possible output values will be available at the same time. A typical data set is made up of sets of examples, so the examples of the many possible outputs for a given input may be spread across the training set. Secondly, if a single input value leads to too many possible output values, the method fails. If we extend the robot arm problem so that three joints are used, there turn out to be an infinite number of joint angle combinations which would lead to each hand position. Clearly an output unit for each is unfeasible.

Carve up the data set

If it is possible, splitting the data set into several parts and training a different network on each set can provide a simple solution. This is only feasible for a 1:m mapping

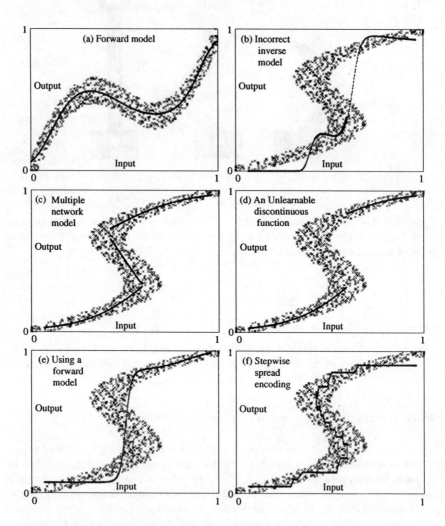

Figure 5.3: (a) The well posed forward model. (b) A poor solution to the ill posed inverse model. (c) Using a different network for each section of the curve. (d) An example of an ill considered constraint which minimises the output and causes a discontinuous, and consequently unlearnable, function. (e) Creating constraints using Jordan's forward/inverse model. (f) Representing more than one output value with stepwise spread encoding.

when m is low. Just as in the previous example, we cannot train sufficient networks to cover every possible combination of three joint angles. Figure 5.3(c) shows the results of splitting the data set into three well posed regions.

Data re-coding

It may be possible to re-code a data set so that it becomes a one to one mapping. This can be done in either of two ways, each method relying on the assumption that you only need a single answer in the end. One way is to throw away contradictory examples. Simply keep training examples which are consistent and discard all others. This is possible if the problem requires a single answer and it is of no importance which is chosen. Care should be taken, however, when using such a method: a lot of problems are not well suited to such a brutal approach. For continuous valued functions, it is necessary to split the output range into bins of values over which it would be harmless to take an average. Examples can be classed as contradictory if they fall into more than one bin. The problem here is that you need to be consistent in what you discard: you must keep all examples of one case and none of the others. A computational method for achieving this is described below.

The second method relies on the assumption that extra information can be used to transform the mapping into a one to one format. In the case of the robot arm, an extra constraint is that the arm should move smoothly without flipping back and forth. By using the previous arm position as an extra input, it is possible to define a single new position for the desired output which satisfies the smoothness constraint. In this way, an ill posed problem may be transformed into a well posed one by adding temporal constraints.

One method for constraining the network behaviour is to add an extra term to the network error function. Poggio [76] showed that it is possible to take an ill posed problem and constrain it into to being well posed by using a regularisation term on the error function.

Extra terms or constraints may take the form of a cost function. The robot arm, for example, will have some positions for which less power is required to support the extended arm. In such cases a constraint term could be used to penalise outputs for the power they require.

Jordan [52] provides a method for incorporating such constraints at the output of the network. His method involves calculating the error of the current input with respect to a set of constraints functions rather than the target output. The output of the network is passed through the constraints function to produce a final output value. The derivative of the error on the final value must be calculated in terms of the network outputs so that the weights can be changed. Care is needed when choosing extra constraints: if your constraint was *"Make the output as low as possible at all times"*, for example, then there may need to be a large jump in your function where the lowest possible value suddenly falls within the top part of the curve. This is hardly a fair request as you can see in figure 5.3(d).

Learning a one to many mapping via its inverse

So choosing a constraint is not easy. There is an interesting set of facts, however, which helps us here. The first is that $f(f^{-1}(x)) \doteq x$. Or in words: put a value through a function, take the output of that function and put it through the inverse of that function, and you end up with the number you first thought of. Clearly, glueing a function and its inverse together in this way produces a one to one mapping. As Jordan points out, if we try to learn this mapping, we will end up with a well posed problem. So we have to build a network which, when given x as its input, produces an intermediate value, passes that value through the inverse of the function to be learned, and produces x.

The errors made by this network will occur in two places: firstly on the output layer of the network, and then on the output of the inverse function. Now we know that all we need in order to calculate the weight change is a derivative of the output which describes the error made by that output. So if we can differentiate the second function, we can calculate the error on the output of the network. The second function is both the inverse of the network we are trying to build and at the same time, the constraint function. Obviously this function has to be known, and differentiable.

Here lies the neatest part of all: a neural network is differentiable. You can calculate the derivative at the output layer, as is required for back propagation, and similarly calculate the derivative for each lower layer, right down to the input layer. So if we can learn our function in the direction for which it is well posed, we have a differentiable model to use as the constraint function. Note that this model is learned first, and then used with fixed weights; it is not altered while the inverse network is being built.

Figure 5.3(e) shows the result of carrying out the following steps during training. Let o = network output, n = output of the double model, and i = network input. The double model refers to the concatenation of the forward and inverse functions.

1. The output of the network being trained to build the inverse function is put through the forward function, $n = o + 0.3\sin(2\pi o)$.

2. The error is calculated as $n - i$ because the output of the double model should equal its input.

3. This error is multiplied by the derivative of the forward function, $1 + 0.6\pi\cos(2\pi x)$ in order to produce the error on the network output layer. Note that the derivative is stated, and used, in terms of its input (x) rather than its output. It is not important which is used in this case, as long as the correct value (input or output) is used with the correct form of the derivative. The input to the function is simply the output from the network below. If the output of the function is to be used, then the function must be re-written in terms of its output (as with $o(1 - o)$ for the sigmoid).

4. The error on the network output is passed through the derivative of its activation function, $o(1 - o)$ in order to update the weights in the normal way.

It is only fair to point out that the function in this example is particularly difficult as there is no clear constraint which could be attached. As we pointed out before, fitting any constraints for this function perfectly would require a discontinuous function and neural networks are not able to build such functions. Figure 5.3(e) shows how the double model attempted to approximate the discontinuous function shown in graph (d) of the same figure.

If the function was $\subset$ shaped however, this type of solution would be able to restrict its model to a single side of the curve, consistently choosing one possible value from the two. The simple explanation for this is that the sign of the derivative as calculated in step three above cannot change once the model has started to learn. This means that the errors will always cause a movement of the weights in the same direction each time regardless of which half of the curve the inputs are in.

As structural changes to the back propagation process are required for this type of solution, problems may be encountered when using software packages which do not support such a function. In such cases, constraints must be added in one of the ways discussed here in order to eliminate the ill posed nature of the problem.

Spread encoding

Another possible way around ill posed problems is to use spread encoding. This involves splitting the output range into a number of bins, each covering a small range. Each bin will have an output unit assigned to it which contains a value of one if the output value being coded is equal to the centre point of the bin. When a value falls between two centres, each of the two units involved takes a value proportional to the distance of the value from the unit centre. The two values must sum to one. It is now possible to explicitly code a one to many mapping—as long as the different possible outputs fall into different bins. If a $1{:}m$ mapping required an output of 0.3 or 0.5 for a given input, then a network with a single output would yield the average of the two: 0.4. A network with bins covering a range of 0.1 would also average over the results, but this time produce a value of 0.5 in each appropriate bin, thus making explicit the duality of the answer. See section 2.6.6 for a more detailed examination of spread encoding.

Figure 5.3(f) shows the result of fitting a stepwise spread encoded output to the data. By stepwise, we mean that values are not spread over more than one bin which leads to the step-like function seen in the figure. The use of such steps is not recommended and is only included in the example so that the reader may have a better idea of how the coding is split up. The plot was produced by pairing each input value with every value contained in the spread encoded output produced by that input and would normally be smooth when the output values are properly decoded.

The astute reader, at this point, will cry *"Hold on!"* and point out that spread encoding suffers the same confusions as a single valued coding. If a coding system has centres at steps of one and we wish to code 4.5, then the units representing centres 4 and 5 will each be activated to 0.5. Exactly the same result would occur if the output to a certain pattern was four for half of the training examples and five for the rest. All we have done is localised the confusion. Fortunately, as a coding will only ever cover two units and those units will always be adjacent, we can set the level of confusion by choosing a sufficiently small step size. An input pattern may be associated with different output patterns in the training set for one of two reasons: the first is an ill posed data set, the second is noise. Step sizes must therefore be small enough to ensure that the distinct outputs are not confused. Noise on the other hand, needs to be averaged away so it is desirable for the coding pattern to not capture its details. This leads to the intuitive observation that a finer coding system requiring more output units will lead to a network model with a larger number of weights and so a finer scaled model. As we have seen, network size contributes to determining the extent to which noise is averaged away by a neural network model.

Spread encoding gives you the advantage of being able to impose constraints at run time rather than during learning. This is because it expresses each different possible value explicitly, allowing the choice of a single final answer to be made at run time. However, it has the disadvantage of adding extra weights and complexity to your model. A single value spread over s output units will multiply the number of weights in the top layer of the network by s, thus affecting the decisions made on hidden layer size. Notice must also be taken of the frequencies with which different output codings are targeted which will be reflected in their final activation values. A properly balanced and trained spread encoded output will produce the probability distribution which tells us the probability that each possible output value will be the correct answer.

Multiple outputs from categorisation tasks

Contradictory codings in categorisation tasks can be viewed as overlapping classes. Such cases are dealt with in chapter 6 on classification errors. Suffice to say, however, that the principles already discussed here apply equally well. Where the data set itself provides insufficient constraints, external ones must be supplied. In the extreme case these constraints may even be random: take the example of a navigational robot which finds itself facing an obstacle. Direction control outputs for *left* and for *right* may both register equal values as there is nothing to choose between the two. Choosing one at random would be the correct decision. Taking the average would not. Such tasks are less of a problem as they are stochastic by nature: the system choices are random, but weighted by the network outputs.

5.3.5   Using conditional entropy to detect ill posed problems

As we have seen, conditional entropy is a measure of the uncertainty about a given event which remains after the occurrence of a related event. It is a measure, given the fact that a certain event has occurred, of how many different possible events might follow. Conditional entropy is not a symmetrical measure: the entropy left when we observe X and wish to predict Y is not necessarily the same as that left when we observe Y and want to know the value of X most likely to have caused it.

Figure 5.4 shows the result of taking the data set from the previous example and grouping nearby values into small steps. It is now clear from looking at the graph

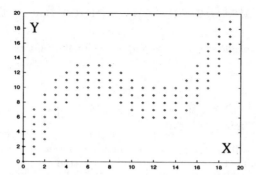

Figure 5.4: Splitting the data set into discrete bins in order to calculate conditional entropy.

that the conditional probabilities on y values, given a value on x are larger than those of x given y. If we know $x = 10$ then y can only be 7,8,9,10, or 11, each with a probability of 1/5. If we know $y = 10$ however, x might be anything between 3 and 17, each with a probability of 1/15. Clearly, the measure we really need must be the weighted average of all the uncertainties between x and y. That is, the average across all values of x, of the entropy between x_i and Y. As we have seen, this is exactly what conditional entropy measures.

For the data set in figure 5.4, the following values were computed:

$$H(X) = 2.995$$
$$H(Y) = 2.613$$
$$H(Y|X) = 1.540$$
$$H(X|Y) = 1.921$$

$I(X;Y) = 1.074$

Each dimension in the data set was split into 20 bins, so the maximum possible value of $H(X)$ or $H(Y)$ is $\log 20 = 2.996$. Clearly, we can guess little about X or Y before we know either. If we take X as our input, and try to predict Y, the uncertainty we have to contend with is reduced by almost 50%. In the case where we would take Y as our input and wish to learn to predict X, we could only reduce the initial uncertainty by a quarter. Clearly, one direction is a far easier prospect than the other, and therefore provides an indication of the ill posed nature of the problem. The noise in the data accounts for the rest of the entropy which remains after the input is known.

A final point worth making is that inverse mappings are not the only type which could be ill posed. Many systems have several possible correct outputs for any single input: so called one to many mappings. Any such mapping will still have lower entropy in the reverse direction (i.e. the entropy of the inputs, given the outputs) and may be solved with any of the methods presented above. If it does not, however, then noise or lack of predictability is to blame and your problem is at a rather more fundamental level!

5.4   Calculating entropy values for a data set

The entropy of a single set of events (either the input events or the output events) is calculated as

$$H = \sum_{i=1}^{n} P_i \log \frac{1}{P_i} \tag{5.2}$$

Where P_i is the probability of event i occurring out of the possible n events. H always falls in the range from 0 to $\log(n)$.

The conditional entropy of one set of events, X, given that a single event y_j has occurred is calculated in exactly the same way as the entropy for a single variable, except we need to replace $P(x_i)$ with the conditional probability $P(x_i|y_j)$:

$$H(X|y_j) = \sum_{i=1}^{n} P(x_i|y_j) \log \frac{1}{P(x_i|y_j)}$$

Replacing $P(x_i|y_j)$ with $P(x_i, y_j)/P(y_j)$ gives

$$H(X|y_j) = \sum_{i=1}^{n} \frac{P(x_i, y_j)}{P(y_j)} \log \frac{P(y_j)}{P(x_i, y_j)}$$

$$H(X|Y) = \sum_{j=1}^{m} \left(P(y_j) H(X|y_i) \right)$$

Replacing the conditional entropy with probabilities gives

$$H(X|Y) = \sum_{j=1}^{m} \left(P(y_j) \sum_{i=0}^{n} \frac{P(x_i, y_j)}{P(y_j)} \log \frac{P(y_j)}{P(x_i, y_j)} \right)$$

Taking $P(y_j)$ inside the second sum gives

$$H(X|Y) = \sum_{i=1}^{n} \sum_{j=1}^{m} P(x_i, y_j) \log \frac{P(y_j)}{P(x_i, y_j)}$$

Note that
$H(X|Y) \leq H(X)$.
$H(X|Y) = H(X)$ when X and Y are independent.
$H(X|Y) \neq H(Y|X)$.

Here, n is the number of possible distinct input events, m is the number of possible distinct output events, and n does not necessarily have to be equal to m. This final value tells us the uncertainty which exists between the input and the output data in a training set. As stated, mutual information is simply $H(X) - H(X|Y)$:

$$I(X;Y) = \sum_{i=1}^{n} P(x_i) \log \frac{1}{P(x_i)} - \sum_{i=1}^{n} \sum_{j=1}^{m} P(x_i, y_j) \log \frac{P(y_j)}{P(x_i, y_j)}$$

As $\sum_{j=1}^{m} P(x_i, y_j) = P(x_i)$, we can rewrite the equation as

$$I(X;Y) = \sum_{i=1}^{n} \sum_{j=1}^{m} P(x_i, y_j) \log \frac{P(x_i, y_j)}{P(x_i)P(y_j)}$$

$I(X;Y) = I(Y;X)$.
$I(X;Y) \leq \frac{1}{2}(H(X) + H(Y))$.
$I(X;Y) = 0$ when X and Y are independent.
$I(X;Y) = H(X) = H(Y)$ when X and Y are perfectly related.
However, $H(X) = H(Y)$ is *not* sufficient to allow us to imply perfect relationship.

Given that it is desirable to have a large value for $H(X)$, it is sufficient to say that we require a low value of $H(X|Y)$ to yield high information content. The ranges over which the measures fall may cause confusion, so it is good practice to use ratio values instead. These are listed below.

5.4.1 Summary of the application of information theory to data set analysis

- A well balanced training set is one where $H(inputs) \approx \log n$ and $H(outputs) \approx \log m$.

- Conditional entropy of the outputs given the inputs, $H(output|input)$, should be as low as possible. If it is high (maximum = $H(inputs)$), then the data is not learnable. This could also be an indication that the data set is ill posed.

- The above two points dictate that a good training set will have a high mutual information value between input and output. Mutual information ranges from 0 to $H(input) = H(output)$, a low score indicates little chance of success for a neural network.

- Looking at ratios:
  $H(input):\log n$ ranges from 0 to 1 and will be high if the input data is evenly distributed.
  $H(output):\log m$ ranges from 0 to 1 and will be high if the output data is evenly distributed.
  $H(output|input):H(output)$ ranges from 0 to 1 and a low value indicates that the task is learnable.
  $I(input;output):H(output)$ ranges from 0 to 1 and will be high if a data set is learnable.

- As with the use of all probability based statistics, continuous valued functions must be split into small sub-ranges, just as you would when building a histogram. The number of divisions the data is split into at this stage determines the resolution to be used when calculating the training set size (see section 5.1.1). Calculating entropy values at different resolutions (using different sized sub-ranges) is a useful method for determining the resolution at which a learnable relationship exists. Such a measure can consequently contribute to the decisions on network and training set size.

- When a data set has more than one input or more than one output, each combination of input values must be coded as a single event, as must each combination of output values. The number of calculations required then, grows exponentially with number of network units.

5.5   Using a forward–inverse model to solve ill posed problems

The following steps must be carried out to build a well posed version of an ill posed problem by propagating the error through an inverse model. Let: o = the output of the network being trained, n = the output of the double model, and i = the input to the network being trained. The double model refers to the concatenation of the forward and inverse functions.

1. If the equations describing the forward dynamics of the system are known and differentiable, then they may be used. If they are not, then train a network to solve the problem in the direction in which it is well posed. Once this network has been trained, its weights should no longer change.

2. Build a second network which is to learn the ill posed version of the problem. This is the network you will finally use to carry out the desired task.

3. To train the new network:

   (a) Present each input and produce an output from the network being trained.

   (b) Pass the output of the first network through the inverse network.

   (c) Because the output of the double model should equal its input, calculate the error as $n - i$.

   (d) Propagate the error through to the input layer of the top network, as described below.

   (e) Use the error at the input of the top network instead of the error at the output layer of the network being trained. Do not use the actual error at the output of the first network.

   (f) Update the weights in the first network in the normal way. Do not update the weights in the top network; these remain fixed.

4. When the new network has been trained, you may discard the first network as it is no longer needed. The newly trained network is used in exactly the same way as a normal multi-layer perceptron. Its structure is identical to a normally trained network and you may apply any of the analysis techniques described in this book.

Figure 5.5 illustrates the process.

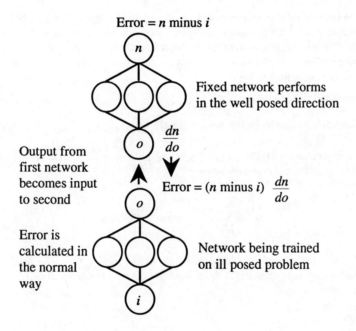

Error = n minus i

Fixed network performs
in the well posed direction

$\dfrac{dn}{do}$

Output from
first network
becomes input
to second

Error = (n minus i) $\dfrac{dn}{do}$

Error is
calculated in
the normal
way

Network being trained
on ill posed problem

Figure 5.5: Learning an ill posed problem using an inverse, well posed function. The top network is trained in isolation and then fixed whilst the other is being trained.

5.5.1   Propagating the errors through to the input layer

In order to calculate the error on the input to the second network we pass the error at the output of the network back through the derivative of the network. The following equations are based on a network with sigmoidal activation functions.

At first glance it may seem that a lot of work is required in order to calculate these derivatives. Each unit must be differentiated with respect to its input which, in turn, may depend on the output of units below. However, if we know the output values of each unit, we may ignore the inputs, including those from the bias, and simply base our calculations the output values. This is only possible, of course, if it is possible to re-write the squashing function in terms of its output, as is the case with the sigmoid.

In order to make the following calculations, first pass the inputs through the network in the normal way. Ensure that the hidden units are not reset when the output is produced. The following equations us the logistic squashing function. If your network uses a different function, be sure to substitute the correct derivative where you find $x(1 - x)$ in the equations below.

Networks with a single input and a single output

The top network has a single input o, a set of hidden units h_i $i = 1 \ldots m$ and an output n. It is differentiated as follows:

$$\frac{dn}{do} = \sum_{i=1}^{m} h_i(1 - h_i)w_i\ n(1 - n)u_i \tag{5.3}$$

where h_i is the activation of hidden unit i, w_i is the weight from the input unit to hidden unit i and u_i is the weight from hidden unit i to the output unit. There are m hidden units.

5.5.2   Dealing with more than one input or output

If a network has more than one input or output, we only compute the partial derivatives of each output unit with respect to each input unit in turn. For a network with j inputs and k outputs, this will produce a $j \times k$ matrix of derivatives, known as a Jacobian matrix. To calculate the derivative of each output unit o_j with respect to each input unit i_k use the following function for all j and k.

$$\frac{dn_j}{do_k} = \sum_{i=1}^{n} h_i(1 - h_i)w_{i,j}\ n_j(1 - n_j)u_{i,k} \tag{5.4}$$

where h_i is hidden unit i, $w_{i,k}$ is the weight from input unit k to hidden unit i and $u_{i,j}$ is the weight from hidden unit i to output unit j.

5.5.3   Calculating the training error

Having found the derivative of the top network at the given point, the error for the first network output layer is calculated as the error $n - i$ times the derivative of the function (or network) above:

$$e = (n - i)\frac{dn}{do} \tag{5.5}$$

Chapter 6

Output and error analysis

We should be careful to get out of an experience only the wisdom that is in it—and stop there;...
Mark Twain

6.1 Introduction

Having been told that computers don't make errors and then been sent a gas bill which only a small country might have accrued, I have approached this chapter with some caution. The chapter investigates methods for analysing the accuracy of a multilayer perceptron once it has been trained. Errors are not considered as a means of improving the model as during training, rather as a measure of the confidence we should place in an answer. Sometimes, apparent errors are not errors at all; they are simply uncertainties. This is often the case when attempting to classify objects from overlapping classes. It is perfectly acceptable to say "The input has a 70% chance of belonging to class A", which means that seven out of every 10 objects with similar characteristics to the one under consideration belong to class A. We are less concerned by the fact that the target output was one and the true output was only 0.7 than we are by the fact that there is a 30% chance that the object belongs to some other class. Network accuracy measures may be made for the network as a whole or on a case by case basis: the network may be more accurate for some inputs than it is for others.

A network error, or rather, an output from a network which is not equal to the output one would have liked, may be caused by one of three different factors. Firstly, the data with which the network was trained may not carry the information required to complete the task. Secondly, the data may be sufficient but the network model may be wrong. Finally, you may have good data and a good model but either be operating outside the range which the network has learned or simply be using noisy data. In the final case, the errors lie in the data rather than in the network itself, and should be thought of not as mistakes, but as indications of limits or inconsistencies in the system which is being modelled.

Given that we have identified the nature of any errors, we must either remove them in the case of poor data or a poor model or, in the case of noise, quantify them along the range of the system's operating space.

6.2   What do the errors mean?

We saw in chapter 3 how the error rates for the test and training data change during learning. We also saw how one can get an idea of the level of error to expect from a data set. In this section we investigate methods for analysing and removing network errors and present some useful pointers on deciding whether an error level is acceptable.

It is important to point out here that an error is not necessarily a bad thing. For many noisy or overlapping problems, it would never be possible to achieve a zero error level. The errors a network makes can tell us a lot about the task we are trying to make it learn; it is important to look at the results a network gives even if it does not reach its training error criteria in order to discover the type of error being made. In the case of a network (or indeed, any statistical model) trained or tested on noisy data, errors may be thought of as variance around the mean.

6.2.1   Structured or uniform errors

A neural network model is designed to give the right answer, on average, over the entire training set and this restricts the way in which errors can manifest themselves. If the output of the network is the same regardless of the input, then you have simply averaged over your training set; indicating that the task you are attempting is inappropriate for the current network and you must start again. If the errors are more systematic than that, for example all falling within certain regions of input space, then there are more sensible ways of improving the network's performance.

A network which makes errors in some cases and not others indicates several possible problems. Such errors might be caused by insufficient examples of certain regions or categories in the training data. Chapter 2 discusses methods for ensuring a data set is properly balanced. Errors might also be caused by data which falls outside the experience of the network. Techniques for detecting such occasions are presented below. Another cause of variability in the errors produced by a network is variability in either the level of noise or predictive power in the training data. This chapter also investigates methods for detecting such errors.

6.2.2   Error measures

There are several possible criteria to which we could train a network: one approach is to wait for the maximum error to fall below a certain limit. When training a classification network however, you could see a maximum error of 1 if just one training pair was wrongly classified. The average error, or better still, the total distribution of errors is a better measure. A useful exercise is to calculate the level of error you would expect before training the network. We have seen how information theory may be used to give a measure of how well a network will be able to learn a given data set. Section 3.2.10 describes a series of error measures which can be used to gauge the success or otherwise of an attempt to train a neural network.

6.3 Error bars and confidence limits

If the answer derived from a neural network model influences the decisions we make concerning the real world process being modelled, then it would be useful if we knew how much confidence to place on a result. If the variance or reliability of the training data is not consistent across its entire range, then we need to be able to model not only the system's behaviour under a range of conditions, but its predictability under each condition too.

6.3.1 Classification errors

As we saw in chapter 2 on data preparation, an MLP classifier maps a set of (possibly overlapping) regions in input space onto a set of regions in output space. If it is not possible to match every input to the correct region in output space due to contradictions in the training data, then the best we can do is to firstly produce a measure of how well a given input maps to a given region. Secondly we must look at the probability of an object in that region belonging to the class that region denotes.

It is easy to calculate the probability of an object, which falls into a given region, belonging to the set denoted by that region. The single probability value for each region is calculated by passing the training data through the network and comparing the outputs given with the target values. The probability of success for each is simply the proportion of examples which are correctly identified as belonging to that set. The same calculation can be carried out in stricter terms using an independent validation set.

Assigning thresholds

Given that a network classifier produces values between zero and one which, under the right conditions, correspond to *a posteriori* probabilities, how should we make a final decision which specifies the answer? In other words, how do we decide which category the output data is really from? The obvious answer is to choose the output with the highest value. There is, however, a method which allows us to use a finer degree of control over the process by which network output probabilities are converted into final categorisation answers. The technique uses *thresholds.*

Setting thresholds on the output units which force their output (after all neural processing) to zero or one provides a method for making such decisions. Thresholds may also allow for regions of doubt where no answer is given. Foster [36] demonstrated how it is possible to train a neural network to recognise the overlap region in two distributions, although this is unnecessary as setting a threshold on the output, below which a value is discarded, will produce the same results. It is, however, worth noting that the same method can be used to learn the error associated with each area of input space the network has delimited. Such as approach is discussed below in section 6.3.2.

It may be the case that you know the level of error you are willing to accept and are able to set the threshold accordingly. For example, a safety critical system may need to err totally on the side of false alarms–not missing a single potential dangerous situation. On the other hand, a system designed to spot good investments may be required to be almost certain before making a recommendation. Finally a system which reads postcodes will want to classify each input as either a certain character or as unreadable. There are two types of problem for which prior knowledge is of use when choosing output thresholds: the first is concerned with the error–reject trade-off as described below. In the second case we reject no inputs but set the decision threshold somewhere other than at the centre of the network output.

Two threshold values may be applied to each output unit:

t_u = upper threshold value
t_l = lower threshold value

Note that $1 > t_u > t_l > 0$

The error–reject trade-off

The doubt region for non-uniformly distributed, overlapping classes is not bounded by a solid line. As we travel further towards one of the two classes, the measure of doubt diminishes. If we do want to fix a solid line between our doubt region and our acceptance region, we must choose some threshold for the output: values below which we will reject. Here is the dilemma: where do we put the threshold in order to minimise both the classification error and the amount of good data which is discarded? This is the error–reject trade-off.

Let us use an example in which two classes are coded in a single output unit where an output of 1 = class A, and 0 = class B. If we use thresholds of $t_u = t_l = 0.5$ we achieve a perfect split between two classes, zero reject but high error. Moving the thresholds together in either direction will assign more doubtful examples as belonging to one class rather than the other, but while $t_u = t_l$ no data will be discarded.

By moving the thresholds apart, we are left with a region between the two which belongs to no class. This is the reject region. Hansen et al. [44] showed that one experiences diminishing returns the further apart the thresholds move. With normally distributed data, for every extra error you want to eliminate by moving the thresholds, you must reject exponentially more input queries. This can be seen from figure 6.4(a) in section 6.7; the further you move into either one of the distributions, the harder it is to spot a point from the other.

Note that for n class problems, the centre point will be at a threshold value of $1/n$ rather than 0.5. Hansen postulated that the error–reject relationship described above often works for n class problems as these problems are often binary in nature. A problem is binary in nature if any conflict in output decision is restricted to two possibilities: the correct answer and one other.

Practical uses of the error reject trade-off

Because the error reject curve describes the effect of moving a threshold, it can be incorporated into a run-time monitoring and tuning system which allows an operator to set the level of either the error or the reject and see how one affects the other. The costs in terms of time or money of a change in either can easily be assessed before being implemented. Combined with measures of confidence, the error reject curve provides a useful and simple tool for controlling the run-time operation of a neural network based system.

6.3.2   Calculating *a posteriori* probabilities from artificially balanced networks

We saw in section 5.2.2 that it was important to balance the number of training examples from each class of a categorisation task. We saw that a bias in the training distribution introduced an undesirable bias in the network operation which could be removed by artificially balancing the training data. We might still be interested in the effect of the prior probabilities however, in which case we must re-calculate the network output probabilities with respect to the original priors. These new probability values are called *a posteriori* probabilities and they reflect the fact that some events are more likely than others, regardless of the inputs. Remember that balancing the training data removed any information reflecting such facts.

The DTI best practice guidelines [31] present a set of equations for calculating the *a posteriori* probabilities from a balanced network. These equations are listed in section 6.6.1. The danger with these equations is that they become very sensitive to even the slightest error on the network output as the original data distribution becomes more imbalanced. Consequently, the network model must be very accurate for the results to be meaningful in such cases.

Figure 6.1 shows how quickly the *a posteriori* probability, as calculated by these equations, drops with a small decrease in the output value given by a neural network. Note that as the original distribution becomes more even, the less sensitive the final probability score becomes. This fact introduces problems with accuracy when data sets are very unevenly distributed. It becomes important to be sure that the output of 0.99 is due to lower accuracy in the data set and not to the fact that the network wasn't allowed to completely converge. This problem is compounded by the fact that to cause a sigmoidal squashing function to output a value of one you must, given perfect accuracy, provide an infinitely large input. Output will be rounded up to a given accuracy to produce output values equal to one. This same, high, accuracy must be used when calculating the *a posteriori* probabilities of unevenly distributed data sets.

The DTI guidelines, for example, quote a value where a network output of 0.99 leads to a *a posteriori* P value of 0.09 when a data set is distributed with 1000:1 examples

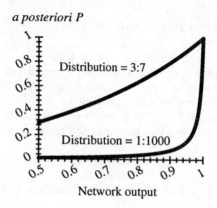

Figure 6.1: The relationship between network output and *a posteriori* probability for data sets with varying original distributions.

from each of two classes but training data is distributed 50:50. Carrying out their same calculations with a network output of 0.999 produces $P = 0.5$. Clearly, it is important to consider the accuracy of the model in such cases.

Empirically calculating the *a posteriori* probabilities

A different way of considering the *a posteriori* probabilities from a balanced neural network is to think of them as an error measure. By treating the network outputs as probabilities (which we can do, as we balanced the training set in the first place) we can consider the error not as the distance that each output is from the desired values of one or zero, but as the distance of the output from the true *a posteriori* probability.

Such an error measure may be calculated in one of two ways, both of which work with reference to the original training and test data. In the simplest case, we can simply calculate the average error associated with each network output category as a probability of error. This provides a simple measure of the probability, on average, that any classification is correct. A network which outputs a probability of p for membership of category C, which has an error probability of e associated with it provides an *a posteriori* probability of $p(1-e)$. The errors must be calculated from the thresholded output values (i.e. the outputs must be forced to one or zero so that all but one contain zero) and are calculated as the probability of an error, i.e. the number of errors (a zero when a one was required or vice versa) divided by the number of tests.

A more advanced approach, based on the same method, would be to calculate local errors. We know that a neural network performs classification tasks by splitting the input space into a number of regions. Each region may have a different error associated with it. These errors can be learned in the same way as the membership probabilities for the same regions may be learned. By training a second network to predict the error values for the first, we can obtain a local error measure for each input presented to the classification network. The next point is important: the errors with which the second network is trained are *not* the same errors with which the first network was trained. That is to say that they are not the distance between the network output and the category target of one or zero—that will just produce the inverse probabilities. The error values to be predicted (i.e. the target values for the second network) are calculated using the thresholded outputs and coded in a binary fashion as *error* = 1 and *correct* = 0. The new training set must be balanced to contain an even number of each *error* or *correct*, and the new network trained in the normal way.

Once the second network has been trained, it will predict the probability that the thresholded output of the classification network will choose the incorrect class (reversing the coding so that *error* = 0 and *correct* = 1 produces the probability of a the answer being correct). The output of this network, e may then be used as the error measure in the same way as in the simple method above, i.e. $p(1 - e)$ (or pe if the coding scheme is reversed). These techniques may be thought of in the light of the observation that the network is classifying *regions* of input space and so producing a probability that a given input falls within a given region. We may also wish to know the probability of a point which falls in that region actually belonging to the category associated with it.

Both techniques are detailed at in sections 6.6.1 and 6.6.3.

6.3.3   Deriving error bars from mapping functions

Detecting errors—or, as we should call them, answers given with less that 100% certainty—in a continuous valued mapping function is harder than it is for classification tasks as there is no clue in the output value itself as to whether we are in a doubt region or not. Points from different areas of input space could give rise to different levels of error for several reasons: firstly, it has been shown [91] that some parts of complex non-linear functions are easier to learn than others. Areas of high curvature are harder to learn for example. Secondly, the training data may represent some parts of the function to be learned better than others. Thirdly, there could be more variance in some parts of the training data than in others. Poor generalisation could result from areas where the system is very complex, data is very sparse or variance is very high.

Jepson et al. [51] present a simple method for assigning confidence limits to neural network models based on training data distribution. Using an independent validation set (IVS), and correlating the network output with the target results, one is able to measure the degree of accuracy of the model and also apply standard statistical techniques to determine whether the fit is significant. If there is any noise in the data then the correlation will be less than one. Assuming that the correlation is significant, plotting the network output against the target values should reveal a cluster of points about a straight line.

This works by assuming that the regression line through the IVS pivots about the average of the network output over the entire test set so that the further away you are from that point $((o - \bar{o})^2)$, the more scope for movement there is. This scope is also limited by the variance of the network output (accounted for by σ_o^2). Equation 6.13 says that the further towards the extremes of the distribution of network outputs and expected values we go, the less confident we can be.

If we want a 95% confidence interval, equation 6.12 tells us that whilst the actual value will most probably be y_c, we can be 95% confident that it will fall within S_{y_e} either side of the expected value y_c. The narrower this range, the more confident we can be about our prediction. This method only works if network output is unimodal; the calculations become more complicated if there is more than one cluster of network outputs.

6.3.4   Extracting structured errors

It has been suggested [87] that it is possible to learn the structure of the errors a neural network makes. This hinges on the assumption that there is structure to the errors. This structure could determine areas of low predictability, or it could be a function which describes the distribution of errors over input space.

If we want to learn this structure, we must start with the following:

- Assume there is structure to the errors. If there isn't, we can only calculate statistics based on the average error.

- Assume that the network has built its model by drawing a curved line through the data set which minimises the squared error over the training set.

- It is absolute error we want to predict (if the errors are distributed evenly about the function, they will have a zero average due to the point above).

- Given that large errors in a region are equivalent to large variance in that region, if we teach a network the error distribution, then we are teaching it the changes in variance over the training (or test) set.

A second neural network which predicts the errors made by the first can be built in the following way:

1. Creating a training set with the same input vectors as the original network.

2. Creating a target output set consisting of the *absolute* values of the errors from the original network. This data may need to be scaled up so that it fills the 0–1 range of the output units.

3. Training a new network on that data.

4. Using the new network to provide confidence levels for new input vectors presented to the original network, remembering to re-scale to the original range if the values were scaled up to fall between zero and one for training the second network.

Satchwell [87] states that setting the target output of the second network as the squared error of the first will produce a network which predicts the variance of the model at each point. Replacing the square with a cube calculates the third moment, or skew and use of a quartic calculates the fourth moment, or kurtosis. This can be seen as a consequence of the fact that a neural network produces a least squares fit to a data set. With noisy data, such a fit (or regression) requires the network to output a local average value given each input. The variance is simply the average squared distance of the network output from each target which is required by the same input pattern. Just as a network produces local averages of output, training a network to predict variance, or squared error, will produce an average measure of variance for each output point.

This method can be extended over more than one output unit in one of two ways. The error on each unit could be calculated, or a single distance metric could be learned which measured the overall distance of the network output point from the desired point. Equations describing this process are included at the end of the chapter.

6.3.5 Accuracy measures from spread encoding

Spread encoding, as discussed in chapter 2 on data preparation, spreads the representation of a single value proportionately over two or more units. The sum of the resultant activation is always one. By using spread encoding on the output layer of the network, it is possible to transpose the problem into something more akin to a categorisation task. I will presently show that a consequence of this scheme is that each output unit, when properly trained, will hold activation values which represent the probability of the answer being equal to the bin centre associated with that unit.

As we have seen in the section on ill-posed problems in chapter 5, spread encoding can allow us to distinguish between the case where a network predicts that the output value could be either a or b and the case where the output is the midpoint between a and b. As a single valued output in a spread encoding scheme should involve a known number of output units (normally two), a measure of accuracy may be gained by investigating the spread of activation across the output layer. The network output will represent a set of probabilities relating to the expected final answer; the expected value must either be calculated as an average or discarded as nonsense.

The expected value may be determined from the highest set of adjacent units over which values are coded—which we will call the winning units (this amounts to decoding the spread code of the most probable output, or calculating the mode of the output). If values are coded over two adjacent units, then the highest two are used to determine the expected value. Care must be taken when decoding the outputs as the probabilities will not sum to one if any unit other than the winning units has an output greater than zero. The output values must be scaled up so that they sum to one whilst maintaining a constant ratio to each other. This ensures that the correct modal value is calculated.

An accuracy measure for the prediction may be calculated based on the fact that the sum of the outputs in a spread encoding scheme should be one. The sum over the winning units will consequently vary over the range from one down to a value just greater than that which would see all the units with an equal score, i.e. s/n where s is the number of units over which the coding is spread (normally two) and n is the number of output units. The greater the sum, the greater the confidence which may be placed on the prediction.

The mean, rather than the mode, of the output can be calculated by decoding every unit and taking an average. This treats the output, as stated above, as a set of probabilities that the expected value will fall upon each bin centre. Calculating the accuracy with respect to the sum of the winning activation makes less sense in this case as more than one group of units is involved. In this case, it is the number of outputs over which the answer is spread, and the distance between them which indicates the level of accuracy. In other words, the variance across the output activation values reflects the variance in the training data and consequently reflects the accuracy of the prediction. By treating the output layer as a set of probabilities, we may also calculate higher order statistics such as skew and kurtosis in the standard way.

The spread of activation across the output layer will have different implications depending on the nature of the task, and averaging across them will consequently take on different meanings. In some cases, the mode will make better sense than the mean, and in others the converse will be true. The same rules apply in this case as those relating to averaging across any set of numbers. The mode is less sensitive to outliers than the mean but the mean takes better account of evenly spread data. As the variance of the outputs is known to us, we are able to make the best choice of average on a case by case basis.

Srivastava and Weigend [95] used a similar coding scheme to predict errors but centred the bins so that each bin contained an equal percentage of the output codes. This was done by sorting the output data into ascending order and splitting the resulting list into a number of equally sized bins. The coding was spread over the bins with respect to their means (where the mean is equivalent to the centre in the previous method). The advantage of this latter method is that quantisation errors (the confusion between membership of two adjacent bins and a single value coded between the two) is minimised. The bins must, of course, be sufficiently small that the confusion caused by two values falling in the same bin is insignificant when determining the final answer.

Pre-scaling the data to within the range from zero to one before choosing bin centres is a good method for ensuring that the correct number and range of bins are chosen and that the data is evenly spread across the bins. A non-linear scaling function (for example softmax) will ensure that values are never too large or too small for the range of bins.

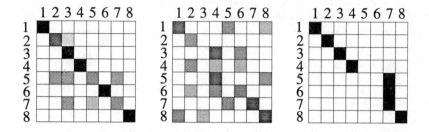

Figure 6.2: Three typical grey level confusion matrices: (a) shows a good model, (b) shows a poor model and (c) shows a model with structured errors. These errors give clues as to which aspect of the network's task needs more work. Rows indicate target values, columns indicate actual network outputs. Grey levels indicate the number of times each row was mistaken for each column.

6.4 Methods for visualising errors

6.4.1 Confusion matrices

Categorisation tasks

A categorisation task in its simplest—and yet most common—form requires an output which indicates a single class membership. By means of a threshold or some other mechanism, the final answer taken from the network tells us the single class of which input vector is most typical. When testing such a network, we have the answer and the target with which to judge the network's ability. These two measures can be used to build a *confusion matrix* of the network's behaviour by building a square matrix with a single row and a single column for each category defined in our data set. The matrix is built by labelling the rows as network targets and the columns as network outputs, and entering at each cell, a count of co-occurrences. The intersection of row B and column C will contain a count of the number of times the network was required to give an output indicating class B but in fact labelled the data as belonging to C. A perfect network then, would have high scores along the leading diagonal (A, A; B, B;...) and zeros elsewhere.

Figure 6.2 shows how it is possible to plot the confusion matrix using grey levels to indicate frequency. The darker the shading of a square in the grid, the more frequently the network produced an answer listed on the same row as the square when the correct answer was that denoted by the square's column. Clearly a black diagonal indicates a perfect set of outputs, but it must also be remembered that unless the categories are ordered by some aspect of similarity, a black square just off the diagonal is just as bad as one in a far corner. A near perfect model produces a confusion matrix with a very dark right hand diagonal and very pale entries elsewhere.

The confusion matrix not only tells us how well the network is doing over the entire test set, but also gives clues as to where the errors are being made. As we have already seen, if the errors a network makes contain structure, then we can learn that structure and reduce the uncertainty associated with the outputs. Investigating the parts of input (or output) space in which a neural network performs badly is a useful method for determining which type of data to collect if more data is deemed necessary.

Mapping functions

For networks with a single output unit, plotting the actual output against a target output value will produce a scatter plot which describes the network's accuracy. The closer to a straight line the scatter is, the better the network's performance. As we have seen, the correlation coefficient of this plot is a good measure of the network's accuracy and can be used for building confidence intervals. For networks with more than one output, several such plots must be produced.

6.4.2   Error histograms

For networks with several outputs or in situations where the size of the errors is more important than their type, an *error histogram* provides a quick method for visualising the distribution of errors a network makes. An error histogram shows a count of the frequency with which an error falls within a set of bandwidths. With a continuous output or a classification probability score from zero to one, these bands must be split into a set of small bins. This is in contrast with the confusion matrix which required the categories to be thresholded; here the distance between a given input and each category at the output layer is used. A healthy network would show a peak at zero, quickly falling off as the number of errors of greater magnitude diminishes. For a data set with normally distributed noise, you would expect a normal distribution on the error histogram.

Figure 6.3 shows the error histogram for the categorisation task used in section 6.5.1 below. The chart was constructed by splitting the real valued network errors into 21 bins and counting the number of errors in each bin. As you can see, the majority of the errors are made in the small error bins, thus signifying a healthy network.

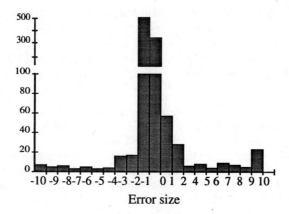

Figure 6.3: The error histogram of a well trained neural network. The vertical axis shows the frequencies of errors of each size on the horizontal axis.

6.5   Novelty detection

In the examples we have investigated so far, there has always been some type of target output for the neural network; always some type of discrimination task to be done, be it that of classifying an input pattern, or that of re-mapping one. There are many cases however, where no such output target exists, or no such discrimination may be made. Such cases usually take the form of a single set of examples of a system behaving in its normal manner, which we wish to characterise. We would like to build a model which knows what it means to belong to the training data set even though we have no examples to the contrary. Having built the model, we then wish to know if a new data point is likely to have come from the system which produced the original model. We wish to detect novelty or measure deviation from the norm.

Such a network has many applications, especially in the field of condition monitoring where the aim is to detect when some system, be it a machine or a medical patient, starts to behave in an abnormal manner. As it may not be possible to collect sufficient data describing what happens to a power station just before melt down, or a patient just before a heart attack, we require a method for building a model of a working power station which is able to detect a deviation from that working state.

An additional advantage to be gained from being able to measure the novelty of a given input vector is that we may know whether or not we are asking a conventionally trained MLP to extrapolate. As we have seen, generalisation from a neural network means interpolation only. A method which is able to determine whether an input vector would force the network to make an invalid extrapolation to a point outside the space on which it was trained would reduce the risk of such an error.

6.5.1   Spotting data outside the experience of the network

One type of test error occurs when a network is given an input vector which falls outside the experience of the network. This is illustrated in the current section by a simple set of experiments and followed by an explanation of a method for overcoming the problem.

As we have seen, an MLP classifier learns *decision boundaries* and not, as is often claimed, a model describing what it means for a pattern to fall in a certain category. As a consequence a network will only need—and indeed, only be able—to define the class boundary where the classes need to be split. This can lead to the network extrapolating to areas outside its training experience and so giving erroneous classifications. Neural networks share a limitation with all function approximators in that they cannot extrapolate sensibly.

Roberts and Tarassenko [84] present a method for detecting novel inputs for an EEG monitor where they build a network from a number of gaussian kernel functions. The learning algorithm looks at each training point and either assigns it to an existing kernel or, if it falls outside the current model, adds a new kernel. The same threshold which is used to determine whether to add a new kernel to accommodate training points is used to decide whether a test input falls within the training experience of the network or not. This method involves building probability density networks and is outside the scope of this book. However, we now present a series of examples designed to allow one to process outliers using a straightforward MLP.

Bishop [15] approaches this problem from a Bayesian viewpoint by showing that the back propagation algorithm settles on the model which has the highest probability of describing the training data. By building other models with smaller probabilities (of describing the data) and then integrating over them all, we gain a greater level of uncertainty in regions of sparse data. There are, however, practical problems involved in training the large number of networks required to span the space of all network probabilities.

The random noise method

One method for allowing a network to spot data points which it should not attempt to process is to build a random data set which covers the entire data space in all dimensions. The new random points must then be assigned to one of two classes: either usable by the network, or noise. This may be done by any one of a variety of statistical methods, the easiest of which is perhaps k nearest neighbour. The k nearest neighbour approach involves selecting each point in the random data set and counting the number of data points in the original training data which lie in close proximity to that point. If sufficiently few proximal points are found then we assign the random point to the noise category. If there are sufficient proximal points, the point is assigned to the usable data category.

We now have two choices as to how the noise data is used. If we are teaching the network a categorisation task, the noise data may be interspersed with the training data and related to a new category, *noise* on the output layer. If this method is used, the new data set which this process produces should contain an equal number of examples as each real category in the network training data set does. We can now add an extra output unit to the network which has a target value of one if the data is noise and of zero otherwise. The network is now trained on the new data set with the noise data mixed in as an extra category to be identified.

Adding an extra category to a network adds to the network size and complexity. It is also not easy for function mapping tasks. In such cases it is probably wiser to build a second network which performs a two-choice categorisation task on each data point presented to the actual mapping network. The output of the second network should indicate whether or not the input to the first network falls into a usable part of input space. This network should be trained on an equal number of examples of data points which are good as those which are not.

This process, whilst working well for small dimensional problems, suffers from exponential explosion as the number of input variables increases. If, for a one dimensional problem, we use N random data points to build our outlier model, then we would need N^d data points for a d dimensional problem. It may be possible, however, to intelligently generate an outlier set; some problems even provide such data for free.

Bromley and Denker [19] used a category they called "rubbish" in order to allow their digit recognition network to eliminate non-numeric inputs. Their network was trained to recognise the digits 0–9 from American zip codes which had been handwritten on envelopes. The segmentation process produced single digits but was not perfect and so also produced strange shapes by cutting digits in half, picking up noise, and so on. By adding an extra target output of *rubbish* which would be activated if such an input was presented, they were able to reduce the number of mis-classifications from 10% to 3%.

It is worth noting that Bromley and Denker had 1642 examples of rubbish against around 2700 examples of each digit; just over half as many. It is often best if the examples from each class are fairly equal in number. If this is not the case, or if you do not have such a set available, then it is a good idea to build or artificially extend such a set. In the case of character recognition, such examples could simply be drawn by hand and entered in the same way as the rest of the training set.

6.5.2 Auto-associative models

The task given to an auto-associative network is to reproduce, at the output layer, the input pattern it receives. The task is made a little more difficult by the use of a hidden layer which contains less units than the input layer. The task for the network becomes that of finding a representation of the structure of the training data which requires less variables in order to code a single point. It must be able to re-code a given input at its hidden layer and decode that representation at the output layer. Such a method has been used for data compression by Cottrell et al. [26]. That is to say that the hidden layer contains a projection of the input representation in fewer dimensions.

The fact that the hidden layer contains an abstract representation of the input may be used to detect input patterns which fall outside the experience of the network. One advantage of trying to map the input pattern to a copy of itself is that errors are very easy to detect. As the target output of an auto-associative network is simply the input with which it was presented, one has all the data required to take a measure of how well the network performed. An input vector from within the network's area of experience will produce an error on the output which falls within a certain range. This range will be known from the training process. The error produced when attempting to process a point from outside the span of the training set will be greater than that produced by an inside point as such a process requires extrapolation on the part of the network. A high error on the output (i.e. a discrepancy between the input and output values) indicates a novel value.

6.6 Implementation details

6.6.1 Calculating *a posteriori* probabilities

The DTI best practice guidelines [31] tell us that if we train a network on an even distribution, but want the answer in terms of an *a posteriori* probability, we must train with an even distribution and apply the following transformations:

$$A = (Network\ output) \times \frac{Actual\ class\ probability}{Probability\ of\ class\ occurring\ in\ training\ set} \quad (6.1)$$

$$B = (1 - Network\ output) \times \frac{(1 - Actual\ class\ probability)}{(1 - Probability\ of\ class\ occurring\ in\ training\ set)} \quad (6.2)$$

The *a posteriori* probability associated with the network output is then calculated as

$$P = \frac{A}{A + B} \quad (6.3)$$

6.6.2   Treating *a posteriori* probabilities as errors

The average error, e, for each output unit in a classification network is calculated from a training (or test) set as

$$e = \frac{\sum_{i=1}^{n}(t_i - \Gamma(o_i))^2}{n} \tag{6.4}$$

where o_i is the output produced by training point i, T_i is the binary target output for o_i, $\Gamma(o_i)$ is the thresholded output (i.e. set to zero or one) shown in equation 6.8, and there are n test points.

An error prediction network for classification tasks may be built as follows:

1. Generate a test set in which the inputs are the same as the original training (or test) set and the single output unit is calculated as the binary value

$$(t_i - \Gamma(o_i))^2 \tag{6.5}$$

2. Train a network on a balanced number of examples of both correct and incorrect thresholded classifications.

3. Use the classification network to calculate the probability of the input vector belonging to each class region and the error network to calculate the probability of the original network making an error. With a classification probability of p and an error probability of e, the *a posteriori* probability of class membership is calculated as

$$p(1 - e) \tag{6.6}$$

6.6.3   Setting thresholds

Upper and lower thresholds, t_u and t_l are specified on each output o, indicating membership of class A so that

$$Class = \begin{cases} A & \text{if } o > t_u \\ Not\ A & \text{if } o < t_l \\ Discard & \text{if } t_l \leq o \leq t_u \end{cases} \tag{6.7}$$

Setting a threshold such that $t_u = t_l$ will result in no data being rejected.

The output, $\Gamma(o)$, from a thresholded unit with an output of o, and a threshold of t, will be

$$\Gamma(o) = \begin{cases} 1 & \text{if } o > t \\ 0 & \text{if } o < t \end{cases} \tag{6.8}$$

6.6.4   Confidence limits from training data distribution

The expected value from an output unit with a value of o can be calculated as a regression line through the target values and expressed as

$$y_c = a + b(o) \qquad (6.9)$$

where a is the y intercept value and b is the gradient of the line. A good fit will have a gradient close to 1 and an intercept at $y = 0$. The value y_c is the expected value.

This equation is calculated using the standard linear regression technique.

These confidence limits depend on the following factors:

- y_c = expected value from equation 6.9;

- t_α = t statistic with $n - 2$ degrees of freedom and $\alpha\%$ confidence;

- n = number of {network output, actual value} pairs;

- σ_y^2 = variance of the expected values from equation 6.9;

- σ_o^2 = variance of the network outputs;

- r^2 = correlation coefficient between the network output and the required output, squared;

- $\bar{o}$ = mean of the network outputs;

- o = network output value.

$$\bar{o} = \frac{\sum_{i=1}^{n} o_i}{n} \qquad (6.10)$$

$$\sigma^2 = \frac{\sum_{i=1}^{n}(o_i - \bar{o})^2}{n} = \frac{\sum_{i=1}^{n} o_i^2 - \frac{\sum_{i=1}^{n} o_i^2}{n}}{n} \qquad (6.11)$$

and is described by the pair of equations:

$$Y = y_c \pm t_\alpha S_{y_e} \qquad (6.12)$$

$$S_{y_e} = \sqrt{\frac{n-1}{n-2}\sigma_y^2(1 - r^2)\left(1 + \frac{1}{n} + \frac{(o - \bar{o})^2}{(n-1)\sigma_o^2}\right)} \qquad (6.13)$$

6.6.5   Training an error predicting network

The following steps should be followed when training a second network to predict the errors made by an existing model:

1. Creating a training input set with the same input vectors as the original network.

2. Creating a target output set consisting of the any number of the measures listed in equations 6.14 to 6.18 below. This data may need to be scaled so that it fills the 0–1 range of the output units.

3. Training a new network on that data.

4. Using the new network to provide confidence levels for new input vectors presented to the original network, remembering to re-scale to the original range if the values were scaled up to fall between zero and one for training the second network.

For the network to predict the variance of the output for any given input:

$$(target - output)^2 \qquad\qquad (6.14)$$

For the network to predict the standard deviation of the output for any given input:

$$\sqrt{(target - output)^2} \qquad\qquad (6.15)$$

For the network to predict the skew of the output for any given input:

$$(target - output)^3 \qquad\qquad (6.16)$$

For the network to predict the kurtosis of the output for any given input:

$$(target - output)^4 \qquad\qquad (6.17)$$

Root squared error

A single error over n output units is calculated as a root squared error over the output units, i.e.

$$\sqrt{\sum_{i=1}^{n}(d_i - o_i)^2} \qquad\qquad (6.18)$$

where d_i is the desired value for each output unit, o_i.

The power to which the difference is raised may be changed to reproduce the equations above.

6.6.6 Accuracy measures from spread encoding

6.6.7 Calculating activation values for spread encoding

The following is based on the premise that the bin centres range from zero to one, i.e., the data must have already been scaled for the methods to work properly. Equations are given for single and multiple dimensional coding schemes. Dimensionality should be kept low as the number of units required to assign m bins to n dimensional data is m^n.

An n dimensional point to be coded is represented by the vector $P = p_1 \ldots p_n$. The network layer has m units, $O = o_1 \ldots o_m$, each referring to a bin centre. Each unit represents an n dimensional centre. A point will be coded across a set of m, n dimensional units, $C = c_{1,1} \ldots c_{m,n}$. Where only a single value is being coded, $n = 1$, O and P become single values, and C becomes a single vector $C = c_1 \ldots c_m$ of bin centre units.

The Euclidean distance in n dimensional space of a point P from a centre C_i is calculated as follows.

- In one dimension:

$$\text{dist}(P, C_i) = \sqrt{(P - c_i)^2} \equiv |P - c_i|$$

  i.e. the positive difference between the two.

- In n dimensions:

$$\text{dist}(P, C_i) = \sqrt{\sum_{j=1}^{n} (P_j - c_{i,j})^2}$$

To code the point P, the output of each unit is calculated as follows.

- In one dimension:

$$o = \frac{1 - \text{dist}(o, C_j)}{\sum_{i=1}^{n} \text{dist}(P, C_i)}$$

- In n dimensions:

$$o_j = \frac{1 - \text{dist}(o, C_j)}{\sum_{i=1}^{n} \text{dist}(P, C_i)} \quad \text{for } j = 1 \ldots m$$

The sum is taken over all the units which are to be used in the coding. All other units take values of zero.

A set of m bins will place a centre at values from zero to one in divisions of $1/m - 1$.

6.6.8 Calculating the expected value from spread encoding

The mean

The mean output, μ, is calculated as the sum of each bin centre multiplied by its output activation.

In one dimension:

$$\mu = \sum_{i=1}^{m} o_i c_i \qquad (6.19)$$

For multi-dimensional data, the mean value for each single variable, μ_j is

$$\mu_j = \sum_{i=1}^{m} o_i c_{i,j} \quad \text{for } j = 1 \dots m \qquad (6.20)$$

The mode

The mode of output is calculated by choosing the set of s adjacent units which have the highest summed activation, and re-scaling their outputs so that they sum to one. s must be equal to the number of bins a value is spread across when initially coded (usually 2). All other network outputs are then set to zero, and the mean calculated as above.

To re-scale each network output in the winning class, $\{w\}$ from their original values o_i to a new set of values which sum to one, $\hat{o}_i$, use

$$\hat{o}_i = \begin{cases} o_i \dfrac{1}{\sum_{i \in \{w\}} o_i} & \text{if } i \in \{w\} \\ 0 & \text{otherwise} \end{cases} \qquad (6.21)$$

Once the values have been re-coded, the expected value may be calculated by substituting $\hat{o}$ into equation 6.19 above.

6.6.9 Calculating accuracy measures from spread encoding

Having calculated the mean

If the mean value is calculated, then the variance provides a measure of accuracy. The variance of the output is calculated as

$$\sigma^2 = \sum_{i=1}^{m} o_i^2 c_i - \mu^2 \qquad (6.22)$$

Having calculated the mode

If the modal expected value is calculated, then an accuracy measure derived from the proportion of the total output activation which contributes to that modal value, A, may be used:

$$A = \frac{\sum_{i \in \{w\}} o_i - \frac{s}{n}}{1 - \frac{s}{n}} \tag{6.23}$$

where $\{w\}$ is the set of winning units and o_i is the output of unit i. Do not calculate the variance across the winning units as the re-scaling will render it meaningless.

6.7   A simple two class example

As a simple example to illustrate several points from the current chapter, let us build a network to classify points from the two overlapping Gaussian distributions shown in figure 6.4(a). Figure 6.4 illustrates the following discussion in terms of a binary decision task: is the input in class A or class B? Figures 6.5 and 6.6 show the level of certainty with which the network produces its answer and represent a cross section through the data three quarters of the way up the input map (a). The three figures are worked through concurrently.

An MLP with two inputs and one output which scores 1 if the input is in class A and 0 for class B easily learned to divide the two classes. If we use a threshold on the network output of 0.5 to force output to 1 or 0 and so convert the task into a binary decision, then the dividing line drawn by the network falls as indicated in figure 6.4 (b). This figure demonstrates the problem of a network learning a task in terms of a decision boundary rather than the actual probabilities of points falling in certain places; the network model of the two classes as shown in (b) does not well reflect the original distribution shown in (a).

Similarly, figure 6.5(a) shows the level of certainty which a Bayesian model would assign to a cross-section through the input space and (b) shows the network's level of certainty for the same cross section. Note that certainty is still high even at the extremes of the distributions where data was sparse and the Bayesian probability is low.

In order to improve our model, let us generate a set of points which are evenly distributed over the entire input space, and assign each point to one of two new classes: *data point* or *outlier*. An outlier is a point with sufficiently few near neigbours in the training set. If we train an MLP to learn this new classification, as shown in figure 6.4 (c), then we can use its output to decide whether or not each test point is within the learned distributions.

Figure 6.5(b) shows the certainty the network has of a point being in at least one of the classes to be learned. By multiplying the outputs of the two networks together, we end up with the distribution map shown in figure 6.4(d) with certainties show in figure 6.6(b).

Figure 6.7 shows the error–reject trade-off for the network output from figure 6.4(b). The exact shape of the curve is determined by the shape and overlap of the training distributions. Looking at figure 6.7, we can see that we can almost halve the original error of 1000 that a threshold at 0.5 (i.e. no rejects) returns by rejecting 10% of the input vectors. To reduce the error to 10, we must throw away half of our data and any decrease in error after that will leave us with barely an accepted input to process. Such a curve is easily derived by changing the value of the threshold over the range $t_u = 0.5, t_l = 0.5$ to $t_u = 0.999, t_l = 0.001$ and counting the number of outputs which fall into the categories of *error* or *reject*. The size of the reject region for any specific problem will depend on the overlap in class membership. The acceptable reject rate will depend on how critical it is that the system is correct balanced with how expensive it is to process rejects manually.

6.8 Unbalanced data: A mail shot targeting example

A good example of a task based on an unevenly balanced data set is that of mail shot targeting. Imagine a bank wanted to build a model which was able to predict the type of customer who was most likely to respond to a certain type of marketing mail shot. Data from a previous mail shot might provide a data set where 92% of all clients did not reply. Training on the full, unbalanced data set would result in the network learning that any given person had an approximately 92% chance of not responding. The subtle features which distinguish those who did or did not respond are lost to this far easier method of achieving a 92% success rate. Manipulating the data so that the prior probability of a client responding becomes 50% ensures that any reduction in error must be due to features which distinguish respondents from their counterparts rather than to any bias in the data.

In the following examples, the following distinctions are made.

- Class *one* is the class into which most data points fall and is of no interest. This corresponds to non-respondents in the mail shot example.

- Class *two* is the class of interest into which only a small proportion of the inputs fall. This corresponds to respondents in the mail shot example.

- Region *two* is the region of interest. It is the part of input space into which class two members consistently fall. It describes some features which class *two* members have in common.

- Region *two* is also referred to as the region of doubt in cases where not every input which falls into the region belongs to class *two*. In this case, probability provides the only method of guessing whether a resident of region *two* will be a member of class *two* or not.

- Region *one* is the rest of input space.

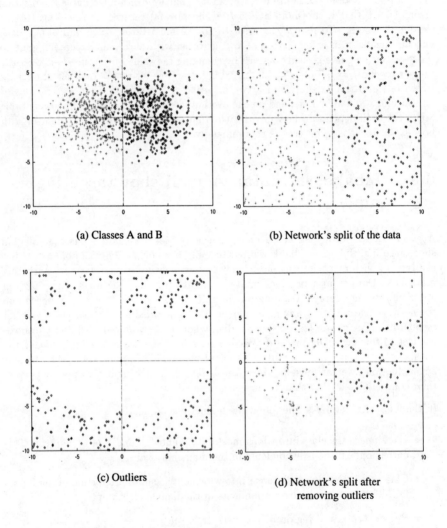

(a) Classes A and B

(b) Network's split of the data

(c) Outliers

(d) Network's split after
removing outliers

Figure 6.4: (a) The original training distribution; (b) the network outputs when tested over the entire data space; (c) the learned outlier set; (d) the combination of the category network and the outlier network.

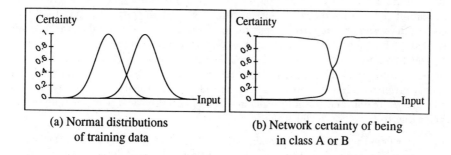

(a) Normal distributions
of training data

(b) Network certainty of being
in class A or B

Figure 6.5: Network certainty for the plots from the discussed example.

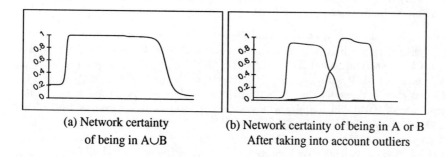

(a) Network certainty
of being in A∪B

(b) Network certainty of being in A or B
After taking into account outliers

Figure 6.6: Training data distributions and network certainty for the plots from the
discussed example.

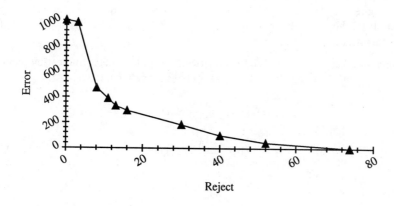

Figure 6.7: The error–reject trade-off from the discussed example.

It is essential to realise that the output of a neural network classifier describes the probabilities (or some other measure of certainty) that the given input will fall into each of the designated *regions* in input space. These regions are shaped by the network so that each region contains as many examples as possible of the class to which it is assigned. An error will result from any region containing a few examples from classes other than its own. If we want to know the true probability of a given input falling into a given output class, we must first calculate the probability that it falls into the correct region and secondly calculate the probability of a point in that region belonging to the class to which the region is assigned.

In cases where the training set contains an equal number of examples from each class, the output of a well trained network will fully reflect the probabilities of class membership as any confusion or contradiction will result in a probability of membership of a region in proportion with the training data. In cases where some examples have been artificially duplicated, these probabilities will become distorted and the true values will have to be calculated.

Figure 6.8(a) shows a two dimensional version of the mail shot problem. Ninety two percent of the data points in the plot belong to class *one*, the rest to class *two*. The points in the second, small class are grouped in the area bounded by 0.6 and 0.7 on each axis. An MLP with four hidden units and one output with a target of zero for the first class and one for the second was trained. The network settled on an average error rate of 0.016 which appears successful until you calculate that as 1269 of the 1280 data points fall into the category where an output of zero is required and only 11 require a one, then simply outputting zero to every input would yield an average error of $11/1280 = 0.009$. As expected, this is what the network did. Regardless of the input, the output was around 0.006. There was still slight variance in the network output which was due to the network giving a slightly higher response for higher inputs. The variance did not reflect the classes in the data.

Figure 6.8(b) shows the results of training the same network on the same data having extracted the 11 small set members and duplicated them so that the network saw an equal number of examples from each class. Height indicates the probability of a point belonging to the small class. Examples from each were mixed randomly for presentation to the network. This time the network has successfully separated out the two classes.

Applying equations 6.1, 6.2, and 6.3 to a network output of 0.999 (indicating membership of the small set) results in the final probability value of 0.9:

$$A = 0.999 \times \frac{0.009}{0.5} = 0.018$$

$$B = 0.001 \times \frac{0.991}{0.5} = 0.002$$

$$P = \frac{0.018}{0.020} = 0.9$$

This allows us still to be sure that the input is in the chosen category. As the network output becomes any less than 0.999, the *a posteriori* quickly drops, thus illuminating

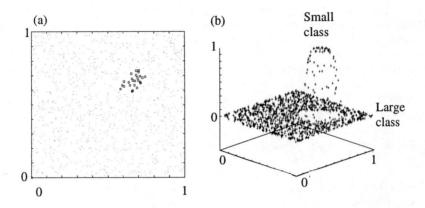

Figure 6.8: (a) The unevenly distributed training data which, if used in its current proportions leads to a network with a flat response function; (b) the response function of a network which has been trained on the same data with the examples of the smaller class duplicated so that the examples from each class are equal in number.

the mid-range responses seen on what appear to be walls around the decision region in figure 6.8.

A second experiment demonstrates how sensitive to changes in the distribution this method is. This time, the small area which bounds the second class is not filled exclusively with points which belong to that class. In this case a random 50% of those points really belong to class *one*. The data set is still balanced 50:50, but the area bounded by region *two* contains contradictory data points. Half of the data points in region *two* belong to class *one*, the other half to class *two*. However, as the examples of class *two* members were duplicated to even out the training set ratio as a whole, the proportion of examples in region *two* alone becomes approximately 100:1. The same neural network which was used to learn the balanced set in the previous example was trained on this new data set. For an input class to which the first network would produce an output of 0.999; producing an *a posteriori* value of 0.9, the second network produced a value of 0.992 which produces an *a posteriori* value of 0.53.

It is, unfortunately, never clear when such a small difference is due to an imbalance in the training set or an inability of the network to learn the task perfectly. In cases where there is a great imbalance in the number of examples from different classes, more care needs to be taken over data set analysis. In the above example, when the networks had not fully converged, the first, balanced, network exhibited a range of outputs between 0.989 and 1—depending on how close to the centre of the decision region the values fell. The second, confused, data set produced network outputs in the range 0.9 to 0.999: a variance nine times as large as that of the first network.

6.9   Auto-associative network novelty detection

Figure 6.9 shows a very simple example using two class data. An auto-associative
network with two inputs, two outputs, and a single hidden unit was trained on the
data from category A. Figure 6.9(a) shows the data set; class A only was used for
training the network. Figure 6.9(b) shows the network output when tested on data
from classes A and B. The top curve, labelled class A, shows the normal working
range determined by the training data. The lower curve shows the output generated
by data from outside that range. Figure 6.9(c) shows a histogram of the error on
the output layer of the network when presented with random points from class A
and then from class B. The vertical line divides the examples from the two classes.
Finally, figure 6.9(d) shows the error produced by a data set which follows a straight
horizontal line through the centre of class A over the entire range of the data space.
The labelled region defines that covered by class A in the training data. It is clear
that the further from the centre of class A the input point falls, the greater the error
from the auto-associative network becomes.

6.10   Training a network on confidence limits

Figure 6.10 shows the steps involved in training an MLP on the error bars for a
simple function: (a) shows the original distribution with the neural network fitted
line through the centre; (b) shows the absolute error values, again with a neural
network fitted model; (c) shows the original network function with added confidence
intervals. Note that the original model fails to capture the system behaviour at the
bottom end of the data set, a fact which is reflected by the confidence limits.

6.11   An example based on credit rating

The following example was simulated to demonstrate the difference between structured and unstructured errors. The example is based on a credit rating system designed to determine whether an applicant should be granted credit, based on a set
of personal factors. The answer will be of the form *yes* or *no*. A set of rules which
determine whether or not a person with a certain profile would be given credit were
used to produce a set of synthetic data for this example. The rules were of three
types:

1. Rules where a certain profile always led to a certain output.

2. Rules where a certain profile always led to a random output.

3. One final procedure which took a random 10% of the data points and flipped
   their answers so that *no* became *yes* and *yes* became *no*.

A training set and an independent test set were produced and a network was trained
until the error rate reached a level which indicated that only the random variance in

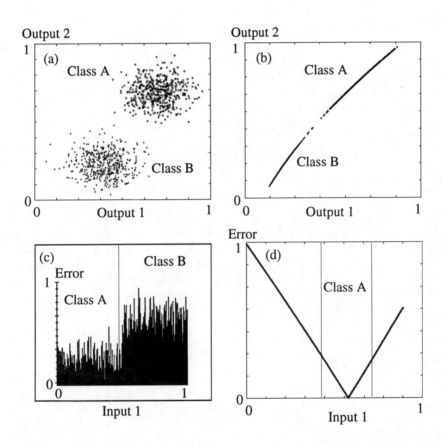

Figure 6.9: (a) The training and test data clouds; (b) the output of a network, trained on A and tested on A and B; (c) the errors made by that network; (d) the errors made by the same network tested on a cross-section of the entire data space.

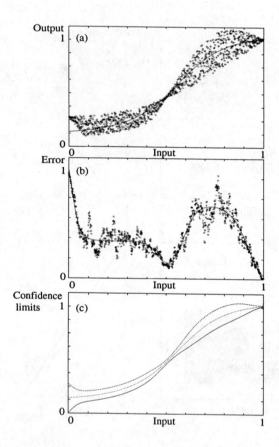

Figure 6.10: (a) The original data to be learned; (b) the absolute errors; (c) confidence intervals. The dots show the training data points and the lines show the neural network model.

the data (the level of which we knew, having programmed the rules) remained. As the network had extracted all of the information present in the data, the errors in the test data could be ascribed to one of two causes: firstly those caused by the profiles which led to a random output, and secondly those caused by the flipped outputs.

Entropy analysis between the input patterns and the errors revealed some predictive structure so a second network was trained to predict the errors of the first. This was done by applying a threshold to the original network output to obtain a definite *yes*/*no* answer and then building a new training set which contained an equal number of examples of correct and incorrect results. We will call the results from the first network successes and errors to avoid confusion. The errors made by the first network were all due to rule types 2 and 3 above. The second network classified the successes from the first network perfectly as they contained no noise. These were type 1 cases. Of the errors from the first network, some were classified correctly and some were not. Those which were correctly classified as being errors were all produced by rules of type 2 above and could be identified as a certain profile always led to an error. The errors made by the second network were all due to rules of type 3 above and, in this case, should not be viewed as errors of the network, for the network is perfectly consistent, but as errors in the training data which is not.

A third network was built in order to attempt to learn the remaining errors. Primary analysis using entropy measures showed the data to be random and, as expected, the neural network settled on a prediction of 50% certainty for both *yes* and *no* answers for each example. So we have deduced, analytically, what we knew to be true at the start: that some profiles lead to an answer, some provide no clue to an answer at all, and some of the errors were due to mistakes in the training data which we can discard. Removing rules of type 3 allowed us to correctly predict all of the successful answers and discard all those which would lead to an error.

Chapter 7

Network use and analysis

... one of the things we cannot answer satisfactorily is how a neural network gets the answer it does. This is important for legal reasons.
Inderjit Sundhu, Senior technical consultant, Barclays Bank.
PC User, December 1994

7.1   Introduction

One of the main criticisms levelled at neural networks is the claim that it is not possible to discover why they produce the answers they do. This belief stems from the fact that neural networks were once touted as miraculous black boxes performing some strange magic which could only be understood in terms of the codings which the black boxes somehow invented for themselves. This is, of course, a complete fallacy. The following sections present some simple methods for deriving explanations of a neural network's outputs which do not require any alteration to the learning procedure or any investigation of weights or hidden unit clusterings. It also demonstrates how a neural model may be used to search or optimise the system it models.

The need for deriving explanations is far greater in America than it is in the UK. In the States, credit providers must, if they refuse you credit, provide a reason why. Medical systems, in order to become approved by the FDA, must be driven by a set of rules or definitions which a human could understand and verify. On a more practical note, understanding why a market model has told us to drop the price of our products or why a process monitoring system has suggested we shut off a machine will not only increase confidence in neural models but further reduce the possibility of error.

7.2   Extracting reasons

It is one thing to use a neural network to prove that your company would sell more widgets if you painted them blue, and quite another to go to the production manager and say *"We need to paint the Widgets blue because the sum of the weights from the input units, taken through these logistic functions ...*". Rule based systems are popular in industry because the rules make sense to the managers. Networks of weighted logistic functions, it seems, do not and managers are understandably reticent about investing large sums of money based solely on the output from such a network.

Decision trees—A common alternative to neural networks

A popular method of deriving rules from a data set involves building a decision tree in which each fork splits the data along a line which accounts for as much of the variability in the data as possible. To classify a new item, we traverse the tree, using the rules to follow the correct path until we reach a leaf on the tree, which tells us to which class the item belongs. A rule base for identifying animals might have the first decision branch asking "Does it swim?" followed by questions concerning legs, wings and so forth. If our object is a tadpole, we will follow the "Yes, it swims" branch. Next, the decision may be "Fresh water or salt?"; And so it goes until the answers take us to the bottom of the tree where, if all goes well, the tag *tadpole* will be found.

Reasons for the answer are easily generated by referring to the path taken down the tree. As the higher branches are concerned with decisions which cause the greatest split in the data (you wouldn't start the animal classifier with "Does it have a red breast?"), the rule which dictates the first decision may be cited as the prime reason for the final choice. Subsequent rules may be cited as more detail is required and the tree is further traversed.

The split of a decision tree is based on separating as much of the training set as possible at each branch, i.e. keeping approximately equal amounts of data on either side of a split. Proximity in the tree is consequently determined by the number of splits which separate two entities. It is sensible to say that a tadpole is similar to a stickleback because they share a set of features, whereas a tadpole and a giraffe will be separated, perhaps, on the very first branch of the tree. Tracing a path back up the tree from two leaf nodes, i.e. two answers, allows us to discover the point at which the two diverged.

Rule based systems such as the one just described are able to produce general rules and explanations of the answer because they build a structure of linear decisions. The split at each branch of the tree subdivides the data into still smaller regions by drawing straight lines through the current sub-division. While this does allow non-linear data to be modelled, it requires the superposition of hierarchically arranged linear decisions. If the effect a certain attribute has at one part of the tree differs from that which it has at another branch elsewhere in the same tree, then the model contains non-linearities. Non-linearities in a system introduce the need for local, ungeneralisable rules.

Extracting rules or reasons from a non-linear model

Non-linearities in a system mean that the effect of a change in the value of one input variable will depend on the values of all of the input variables. This means that setting all but one input constant and varying the value of the one which is left will not tell you anything useful about the effect that input has on the overall behaviour of the system. It will only describe the effect of that input, given that the other inputs do not vary. In consequence, we cannot look at the behaviour of any given example and derive a generalisable rule without adding a proviso based on the state of the system at the current input.

With a wholly linear system it is possible to extract general rules. "Female birds lay eggs" for example, is a linear rule as whatever the other attributes of the creature happen to be, the rule "If it is a female bird then it will lay eggs" will hold true. On the other hand the rule "If it has no shell then it is a slug" only applies when the creature currently under analysis has already satisfied the system on several criteria and the only doubt remains as to whether we have a slug or a snail. The same rule applied to a creature that followed a branch concerning sea creatures and the possession of claws would yield a different answer. In this case the rule is context sensitive, and so non-linear.

In the linear case we are able to extract all-encompassing rules and then cite those rules as explanation for a certain answer. In the non-linear case, we cannot extract all encompassing rules, but we can still give explanations for specific examples by reciting the path taken through the tree.

7.2.1   Neural networks can give explanations

Neural networks are generally used to build non-linear models. Non-linear models do not yield all encompassing rules, but do allow for explanations of individual answers. How then, might we extract explanations from a neural network? Let us take the simple example of house price prediction. We would like to enter the details for a given property and have the system come up with a price to sell at. Furthermore, the system is required to give a reason for its choice. If we assume for simplicity that we are only concerned with properties in Florida and in Alaska and that the only details we have concern air conditioning, the rules would be simple. Figure 7.1 shows a decision tree for the model. Note that Florida is more expensive than Alaska and that air conditioning in Florida has a large effect whereas in Alaska it is of no importance and so is excluded from the tree.

If we were to present a house for valuation, we could ask the reason for the price given and be told "Because it is in Alaska" in one case, but be told "Because it is in Florida and has no air conditioning" for another. We could ask instead, "Does the air conditioning affect the price?" and find that in one case it does not, and in the other it does. All this is possible by traversal of the tree.

A neural network does not have decision nodes we can peer in at, or branches we can traverse, so we must find the equivalent. The non-linear aspect of the given example is clearly the air conditioning: in one case it makes a large difference to the output, and in another case it makes no difference at all. It is the fact that air conditioning has a large effect in one case which allows the system to cite it as a reason for that decision and to exclude it from an explanation of another. The information we must extract from a neural network, when it gives an answer, must relate to the importance

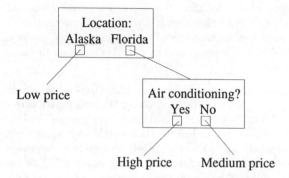

Figure 7.1: A decision tree for house prices according to location and presence of air conditioning.

of each factor at that particular point. This importance is a measure of how much the answer would change if we were to make a small change to the value of each individual input. If it is possible to greatly vary the value of a given input with little effect on the output, then that variable, in this case, evidently contributes little to the decision. This allows us to state the following definition for linearity between any input and any output variable.

A linear relationship exists between any input-output variable pair if, and only if, the effect on the output caused by a constant change on the input is constant throughout the whole network space. Any variance in the derivative of an output unit with respect to a certain input unit as the value in that, or any other, input unit changes indicates a non-linear relationship between the two.

Spotting non-linearities

If the relationship between any input variable and any output variable is non-linear, then we cannot extract a definite rule independently linking the two. By a rule, I mean a proportional relationship between two variables[1]. *The more it rains, the more umbrellas we sell* is such a rule.

Pilkington [75] suggests that non-linearities between input and output variables may be spotted by calculating the correlations between the value of each input value and the sensitivity of each output unit at each point in the network's operating space. Non-zero correlations reveal non-linearities. This is because, in a linear relationship, the sensitivity of an output unit—i.e. its derivative with respect to the chosen input—will remain constant as the value of that chosen input variable changes. Variation in one variable which leads to none in another is indicated by zero correlation. Any change in the gradient of the output should lead to some correlation with the input—thus

---

[1]In the case of a monotonic relationship which is non-linear with respect to the input unit concerned, but linear with respect to all other input units, then a non-proportional rule may still be derived.

indicating non-linearities.

Spotting linear relationships

Unfortunately, as correlation is a linear measure, it is possible for a non-linear relationship to lead to a zero correlation. All we can discover from this method is that it is possible that all of the relationships in the data are non-linear, but there are some we can be sure about. As this method requires an exponentially expanding data set size as the number of inputs grow, you might hope for a little more return from your effort. The Pilkington correlation method is based on the need to determine whether the derivative of each output with respect to each input is constant over the entire range of inputs, based only on a measure of how the output changes with respect to a change over all those inputs. It fails because the measure can be zero whether there is a non-linear relationship or not. There are several other ways of determining whether any single variable has a linear effect on each output unit. These methods work because, as we shall see below, it is possible to calculate the derivative of each output unit with respect to an individual input unit without the need to perturb the network inputs.

The methods presented below are based on the derivatives of the network function at the point under consideration. That is to say, the proportional effect on the outputs which any small change to the current input variables would have. Derivatives measure slope, or gradient, in a function and a neural network is a no more than a complex function. The method by which a neural network is differentiated is presented in section 7.4.

A good method of spotting linearities in a network is to measure the variance of the partial derivatives of each output unit with respect to each input unit as random input patterns are presented to the network. Any such partial derivative with zero (or low) variance over a sufficiently large sample of input patterns indicates a linear relationship between the input variable and the output unit concerned. Such linear input—output relationships may be converted into simple rules which state the proportional effect the single input unit has on the single output value. As we shall see in the example below, sudden non-linearities (i.e. large steps) in an otherwise flat relationship may be used to detect sharp decision boundaries.

Investigating the effect of a single input variable over a smaller range

It is now possible to devise a method for altering a single input variable whilst keeping the others constant in order to measure the effect of that variable over part of its range. For such a practice to be valid, the differential effect that all of the input variables have on the output must remain constant. It is apparent therefore that it is only valid to measure the effect that a variation of one input variable has on the output values over a certain range. In this range, the gradient of the output with respect to all of the input variables must remain constant. Put simply, such a method only works in areas of local linearity, or at least where non-linear effects are small.

A quick example will serve to illustrate the point. Let us imagine we have built a neural model which predicts the demand for the watermelons we are selling from a stall on the beach. The network takes factors such as temperature, price of melons, and whether it is raining. One warm day we try a little experiment. We keep the variables indicating no rain and warmth constant, and we vary price. As price rises, predicted demand drops very slightly. Higher and higher we push the price, and still the demand hardly changes. Suddenly, a little more of a price increase, and demand falls sharply. A look at the derivative of demand with respect to price shows no change, so why has demand dropped? Looking at the derivative of temperature with respect to demand reveals that as long as the price is below a certain level, demand is affected by temperature to a constant degree, i.e. the derivative with respect to temperature remains constant. As soon as the price goes above a certain level temperature becomes more important and we can no longer treat the effect of price as we could before.

Non-linearities could manifest themselves in a number of ways on the melon stall. Perhaps, even on the hottest days, demand will eventually fall dramatically if price is pushed too high. In this case the derivative of demand with respect to price will show non-linear behaviour. Perhaps when it rains, nothing is sold regardless of price. In this case the derivative of demand with respect to price will be zero. A change in any of the derivatives as the value of any single input variable is changed indicates that any conclusions drawn from the system's behaviour when the derivatives were constant are no longer valid.

Discovering the relevance of each variable to a given answer

Returning to and extending the house price example across a range of temperatures and a measure of effectiveness of the air conditioning of the given house, figure 7.2 shows the non-linear relationship between the two variables and house price. Note that at the low end of the temperature scale, air conditioning has little effect on price but as the temperature increases, so does the importance of air conditioning, and so does the slope of the function.

Given that we actually know nothing about the structure of the data, if we enter an input representing a house in a cold area with no air conditioning, the network will return a low house price. To find out why, we can look at the gradient on the inputs, calculated by back propagation, and discover that at this point, the slope is steeper along the temperature dimension. Therefore the low temperature is the primary reason for the low price of the house. The slope along the dimension of air conditioning effectiveness is shallow at this point and so can be deemed to have had little effect on the price. This also allows us to ask *"How can I improve the value of the property?"*. Clearly, altering the value in the dimension with the highest positive gradient would yield the greatest increase in price. Unfortunately, in this case, it would involve jacking the house onto a truck and driving it to a warmer climate.

Conversely, a house in a hot climate will show a steeper gradient along the dimension of air conditioning effectiveness, which would now be cited as the primary reason for the answer and as the dimension along which an improvement would have the greatest effect on value.

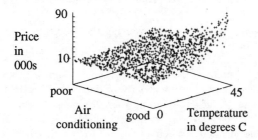

Figure 7.2: House prices plotted against the temperature of the region and the effectiveness of the air conditioning in the house. Note that where temperature is low, the air conditioning is of no importance, whereas further up, it has a far greater effect.

Now we can see more clearly the effect of non-linearities in a system. Another way of defining a linear system is to say that the gradients along each dimension are constant along their entire range. It is this constancy which allows us to derive general rules. As the gradients in a non-linear system change across their range, we can only derive very local rules or explanations.

7.2.2   Deriving knowledge from continuous mappings

We have already discussed how, in the case of the house pricing example, we were able to determine which of the input factors contributed most to a given network output. Methods by which the gradients may help us to understand or explain other aspects of an output are discussed below.

Using the gradients to aid decision making

Knowing about the gradients at the current point in a neural network model aids decision making in two ways: firstly it tells us about the reasons behind the answer given, and secondly it allows us to find out what kinds of changes we should make to the inputs in order to effect the greatest change in any desired direction on the outputs. Another example will illustrate the point. Let us say we have built a neural model describing the effect which a company's marketing mix has on revenue. We might be interested in two different types of question: firstly, how can we increase revenue with only a small increase in expenditure? Clearly we need to identify the input variable with the highest slope as a small increase in expenditure in that area will lead to the largest increase in revenue. Secondly, we might want to reduce expenditure in some area whilst having a minimal effect on revenue. In this case we would look for the variable with the most shallow slope as we can move down in that dimension with the least effect on revenue.

Derivatives are identical to elasticities in economic modelling

In the case of decision support, we are not using the gradients to directly identify a reason for the given output, but deriving an explanation for the decision which the gradients help us to make. We can now say why a decision was taken by referring to the gradients at the current point in the network. When economists talk about gradients, they use the word elasticity. Price elasticity of demand refers to the proportional change in demand one would expect from a small change in price. Cigarettes are price inelastic: you can increase the price considerably before too many people will kick the habit. Cross-elasticity of demand refers to the change in demand for one product given a change in price of a competitor's product. Elasticities may be defined between any set of factors.

Training a network to predict demand from price would produce a demand curve, the elasticity of which would be equal to the derivative of the input (price) with respect to the output (demand). Models with greater numbers of parameters still provide elasticity values between each combination of single input and output parameters. These are the partial derivatives of the network. A system is linear when the elasticity between any pair of parameters remains constant regardless of the values of any of the other parameters. When non-linearities are present, the elasticity of any one parameter against any other will depend on the values which the variables contain.

So what can we tell our managers? Perhaps that we can afford to raise the price by 1% because present conditions in the market have caused price elasticity of demand to fall. The other partial derivatives tell us how closely we need to watch the market before dropping the price again. A steep derivative relating to one of the other factors in the model tells us that if that factor changes by a small amount, the advantage we were trading on may disappear.

Developing a non-linear model of a marketing system allows us to spot anomalies in (say) the demand curve which may have been previously undiscovered. A product might, for example, experience a reversal in the demand curve at high prices due to an ostentation effect. If such an effect is detected, it is important to determine the conditions which must prevail for the effect to persist.

7.2.3   Explanations from categorisation tasks

Continuous valued inputs and probabilistic outputs

Categorisation tasks which map continuous valued inputs onto output categories in a probabilistic manner may also be analysed in terms of the gradient of the model at the current input point. In such cases the slope tells us about how close to the centre of a given distribution we are and how quickly we will move out of that distribution if we change any input value. The gradient is not equal to the probability of class membership, rather it is an inverse measure of membership. A low (or zero) gradient tells us that we are well within the given class and that small perturbations in the input will not take us out of that class. This may seem to be of little help as the output units' values are equal to the membership probabilities, but we are able to derive more interesting facts.

Let us consider the case where an input falls close to the extremities of a class which overlaps several others. Such a case is easy to detect as the largest probability output will be considerably less than one and not much greater than one or more of the others. As discussed in chapter 6 on errors, the variance across the outputs is a good measure of the confidence we can place on a classification. By examining the output units we may know which is the most likely classification, how confident we may be in that classification, and what are the next most likely answers. We cannot know, however, the dimensions along which the classes overlap. In other words, we know that a small change in the input values might cause the classification to change, but we do not know which variables are more sensitive and to what extent this sensitivity exists. This knowledge is held in the derivatives of the network.

The partial derivative of each output with respect to each input tells us how close to the edge of each output class the current input lies along the dimension described by each input variable. The larger the value, the greater the sensitivity along that dimension. Positive gradients tell us that a small increase in the given input unit will move the point further into the given output class and negative gradients tell us that a small increase in the given input unit will move the point further away from that class. Care must be taken over one point: a low gradient may mean one of two things—either the point is well within the class and robust to small changes, or the input variable in question has little bearing on this particular classification and you could change it all you liked with little effect. Care must be taken, when basing assumptions on such points, not to attribute reason for class membership to a variable of no importance.

Binary input or output representations

Tasks which require an input vector which describes the presence or otherwise of a set of features belonging to the item to be categorised require binary codings on both the input and the output layers. Consequently, there is no concept of a small change in any input variable; the feature is either present or it is not. This is reflected in the gradient measures derived from a neural network as the derivative for an output value of one or zero is zero. A small change in the input will cause no change in the output. Of course, with infinite precision the sigmoidal activation function will never reach a value of one, but with the limited precision of a computer representation, such values are easily reached.

In cases where any given output decision relies only on a subset of the input features (in the case of the animals example, whether a stickleback has webbed feet or not is of no consequence, but must be included in a simple coding scheme), an explanation may be derived in terms of a list of those inputs which are important. In such cases, the derivative matrix may be derived empirically by flipping the value of each input unit in turn, keeping all others constant, and noting the change across the set of output

units. Flipping translates ones to zeros and zeros to ones and is implemented with
the function $x = (x - 1)^2$. Input units which cause a change in the output pattern
form part of the derived rule for the given input vector. Those which have no effect
on the output may be ignored.

The result may be expressed as a rule of the form **if** *condition list* **then** *output category*
where *condition list* is a list of the contributing input variables equated with the values they took in the current example and concatenated by **and**s. *output category* is
the category determined by the selected output unit. The conditions are translated
into English rules with reference to the original coding scheme. As chapter 2 describes,
such inputs may be coded to indicate the presence or absence of features, or as one of
several possibilities in a set of feature clusters. For example, *has a tail* may be coded
as a one in a single unit dedicated to the presence of tails, whereas colour of tail may
be coded across a set of units which represent *red, brown, grey* etc. Rules stated in
terms of conditions concatenated by **or**s are not as simple to derive as they rely on
more than one input pattern.

Hybrid representations

As we have seen, it is quite acceptable to build an input representation from a mixture
of binary and continuous variables. In such cases, the calculated derivatives for the
continuous values may be used in conjunction with the measures of sensitivity derived
for the binary values by flipping their values whilst keeping all other inputs constant.
The same matrix is derived, but built from the conjunction of two different methods.

7.2.4   Linear rule generation from perceptrons

Single layer perceptrons are linear neural networks with no hidden units. Each input
variable will have the same effect on the output regardless of the values in the other
input units. For this reason, rules may be derived by varying each input unit across
its entire range whilst keeping the other variables constant and noting the effect of
doing so on the output values.

Weights analysis

Examining the weights in a perceptron is another method for discovering any hidden
rules the network has developed. In a multi-layer perceptron, weights analysis is
confused considerably by the hidden units and so usually avoided. With no hidden
units, it is possible to see the direct effect each input variable has on each output
variable simply by examining the weight which links the two.

7.3 Traversing a network

Having calculated the derivatives at a given point, one might be tempted to follow the function in the correct direction in order to arrive at a different desired output with the intention of reading off the resultant input values. In theory it is possible to move ever closer to the desired output values by making the changes in the inputs dictated by the derivatives at each point. This is, in essence, how the back propagation algorithm works. However, the method meets the same problem as back propagation: it may become trapped in local turning points.

Let us imagine that a neural network trained to aid staff selection[2] tells us that a person is not suitable for a job, but we would like to train that person in the right skills for the job. We could look at the derivatives and see that a small improvement in creative skills would improve matters. We move to this new, slightly better, point, look at the derivatives there and see what small improving change might be made next. If this process is repeated sufficiently, and in all directions, we may eventually end up at a point where the output is a job acceptance and the input pattern relates to the required qualities for the job. We may also, unfortunately, end up at a point which is not the required output, but from which all moves would be bad. There is no way of telling whether this point is the best we can expect or is simply a local turning point which should be skipped over.

Adding momentum to our search path will help us to skip such turning points provided they are not too large. The method is a little like trying to drop from the top of a mountain, somewhere in the middle of a range, to the sea, in a thick fog. But then, so is back propagation so we shouldn't write it off completely. The main difficulty comes with knowing which of the many dimensions to travel in at any given step. A simple rule would be to follow the path which gives the most benefit. A second method is to record the input values and the decision at points where more than one option is open so that one may back track at a later time. Finally a population of different points might be set off in different directions and unsuccessful ones killed off. Such an approach is similar to the use of genetic algorithms. The difference lies in the fact that it is possible to steer the search via the derivatives rather than simply following a random path as in the case of a genetic algorithm.

The advantage of such a method over, say, training a network on the reverse task in order to predict likely inputs from chosen outputs is that the latter method simply learns the average value for each variable from a representation of each class. There is no measure of closeness in the latter method. Traversing the network will not simply give an example of an input which would cause the desired output, but will find one as close as possible to a given input pattern.

The most obvious applications for the techniques discussed in this chapter are determining the marketing mix which maximises profit or a manufacturing process which minimises waste. Such optimal points may be found, or approached, using the search techniques outlined above.

---

[2]See the example at the end of the chapter.

7.3.1   Accounting for the input scaling function

Here is a final point, but an important one none-the-less: the inputs to a neural network are usually scaled to within a fixed range so the scaling function must also be accounted for when calculating the gradient of the network at any given point. This becomes important when we are using the derivatives in order to make decisions about which input values to change, and by how much to change them. Any change suggested by the network will be in terms of the scaled inputs rather than the actual input values that you must, in reality, change.

For example, let us say we have scaled data by a factor of 50 so that it falls between zero and one, and that we have calculated that in order to arrive at the desired output, we need a value of 0.1 at the (scaled) input layer. Clearly, we should actually set a value of $0.1 \times 50 = 5$ in our real world system. The actual required value is simply calculated by passing the required scaled value through the inverse of the input scaling function in order to produce the re-scaled value. Scaling functions and their inverses are listed at the end of chapter 2.

Non-linear scaling functions

As long as we can calculate the inverse of the scaling function, we can calculate the re-scaled values. A slight complication arises however, in one certain circumstance. If we are using the derivatives of the network in order to calculate a required increase or decrease in a given input, rather than a new value, that increase must be translated to be in terms of the re-scaled inputs. However, if the scaling function is non-linear, the inverse of a given change value will always be the same, regardless of where in the input range that change is required. This is not the required solution.

If we wish to calculate the required change to the input of a function in order to produce a known change at its output (which is what we are trying to do in this case), we must calculate the derivative of the inverse of the function at the point of its current output. We should then multiply the required output change by that derivative, thus producing the correct value by which to alter the input. Alternatively, we should add the required change to the current output, thus creating the new required value, and pass that through the inverse of the scaling function.

7.4   Summary

We have seen how the derivatives of the outputs from a neural network with respect to the inputs which caused them may be used in several ways. They can tell us why a certain output value was given, help us in altering the inputs to achieve a desired output, tell us about decision boundaries in classification tasks and provide us with extra the confidence in a network output that goes with understanding how that output was produced. The derivatives also help us to explore a network and point out areas of high or low non-linearity. We have seen that there is far more to using a neural network than simply feeding in an input and receiving an output.

The following types of explanation for a network output may be generated, depending on the nature of the task in hand and the way in which the data is represented.

- For continuous valued mapping functions, the explanation relates to the gradient of each output unit with respect to each input unit. The resultant set of combinations forms a matrix of derivatives known as a Jacobian matrix.

- For continuous valued inputs and probabilistic categorical outputs, the derivatives provide a measure of how close to the edge of the current category an input is, in which direction(s) that edge is to be found, and the change in membership probability which would result in a small movement towards that edge.

- For categorical systems which map binary coded input features onto binary coded output classes (such as the animals example above), we are interested not in gradients, but in which input features led to the given output and which were of no importance.

7.5 Calculating the derivatives

Calculating the derivatives for a given point in a neural network function is surprisingly simple. We follow the same process as that employed during back propagation learning, except that the error term is thrown away and we propagate one layer further back. If we wish to know how the output, o, changes with respect to the input, i, we must calculate do/di. However, the effect of a change in the input depends on the weights and the hidden units' activation functions. We can make use of the chain rule from calculus to overcome this problem. The chain rule allows us to say that

$$\frac{do}{di} = \frac{do}{dh}\frac{dh}{di}$$

which means that the derivative of the output with respect to the input can be calculated as the derivative of the hidden unit with respect to the network input times the derivative of the output value with respect to the value received by the hidden unit. At first glance it may seem that a lot of work is required in order to calculate these derivatives. Each unit must be differentiated with respect to its input which, in turn, may depend on the output of units below. However, if we know the output values of each unit, we may ignore the inputs, including those from the bias, and simply base our calculations the output values. This is only possible, of course, if it is possible to re-write the squashing function in terms of its output, as is the case with both the sigmoidal and tanh functions.

The following sections describe the process by which the derivatives discussed above may be calculated from a neural network. This is obviously done after the output has been calculated.

Networks with a single hidden unit

We will start, for simplicity, with a network with a single input unit i, a single hidden unit h, and a single output unit o. The calculations are made simple by the fact that we can express the derivative of the activation function in terms of the unit output values. As we have seen in chapter 3, the derivative of the logistic function $o = 1/(1 + e^{-i})$ is $1/(e^i(1 + e^{-i})^2)$ which may be expressed in terms of its output, o as $o(1 - o)$. The derivative at the output unit can now simply be expressed as $o(1 - o)w$ and that of the hidden unit as $h(1 - h)u$, where u is the weight from the input unit to the hidden unit, w is the weight from the hidden unit to the output unit, h is the activation of the hidden unit and o is the activation of the output unit. Using the chain rule, we can differentiate the whole network with respect to the input unit, o as follows:

$$\frac{do}{di} = h(1 - h)w \; o(1 - o)u \tag{7.1}$$

Networks with several hidden units

This function generalises to networks with more than one hidden unit by a summation of the different chained products:

$$\frac{do}{di} = \sum_{j=1}^{n} h_j(1 - h_j)w_j \; o(1 - o)u_j \tag{7.2}$$

where h_j is the activation of hidden unit j, w_j is the weight from the input unit to hidden unit j and u_j is the weight from hidden unit j to the output unit. There are n hidden units.

The final case to be considered is that of a network with many input and output units. This time, we only compute the partial derivatives of each output unit with respect to each input unit in turn. For a network with j inputs and k outputs, this will produce a $j \times k$ matrix of derivatives, known as a Jacobian matrix. To calculate the derivative of each output unit o_j with respect to each input unit i_k use the following function for all j and k:

$$\frac{do_j}{di_k} = \sum_{l=1}^{n} h_l(1 - h_l)w_{l,k} \; o_j(1 - o_j)u_{l,j} \tag{7.3}$$

where h_l is hidden unit i, $w_{l,k}$ is the weight from input unit k to hidden unit i and $u_{l,j}$ is the weight from hidden unit l to output unit j.

Flipping binary values

To flip a binary input value, i (1 becomes 0, 0 becomes 1) use

$$i = (i - 1)^2 \tag{7.4}$$

7.6 Personnel selection: a worked example

The following example is based on a fictitious data set describing a set of job applicants and the types of job to which they have proved to be most suited. The training set was built artificially based on a known set of rules [25] in order to test the reliability of the gradient measures in giving an explanation of the network's response. Applicants were scored on the following seven traits, either on a continuous scale or as being of one type or the other:

- Intelligence quotient

- Verbal ability

- Numeric ability

- Creative/rule follower

- Dominant/subservient

- Empathetic/unsensitive

- Extrovert/introvert

and classed as suitable for one of the following five job types:

- Ideas person

- Finisher

- Ideas coordinator

- People coordinator

- None of the above

A set of rules was defined so that different traits became more or less important depending on the type of job the person looked most fit for. Figure 7.3 shows the rules in the form of a decision graph.

The data was coded with a binary representation at the output layer and a mixture of binary and continuous values at the input layer. One thousand training examples were generated at random using a C program and balanced so that an equal number of examples from each job class were produced. A network with four hidden units was trained until the average error fell to below 0.01. During testing, partial derivatives were calculated in order to extract the most salient reasons for each decision.

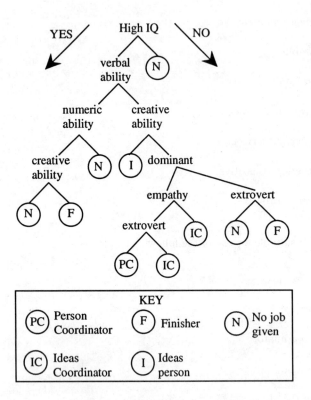

Figure 7.3: A decision tree for determining the best job for a company applicant.

7.6.1 Network analysis

The derivatives from the network at each input point were found to be more useful in some cases than in others. In regions of the network space which were flat, the derivatives told us nothing about the reasons behind the given answer. That is to say that a point which falls well within a decision region so that a small change in any input value will have no effect on the output tells us nothing about why it is there. Only when we are near a decision boundary will the derivatives be of use. In such cases, they will tell us the direction in which the decision boundary lies.

Decision boundaries

Let us examine the case of a low IQ leading to no job offer. As expected, the results showed a steep gradient of IQ score with respect to the *no job offer* class at the cutoff point and zero gradient elsewhere. This indicates the existence of a robust law relating IQ to whether or not a job offer is made. Unfortunately, if the applicant had an IQ which was too low for the job then the entire derivative matrix was full of zeros. A small change in IQ has no effect on the output as it does not flip the binary decision, and any change on the rest of the inputs is irrelevant. This is an extreme case however. It was often found that a small clue was available as to which input variable may be important. Such clues could then be used as the basis for a structured investigation of the reasons behind a decision.

The derivatives must be viewed with respect to the output

A derivative value of two indicates that a small change on the input will cause a change on the output of twice the magnitude. If the output is a probability of class membership and has a value of 0.02, then it is clear than a very large derivative is required before that value will be near to one.

Continuous valued functions

Re-coding the inputs across ranges and introducing overlapping regions to the task so that the output values never reached one allowed an easier analysis of the network's outputs. The cutoff point for IQ, for example, was spread over an area in which a higher IQ gave a higher probability of a job offer. The sudden step in the derivative of that variable was removed and replaced by a sloping region between the flat regions where no doubt lay. Other derivatives correctly indicated many of the assumptions which were made when the data was produced. For example a creative person with verbal ability and sufficient IQ would be best suited to a job as an ideas person regardless of any other qualities they might possess. This was clear from the derivatives which indicated low gradients with respect to the irrelevant variables and positive gradients with respect to the variables which mattered.

In another example, an applicant who was offered no job displayed a steep negative gradient on the *finisher* output with respect to the extroversion score. A look at the rule tree revealed that the applicant had followed a tree to a *no job offer* where the final branch was based on extroversion. An introverted person, at that point, would be given a job as a finisher, but extroverts are considered inappropriate for such a job and, as no other choice is offered at that point, the *no job offer* node is reached.

Searching for a solution

In the previous example, we were given a strong clue as to how an applicant might need to change in order to become suitable for a certain job. The gradient tells us how we might change the inputs in order to obtain a given change on the outputs. By selecting a target output, let us say the applicant wants to work as an ideas person, and altering the inputs with reference to the partial derivative of the chosen output unit, we can step towards the closest acceptable input pattern. Hence we can choose the appropriate training course for the applicant, should we still wish to offer him employment.

Chapter 8

Managing a neural network based project

The following chapter is included as an indication of the issues in project planning and development which are specific to a neural network based project. General issues such as market analysis and raising finance which apply equally to the development of any new product are not covered as the reader would be better advised by a dedicated text on the subject. The chapter is written around the assumption that the reader knows, or can find out, how to write a standard technical project proposal and business plan, and simply includes information specific to neural network based projects. Hecht-Neilson, in his book Neurocomputing [45], provides a useful discussion on planning, proposing, financing and managing a technical project, but does not make specific points on running a neural network based project.

8.1 Project context

The project context describes the system into which the neural network solution will be incorporated. Specifications will include who the users will be, the nature of the platform on which the network will run: will it run on a computer or be incorporated into an electronic system, perhaps on a chip? The source of the inputs and the destination of the outputs should also be specified.

8.1.1 Implementation platform

Incorporating a neural network in a software program

As with any software development project, it is important to establish the type of computer system the final user will run the program on. The actual neural network part of a neural program will often play a small part in the final implementation. A neural network, especially a standard fully connected MLP, may be described by a set of weights and a small number of parameters indicating factors such as the number

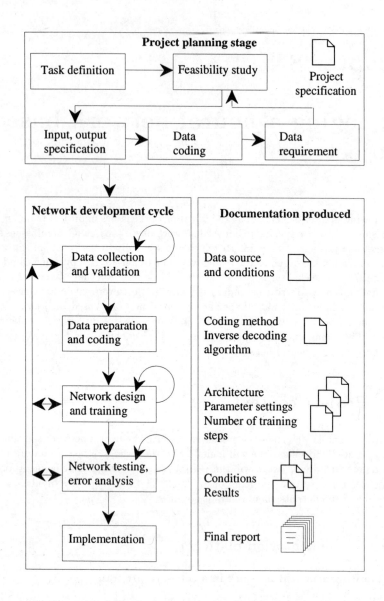

Figure 8.1: The key stages, sub-stages and required documentation for a typical neural network based project. Multiple document icons indicate that numerous trials will be made and recorded at that stage. A circular arrow indicates that the process contains many steps which may be repeated.

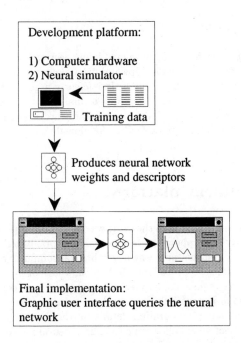

Figure 8.2: A neural simulator is used to build and train a neural network. The network so produced is described purely by the weights' values and some descriptive parameters. A neural interpreter routine may be written to run on any computer in any language, based on the weights and descriptors. In this way, neural networks may be easily incorporated in standard software packages.

of units in each layer and the type of activation function used. The interpreter which converts these factors and weights into a neural network may be written as a very simple program which can be made to run on any type of computer.

All other aspects of a neural network based program may depend more heavily on the type of computer on which the final application will run. Figure 8.2 shows how a typical windows based neural network driven program might be pieced together. The job of the development platform is to produce the neural network weights and descriptor. These details are machine independent, allowing the network which is destined for use on (say) a PC to be developed on a faster computer. Networks so produced may then be embedded in a normal program, written in the traditional fashion, which allows a final user to access the neural network. Developing the user interface for a commercial program can be a time consuming process and should not be thought of as some little extra work to be done once the network has been trained. In the extreme case, the neural network will simply be one function which the program calls in order to perform a certain calculation.

Hardware considerations

Neural networks have a particular advantage of being easy to implement in hardware. There are a number of neural network chips and printed circuit boards on the market, each of which has a number of limitations. It is clearly a good idea to identify the constraints imposed by the hardware on which a final solution will be implemented at the start of the design stage. Most neural hardware is designed to allow off-line development and training with a facility for downloading weights and network descriptors to the chip.

8.2   Development platform

Neural programs run on computers in the same way as any other program and modern PCs have the capacity to support modest neural network based projects. Neural programs are not written in the same way as traditional computer programs however. There are no instructions or procedures and no flow of control. Just as modern programming languages require a compiler or an interpreter to convert the program instructions to machine instructions, a neural program needs a neural interpreter to convert the weights and configuration details into a working neural network. A development environment which allows one to train a neural network is also required. Such systems are often called neural network simulators and there are several on the market. The following points are worth considering when buying a neural network simulator:

- **Required level of expertise.** Packages vary in the amount of neural network know how required from the user. Some have the neural network hidden below an interface which allows a non expert user to train a network on a given set of data. Other packages require a great deal of expertise in order to produce a good model. Some packages have an option which allows the user to choose between novice and expert mode, where in the former the program makes the decisions which are left to the user in the latter. Expert advice from the program on matters such as data collection would also be an advantage to the novice user.

- **Power and complexity.** Very closely related to the required level of expertise of a neural simulator is its power and complexity. Quite often, the more powerful the functions a package offers, the more expertise is required for their use. For example, some packages allow the user to set the activation function on every separate unit in a network, but an awful amount of know how would be required to use that facility to good effect.

- **Pre- and post-processing facilities.** A good neural network development package should provide the user with facilities for checking, coding and scaling the training data and for carrying out error analysis, rule analysis and post-neural processing. Graphical representations of the network output, the errors, and even the network structure are useful analysis tools. Some packages are also able to choose input values in order to optimise some aspect of the output of a trained neural network.

- **Producing usable functions**. Some neural network simulators also act as the neural interpreter, reading in a weights file, asking the user to enter input vectors (or taking them from a file) and producing the appropriate output from the network. In some cases this is the only way in which the network may be used. Other packages produce more useful methods for using the networks they allow one to develop, the most common method being the production of a set of library routines which may be included in any normal computer program. Routines will include data scaling and coding, the neural interpreter itself, and output handling. One step up from this is the production of plug-in modules, such as DLLs for visual C++ on a PC. Such modules are small programs which may be called from any other windows based program, which allow the user to use the neural network, and which return the result to the calling program. A final option, and an extension of the latter method, involves the neural simulator producing a fully functioning stand alone program or application which carries out all the steps required to query the neural network it produces.

The DTI neural transfer program produces a directory of available packages which may be of use when choosing a neural network simulator. As when buying any piece of software, it is important to ensure that the computer on which the software will run has sufficient memory, disk space and power to do so.

A second option is to write an in-house neural simulator which is specific to a given project's requirements. This is becoming increasing less cost effective as the products which are available become more powerful and easy to use. The disk which is provided with this book contains a set of C and C++ programs designed to make this task easier.

8.3   Project personnel

A neural network based project of any non-trivial size will require the expertise of three types of person.

8.3.1   Neural network expertise

Clearly, an expert in the use of neural networks is required. As neural simulation packages improve and books (hopefully like the one you are reading just now!) become more practical in nature, and as the field of neural networks becomes absorbed into the general field of mathematics and statistics, it will become sufficient that the technical staff have an understanding of the general issues involved in building a statistical model from data describing a real world system.

8.3.2   Problem domain expertise

When developing a neural network system, a little knowledge goes a long way, and while I have my dictionary of modern clichés open, I'll add that understanding the problem is half of the solution. We know that blindly training a network on data which we do not understand can lead to results which are at best unexpected. It is important that the neural engineer has access to a domain expert: someone who understands the task which the neural network is being asked to learn.

8.3.3   Project manager

The project manager is responsible for checking that project milestones are met, that the budget is not being exceeded, and that all members of a project team are fully informed of every development. Managers should be able to foresee and pre-empt problems with the project and create an environment in which problems and failures may be comfortably discussed.

8.4   Project costs

The costs of developing a neural project will be incurred in the following areas:

- **Personnel.** Project personnel are discussed above.

- **Development hardware.** Computational speed and storage capacity is an important consideration when running a large scale neural network based project.

- **Neural software.** Professional development packages for neural networks can cost from £200 up to £10,000.

- **Data collection.** If the data for a project does not already exist, the cost of collection must be established. The data must also be entered into a computer if it is not already stored in digital form.

- **Disruption to normal business.** Data collection may require that machinery is run at sub optimal settings or even taken out of service for a time. Testing and installation of the system may require a parallel change over period during which both the old system and the new are run in tandem to ensure that the new system produces sensible results.

- **Usual project costs.** Standard project costs such as office space, heat and light, rates, interest on loans, phones, travel, and so on should be taken into account.

Neural network projects often make heavier demands on the computing facilities of a company than they do on personnel. It is not uncommon to set a network learning on a large data set for several days. This may sound excessive compared to, say, standard compile times for programmed software, but great gains are made due to the small number of man hours required to reach the point where the network is able to learn. Neural networks may be comfortably built on personal computers, but the computer intensive nature of a neural network project means that it is not often feasible to use a machine which is already in heavy use. Whereas when you buy a new spreadsheet, you simply install it on the same PC that holds your word processor and your accounts package, you may find that a new PC will be required to hold the training data and carry out the long training cycles.

8.5 The benefits of neural computing

Neural solutions are often chosen because traditional methods have failed. There are, however, a number of other benefits to be gained from using a neural network based approach to a problem. Firstly, the amount of expert domain specific knowledge which is required to use a neural network is considerably less than that which is required for a rule based solution. The common bottleneck in expert system projects has always been the process of extracting knowledge from the domain experts. Due to this, and other reasons such as the fact that the computer takes on a large proportion of the work, neural network solutions may be produced in less time than those which rely on a more detailed analysis.

The benefits to business of employing neural networks are mostly derived from the fact that neural solutions are often more accurate than either the linear statistical based approaches, or the human estimation which they are replacing. The applications to which neural networks may be applied are often of the nature where a small improvement translates into a large saving. More accurate market analysis can give a company the edge over competitors; more reliable fault detection can save a company on waste, on faulty goods leaving the factory and on maintenance and down time; more accurate demand prediction can improve the efficiency of stock control or production.

8.6 The risks involved with neural computing

Neural computing is still a relatively new technology and as any financier will tell you, high tech is high risk. The main technical risk associated with a neural network based project is that either the data will not contain the information required to carry out the task to the required degree of accuracy, or that the network will be unable to extract that information. Assuming that a solution is possible, there is the risk that it will prove impossible for sufficient data to be collected, or that the balance between generalisation ability and accuracy is difficult to optimise. Most of the risks may be anticipated, circumvented, or removed by an expert in the field of neural computing. There are many pitfalls and traps awaiting the novice neural programmer however, many of which are only manifested in a final incorrect solution. The examples section at the end of this chapter describes a few such pitfalls.

8.7   Alternatives to a neural computing approach

We have established that a programmed or rule based approach to many problems is impossible as the rules are not known. Neural networks overcome this problem by extracting (in some sense) rules from a data set. There are, however, several other methods for extracting rules, knowledge, and generalisable inferences from a set of example data points. A common approach, and one which is discussed in chapter 7 involves building a decision tree. Other statistical techniques such as regression methods or Bayesian methods may also be able to produce working solutions. Neural networks now benefit from the fact that their wide use and research interest has produced an array of books, software packages and consultancy firms which are not available for many of the other techniques. This reduces the technical risks associated with a neural network project as standard methods are widely documented and understood.

8.8   Project time scale

8.8.1   A neural project life cycle

Figure 8.1 shows a typical neural network project life cycle. The two main stages are the project planning stage and the network development cycle.

Task definition

The task definition for a project should state precisely the goal of the project. The exact function which the system should perform should be agreed upon, and any constraints listed. Constraints refer to the finished product and might include examples such as a limit on the number of data sensors to be allowed, or a required speed of operation. A target level of accuracy should be chosen, and any benchmarks established. The processing speed of a trained neural network is not often of primary concern and there are only a limited number of design decisions which will affect that speed. If the network is to be implemented in hardware, on a chip for example, then the number of connections may need to be limited. Such a constraint should be stated at this point.

Feasibility study

Chapter 1 discusses the types of problem to which a neural network solution is applicable. The feasibility study should ensure that the problem to be solved is of such a type. A neural network must transform a set of variables, the values of which we know, and produce a set of values describing a set of different variables, the values of which we want to know. The network simply carries out a transformation from one representation to another. It does not create information (that is impossible) and it does not contain extra knowledge which cannot be derived from the input variables.

It is consequently important that the task the network is to perform is of such a transformational nature. A data source must also be established and costed.

Input-output specification

A more detailed specification of the function the network is to perform must be defined in terms of the input variables and the output variables. It is not always possible to know in advance exactly what variables will be used as predictors or, indeed, which of the variables which we would like to predict may actually be predicted. In this case, a set of possible variables should be stated, along with an indication of any constraints on the number to be used. It may be the case that sensors for collecting data are expensive, in which case it is desirable to use as few as possible, or that examples of some output categories are difficult to collect and might be excluded. Variables should be chosen with their information sharing properties in mind.

Data coding strategy

A data coding strategy which converts the raw collected data into a form which is usable by a neural network should be defined at this stage. Chapter 2 discusses the choices which are available at this stage. Data coding should be designed to make the task which is required of the neural network as explicit as possible.

Data requirement specification

From the data coding strategy, a data requirement specification which describes the quantity and type of data to be collected may be drawn up. Chapter 5 describes the constraints which determine the amount of data required for a neural network to be successfully trained.

Final feasibility

Once the data requirement specification has been drawn up, a final feasibility check may be performed to ensure that the stated requirements may be met. This includes verification that the required data may be collected within budget, that the information required to predict the output is contained within the inputs, and that a usable coding method has been found.

8.8.2 Network development cycle

The network development cycle encompasses the following stages.

- **Data collection and validation.** Data is collected and a series of checks are performed to ensure that it is properly balanced and that it contains the required predictive power.

- **Data preparation and coding**. The data is statistically analysed, outliers are dealt with, a subset of variables are chosen if required, and a set of coding and scaling functions are chosen. Data is coded for input to the network. An independent validation set is set aside.

- **Network design and training**. A number of networks are designed, as discussed in chapter 3 and trained. A record containing the architecture details, training parameter settings, number of training cycles, and final error of each network is recorded along with the weights and configuration descriptions.

- **Network testing and error analysis**. Each network is tested both independently and as part of an ensemble on the independent validation set. Checks are made for generalisation ability, accuracy, and response to stimulus from outside the training experience of the network (i.e examples requiring extrapolation). Confidence limits (or error bars) may be added to the predictions at this point.

- **Network implementation**. The best single network or an ensemble of networks joined by a voting or averaging system is chosen and embedded in the working environment. Final testing is carried out within that environment.

8.8.3   Possible hold-ups

When planning a project timetable, it is wise to allow for possible hold-ups to the project. For a neural network based project, the operation most likely to overrun is the data collection stage. Clearly, network training is time consuming, especially if several models are being built. Judicious use of multiple processors to train more than one network at a time with a set of different conditions can remove some of the burden of the design, train cycle.

If the project is being carried out for a third party, the need for an exact specification is even more important than it is for a traditional software development project. Once the functional specification for a network has been agreed upon and the network trained, it is not necessarily easy to make alterations. Whereas a rule based system allows for the possibility of changing small aspects of the specification even after the system has been installed, a neural network is built upon a representation which is far more distributed and abstract, and which is consequently harder to alter at a later date. It is clearly important that the third party understands the type of problem to which a neural network may be applied, and the type of solution it is possible to produce. Adding an extra variable to the model, for example, could require an additional complete data collection run followed by a new coding scheme, new networks, a whole new project in fact.

The time advantage of a neural network based approach is that much of the time required does not require human involvement. It may take a week to train a large system but, apart from periodic checks, no human intervention is required. Project times are also, on the whole, smaller than those for traditional software development projects as a lot of the hard work is performed by the learning algorithm.

8.8.4   Project methodology

Traditional software development projects are usually approached in one of two ways. The top down approach, also known as divide and conquer, requires that the problem is split into smaller and smaller sub-problems, each being split further, until each is small enough to be solved. The individual solutions—functions and procedures in most programming languages—are then connected, controlled or called upon to carry out their specific tasks by a central controlling system. The controller may be the main program in a traditional approach, or events in an object oriented approach. A second approach is known as the bottom up method. A bottom up approach is rather less structured, rather more holistic, and requires a lot less planning. A bottom up solution will start as a complete solution which is then refined and changed until it reaches a satisfactory level. The advantage to this rather ad-hoc method is that far less planning is required, and problems may be solved as they are thrown up, rather than having to be anticipated in advance.

A neural network, in isolation, may be considered a bottom up solution. We start with a set of weights which provide a poor (random, as it happens) solution, and we continually alter their values until the network performs as required. As this chapter demonstrates, the slightly more encompassing view of a neural network project is a little more structured than that, but is still essentially a sequence of bottom up solutions. Forward planning can allow us to choose a task which is appropriate for a neural network, to collect the correct type and amount of data, and to build a model which should contain the correct level of complexity. As discussed above, it is not possible to reduce the task to steps smaller than that of training a single neural network as a whole.

8.9   Project documentation

Figure 8.1 also shows the documentation which should be produced by each stage of a project. Details are listed below:

- The project specification describes the results of the project planning stage.

- The data source document describes the conditions under which the data was collected, and should be updated if any new data is added to the training set. This document will also include the results of any data validation checks.

- The coding document describes the transformations which are performed on the data before it is presented to the network and should also describe the inverse transformations required to convert the network output back to a meaningful answer.

- Several network descriptions should be produced which describe the architecture details, training parameter settings, number of training cycles, and final error of each network. The weights and configuration description file names should also be recorded.

- For each network, a set of test documents should be produced which describe the behaviour of each network under a number of conditions.

- The final report may include a standard project report, or a user manual for the final product. A final set of weights and configuration details for the network will also be produced. Configuration details will be specific to the software implementation of the neural network.

8.10   System maintenance

Once a system has been installed and is in use, the primary concern is that the conditions in the real world will change from those which were present when the system was trained. In such a case, the system will be predicting outcomes based on a set of outdated observations which will clearly introduce the possibility for error. It is quite possible to detect such situations by keeping track of the system accuracy or by the more advanced novelty detection and accuracy analysis methods discussed in chapter 6. It is, however, considerably more difficult to update a system on-line in real time. For real time updating to work properly, issues regarding the balance and reliability of new data points, the time required to train the system, and re-testing to ensure that the re-training has actually been successful must be addressed.

Part II

Review of neural applications

Introduction to Part II

Now that we have been introduced to a number of multi-layer perceptron techniques, we can investigate some of the real world systems to which they have been applied. None of the chapters in part II is designed to be an in depth guides to any particular field. Instead, these chapters are meant to illustrate ways in which the techniques from part I are used; for that reason very few new techniques are introduced in part II.

Chapter 9 investigates the use of neural networks for signal and image processing. Chapter 10 looks at the different ways in which neural networks have been used to turn a profit and chapter 11 provides a sweeping survey of neural network based solutions to process monitoring and control problems. These chapters are followed by a description of the C++ programs which come with this book.

Chapter 9

Neural networks and signal processing

Well, if I Called the Wrong Number, Why Did You Answer the Phone?
James Thurber

9.1   Introduction

This chapter discusses the use of standard signal processing techniques for neural network training data preparation and the use of neural networks themselves as trainable signal processors. The examples used are taken from the fields of vibration analysis and speech and image recognition and were chosen for their intuitive ease of understanding. The principles discussed apply equally well to many types of data set.

9.2   Signal processing as data preparation

9.2.1   Waveform signals

In this section we consider several options for pre-processing a time varying signal before training a neural network.

9.2.2   Extracting frequency bands from a signal

If we are able to record a window of previous values from a source for input to a time delay network, then we are also able to process the data in that window in order to make explicit the information on which the neural network must base its model. It is often the case that the important information is held in the component frequencies of the signal. There are two popular methods for extracting the frequency bands of interest from a signal: the use of a set of filters, or the use of the Fourier transform.

A filter takes a signal and removes a defined set of frequencies. *Bandpass* filters cut off all frequencies outside a given range, and *bandstop* filters cut off all frequencies within a given range. Filters are rarely square in shape; that is to say that the cutoff point is not sharp, but slopes quickly down, attenuating frequencies in the border area. A filter bank is a set of bandpass filters, each tuned to extract a different band.

The Fourier transform calculates the amount of power in each frequency bandwidth in a signal. It performs the equivalent function of a filter bank containing a single filter for each narrow band frequency in the signal. The width of the bands describes the *spectral resolution* of the transform. A Fourier transform whose output consists of a power value for each integer frequency has a spectral resolution of 1Hz.

A *convolution function* performs a weighted average over a stream of data and so provides a useful method for extracting certain frequencies. The weighted average is taken from a window moving over signal. The same convolution may be performed by first taking a Fourier transform of the data in one window, then multiplying that transform by the transform of the convolution function. The inverse transform of the resultant spectrum is equal to the convolved signal. The convolution function used in the temporal domain is known as the *impulse response* function, and its equivalent multiplication function in the Fourier domain as the *transfer function*. The equivalence between convolution in one domain and multiplication in the other is of particular use when the two need to be combined.

It is clear that multiplying the power bands in the transform by a transfer function with zero output outside the bandpass range will select only the required bands. In order to select that bandwidth from the signal in the temporal domain, we must convolve using an impulse response function equal to the inverse fourier transform of the transfer function. Obviously, once we know the shape of the impulse response functions for the bandwidths required, we no longer need to carry out any Fourier transformations.

As the transform of a pure sine wave is a single spike (known as a *delta function*), the impulse response function required to filter a signal to an exact frequency is a sine wave of that frequency. Convolving a signal with a sine wave of a given frequency is consequently equivalent to filtering the signal at that frequency. The result of such a filtering operation is a single sine wave with a frequency equal to that of the filter and an amplitude equal to that of the same frequency component in the original signal. A flat line indicates that the signal contains no components at the filtered frequency. The convolution function should be a sine wave which covers exactly one cycle from zero, through zero, back to zero again. Its size will clearly depend on sampling rate and frequency. Carrying out such a convolution on a signal in which the power at the given frequency varies with time produces a sine wave of constant frequency and varied amplitude (i.e. an amplitude modulated signal).

The Fourier domain

As we have mentioned, the result of using a Fourier transform (or a fast Fourier transform) is a measure of the power and phase of each constituent frequency in the signal[1] over the chosen window. The part of the transform which represents the power in each frequency is known as the *power spectrum* and is usually of more use than the part which measures phase. The signal is assumed to be periodic—the contents of the window repeating themselves infinitely to either side of the window. The fact that this is not really the case is not of practical concern however as we are only using the Fourier transform to re-code each section of data.

The Fast Fourier Transform (FFT)

In order to apply an FFT algorithm to produce a power spectrum from a signal, a section consisting of N elements must be taken from the data, where N is a whole power of two: i.e. $\log_2 N$ must be a whole number. If this is not possible, the window must either be cut down, oversampled, for example with spline interpolation, or padded with zeros. If the latter option is chosen, it can be a good idea to pass the window through a large Gaussian filter centred on the data and dropping away just where the signal stops and the zeros start. By convolving the data with such a window, the sudden step from data to zero is smoothed and does not appear as a high frequency component in the power spectrum.

Furthermore, the highest frequency an FFT is able to extract is exactly half the sampling frequency. For if something happens x times a second, we must take x samples to see it happening, and another x samples in between in order to witness it not happening! This half sampling frequency limit is known as the *Nyquist interval*. Once the data has been transformed into the Fourier domain, frequencies of interest are available with no extra coding. This can be of great use for several techniques.

Coding power spectra for a neural network

A power spectrum represents the strength of a number of different frequency bands in a signal and each band may be used as an input variable for a neural network. Power spectra can often contain far more bands than the number of input units a neural network can support, so a set of bands may be selected or combined based on numeric analysis or prior knowledge. They may also be transformed onto a lower dimensional space using principal components or an auto-associative network. The power in each band should be normalised with respect to the power in each of the other bands; scaling each into a set range (see section 2.5) is one way of achieving this.

---

[1] Waves of equal frequency but different phase sum to produce a third wave with a frequency equal to its constituents but with a different phase and/or amplitude. Consequently, it is not necessary (nor, indeed, possible) to code for more than one component at any given frequency.

9.3   Pre-processing techniques for visual processing

In what may seem like a sudden shift from the current line of discussion, we shall now consider a few of the considerations related to coding visual images for entry to a neural network. The examples are, of course, simply vehicles for demonstrating some of the techniques discussed throughout the book and are not to be considered as a serious guide to visual image processing. We will discover, however, how the principles of signal processing may be equally applied to visual image processing and investigate the effects of processing an image in such a way.

Binary or grey level coding

The simplest way to code small images is to represent the presence, absence, or degree of light being emitted (or reflected) from each point (known as a *pixel*) on the image. In the simplest case, coding the presence or absence of a point will provide a binary representation which may be used directly as input to a neural network. Pixels in black and white images may be coded with a single value which quantifies the grey level of the point. Colour pixels require a value for each of the red, green and blue components. Quite obviously, the image must be small for such a coding scheme to be practical and this method is consequently often seen in handwritten character recognition systems.

Figure 9.1 demonstrates the principle. Each image is split into 64 squares and the grey level at each square is coded on a scale where white is zero and black is one. For the binary representation, a threshold is set on the grey level scores so that any value above the threshold becomes white and any value below it becomes black. Black squares become coded as one and white squares become coded as zero. Grey levels may be coded in eight bits (a single byte in computer memory) on a scale from 0 to 255.

Data collection

The handwritten character recognition example shown above is useful for illustrating a point made in relation to data collection. Given 64 input units, each varying over a range from 0–255, one would expect to need to collect an enormous amount of data before a reasonable amount of input space is covered. There are 256^{64} possible input patterns which could be built from a grey level image; even in the binary case there are 2^{64} possibilities. Even covering a fraction of those and relying on network generalisation to fill in the rest could take forever.

However, as we saw in chapter 5, a set of related variables has an *intrinsic dimensionality* which can be far smaller than the input space in its entirety. Due to the structured nature of handwritten characters, there are many constraints between pixels in any image. Dark pixels in one area often indicate a high probability of dark pixels in other areas. Common sense tells us that, given 26 letters in the alphabet

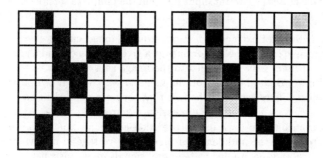

Figure 9.1: Two methods for representing a handwritten letter K for input to a neural network with 64 input units. On the left hand side, each unit would receive a one where a black square was present and a zero otherwise. On the right hand side, the grey level (amount of black present in the square) would be coded between zero (white) and one (black).

plus a few more patterns for numbers and punctuation, we are only using a very small part of the potential 2^{64} patterns. For this reason, we can get away with collecting far fewer training examples than the network size would suggest.

Given the relatively small training set size, however, and the large number of weights in the network caused by using 64 input units, some other regularisation technique must be used to reduce the risk of network overfitting.

Feature extraction

The approach described above is clearly not going to be effective for large images for two reasons. Firstly, the number of input units required to code an entire image is prohibitive and secondly the coding scheme does not attempt to make explicit any important features or qualities which the image might contain. We have just seen how constraints amongst pixels limits the number of possible patterns that a network has to learn. One way of thinking about these constraints is in terms of features. The common features of a set of images are, in effect, a set of constraints on the types of pattern an image is likely to contain. Continuous lines, for example, are a common feature in written text; a related constraint might be that neighbouring pixels must be activated in such a way so as to create continuous lines. A large part of the potential input space suddenly becomes unused under such a constraint, opening the way for some form of transformation or feature extraction.

One way of improving the coding of an image is to extract salient features and describe the image in terms of those features. Early character recognition systems, [64] for example, used a set of features which corresponded to line segments and intersections. Each input unit would represent the presence or absence of a specific type of line in the character and would map these descriptors onto an output layer which represented a measure of how close the current input lay from the template version of each character the network could distinguish.

A standard method for extracting features from an image employs a set of spatial filters which are able to detect edges or lines at a given frequency and a given orientation in the image. Filters may be applied to the image as a whole or to small local areas within the image. Spatial filters work in a similar way to their temporal equivalents, the most salient difference being the fact that they are applied to flat images in two dimensions rather than the single dimension required to process a temporal signal. Transitions from light to dark in any direction across an image may be thought of in identical terms to the undulation of pressure or voltage in a wave or signal. Any technique which may be applied to temporal signals may consequently be applied to images. The Fourier transform of an image may be calculated, and specific frequencies removed or investigated. An image may also be filtered or convolved by any transfer function.

Filtering an image with a high bandpass filter extracts the high frequency components, and these components correspond to lines or edges. Low frequency filters, on the other hand, reveal larger areas of consistent shade. Smoothing an image removes all details which occur at a spatial frequency higher than that of the convolving function. That is to say that details in an image which occur at a finer scale than that of the filter will be averaged away. Filters consequently provide a useful method for reducing the complexity of an image before it is coded for input to a neural network. In his book, *Understanding Vision*, Watt [114] provides a useful description of a range of image processing techniques along with the functions and equations required in their implementation.

9.3.1   Generating image statistics

Filtering an image leaves us with a new image which contains exactly the same number of pixels as our original. Hardly much help to our neural network yet. In the next section, we shall see how small areas of an image may be coded for individual processing. In this section we investigate the simpler course of simply summarising an image with a set of statistical measures.

Image segmentation

A general description of the image as a whole in terms of principal frequencies and axes may be sufficient to carry out the desired task. It is often the case, however, that we are less interested in the image as a whole and more interested in finding and classifying objects within an image. There are several techniques for segmenting an image with respect to areas of similar tone or texture, or based on edges detected by filters and other mathematical techniques such as differentiation.

Segment or object coding

Having segmented an image, we can code each segment in terms of a number of factors. Different factors may be more or less salient to any given application, but the following are often of use: average grey level (or colour if available), variance of that grey level, mass, centre of gravity, area, circumference, degree of curvature on circumference, direction and length of principal axes. Lines should obviously be described by angle, length, and degree of curvature.

Rather than being trained to process an entire image, a neural network may now be trained to process the description of any feature taken from that image. This greatly reduces the required network size and makes explicit the task to be carried out.

Adding context

Useful information about an object in an image may also be gained from the objects which surround it. An extension to single object coding involves presenting the network with a description of the object to be processed along with a description of those which surround it. British Aerospace [121] have applied a contextual coding technique for a neural network based road finding system. The network was presented with segmented scenes which contained segments of road which it was required to identify. The description of the segment, which included statistics on grey level, area and perimeter was appended with descriptions of eight surrounding regions and the angle from the central region at which they fell. The network was found to perform far more successfully when the descriptions of the surrounding regions were included in the input than when they were not.

9.4   Neural filters in the Fourier and temporal domains

Returning to one dimensional signals once more we shall now take the next logical step from our investigation into the use of standard signal processing for neural network data preparation. If a neural network can take a signal or its Fourier transform as input, then it should be able to process that signal and produce a new signal on its output. It should, in effect, be able to learn how to be a filter. As we shall see, this is indeed the case.

9.4.1   Neural filters in the temporal domain

Hecht-Neilson [45] describes a set of experiments into the use of neural networks as noise reduction filters. Hecht-Neilson shows how a simple transversal filter which takes a moving window over a signal may be trained to calculate the noise free component which corresponds to the midpoint value in the input window. The transversal filter is a linear perceptron with a number of inputs equal to the number of elements in the input window and a single output. The weights are altered during training to amplify or attenuate each frequency component in the signal to remove the optimal amount of noise.

Modern signal processing is still based in the linear domain. This is not a great limitation as Fourier theory is based on linear transforms and a linear filter is able to remove any non-overlapping additive noise from a signal. The transversal filter is a linear filter but could clearly be extended to act as a non-linear filter by the addition of a hidden layer of non-linear units. That is to say, by using a multi-layer perceptron. Hecht-Neilson reports some success with training an MLP with a time delay window to remove overlapping noise from structured signals. The two points to note from this research are that the noise overlapped the signal in frequency: a condition under which a linear filter would fail, and that the signal was structured. The consistent structure in the signal allows a *specific* filter to be trained. The filter is not universal; it cannot be trained to remove a given type of noise from one signal and be used to remove that type of noise from a different signal as it is the structure of the signal which allows noise reduction without signal degradation.

As Hecht-Neilson quite rightly points out, almost none of the traditional signal processing methods may be applied to non-linear filters which violate the basic assumption of linearity on which signal processing theory is based. If the output of a filter does not vary linearly with its input, care must be taken that the average power level remains constant. Hecht-Neilson expresses doubt as to whether it would be possible to construct a general theory of non-linear signal processing of this type but points out that, with a qualitative understanding of the application of such methods, their use could provide valuable solutions to a range of existing problems beyond the scope of linear techniques.

Figure 9.2 illustrates how a simple tapped delay line may be fed into a time delay neural network (TDNN) which is able to learn to act as a non-linear filter. The signal,

Processed midpoint of incoming signal

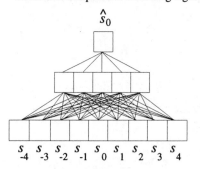

$\hat{S}_0$

S_{-4} S_{-3} S_{-2} S_{-1} S_0 S_1 S_2 S_3 S_4

Recent history of incoming signal

Figure 9.2: A simple tapped delay line is used to produce a processed version of the central input value, S_0. Note that S_0 is not the most recent input value, but the central input value. The network is consequently producing a slightly delayed version of the original signal.

S, takes the value S_t at time t. In order to produce a processed value for a chosen input value, S_0, the network receives a slice of the signal centred around S_0 which incorporates a given number of values both before and after S_0. The processed output, $\hat{S}_0$ is then used to reconstruct the processed signal. Note that the requirement for values which were transmitted after S_0 constrains the network's ability to process in true real time. The required delay will depend on the frequency at which the signal is transmitted and the number of time steps required to perform the task.

9.4.2 Neural filters in the Fourier domain

We have stated that convolution filtering in the temporal domain—which is the type of filtering discussed in section 9.4.1 above—is equivalent to multiplication filtering in the Fourier domain. It follows that, if we can train a neural network to act as a filter in one domain, then we should be able to do so in the other. This indeed turns out to be true. A neural filter may be built which takes as input, and produces as output a power spectrum representation of a signal. Figure 9.3 shows the possible routes from original signal to processed signal via power spectra and a neural network.

As it is possible to process a signal in either the temporal or the Fourier domain, what are the factors which determine which representation should actually be used? The two main principles with which we are concerned when choosing a data representation for use with a neural network are the number of variables used and the extent to which the information the network requires is made explicit. For reasons of speed and complexity, there is often pressure to minimise the number of variables (input and output) that a neural network has to deal with. This pressure also has a bearing on the resolution at which data is represented; the finer the data resolution, the greater the complexity of the network and, consequently, the amount of training time and

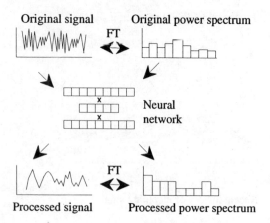

Figure 9.3: A signal may be time windowed and then fed into a neural network as it is, or transformed into a power spectrum using a Fourier transform (labelled FT in the figure). Which ever representation is chosen, a neural network is able to learn to manipulate the data in the associated domain. Data may be transformed from one domain to another using the Fourier transform or its inverse.

data required. This brings us to the second principle of training data representation: explicitness. Given the limit on the number of input variables a network may see, there is pressure to ensure that the variables which are used contain the information required to carry out the task to be learned in a form which is as explicit as possible.

It should be clear that transforming a signal into a power spectrum offers far greater control over both data dimension and explicitness. In the temporal domain, data dimensionality (i.e. the size of the time delay window) may be reduced in one of two ways: one can either reduce the number of steps back in time over which data is taken or reduce the rate at which the data is sampled. The former method obviously reduces the temporal depth of the process, the latter removes high frequency information from the data. In the Fourier domain however, it is possible to control the exact nature of any loss of resolution from the original data. Components at any frequency, not just the highest may be removed and certain neighbouring frequency bands may be combined to produce variable spectral resolution.

The obvious drawback to basing network input on the power spectrum derived from a signal is that the signal needs to be transformed into the Fourier domain. This process not only takes time, but places restrictions on the size of the window of data to be processed. It is also quite clear that such a representation should only be used in circumstances where the frequency components of a signal are known to be of interest.

9.4.3 Recurrent networks as signal processors

We have seen how it is possible to use a time delay window as input to a signal processing neural network and how the contents of such a window may be transformed to make explicit the frequency information contained therein. We have also seen, in several chapters of the book, how recurrent networks have been able to perform temporal processing tasks. Can recurrent networks be applied to the type of signal processing tasks discussed above? In the case where untransformed data is presented to the network, it can easily be seen how a recurrent network could be trained to act in a similar way to a time delay neural network. However, as recurrent networks do not require that a signal is collected into a temporal buffer before processing, there is no simple method for presenting frequency information explicitly to a recurrent network.

Noise cancellation with a neural network

Piché [74] has shown how a neural network may used as an adaptive noise cancelling filter in a system where the noise source is measurable, but where the noise is filtered before it is added to the signal. The nature of the process which filters the noise before it is added to the signal is not known, and so must be modelled with the neural network. Piché used a variation on the back propagation algorithm known as *recursive back propagation* which is shown to be able to learn to act as a non-linear IIR (infinite impulse response) filter. The reader is referred to Piché's paper for more details of the recursive back propagation algorithm.

Channel equalisation with a neural network

The recursive back propagation algorithm shares some common features with the recurrent algorithm discussed throughout this book. It should follow then, that recurrent networks are also able to act as non-linear IIR filters. Indeed, Kechriotis et al. [54] have trained a recurrent neural network to act as a non-linear filter in a channel equalisation system. The network performance was found to be comparable to that of a traditional linear filter based system when channel interferences were linear, but the network significantly outperformed the traditional methods when the interferences contained spectral nulls or severe non-linear distortions.

9.4.4 Managing network complexity

The standard method for using a neural network as a signal processor employs a tapped delay line, i.e. a simple TDNN. The method is straightforward enough; a single input unit is used for each time step, and the output of the network is a single value corresponding to a processed version of the midpoint of the input vector. The reader is referred back to figure 9.2 at this point for a pictorial description of the process. A problem inevitably arises when the required number of time steps (and, consequently, inputs) grows large. The network can easily become too large and underconstrained for the task it is to learn. The resultant overfitting may be particularly unwelcome in signal processing tasks as many require functions such as noise reduction. It is consequently of great importance to constrain the network in some way so that the problem of overfitting may be avoided.

In his recent Ph.D. thesis, Svarer [98] explored a number of methods for reducing the complexity of a neural network for signal processing tasks. One example involved channel equalisation which was achieved by constructing an inverse model for a non-linear transmission channel in order to reconstruct the original input signal. The inverse model was learned by passing a signal down a non-linear noisy transmission line and using the transmitted signal as input to a neural network. The input consisted of the last 25 values from the transmitted signal. The target output for the network was a single value: that of the original input signal from 15 time steps previous. The network contained 10 hidden units. The delay is important; the process would not work if we tried to predict the most recently transmitted value.

In order to reduce the complexity of the network (which contained $25 \times 10 + 10 = 260$ weights), Svarer used a weight decay technique which penalises large weights (i.e. prevents them from growing too large) and a network pruning method which trimmed unnecessary weights from the model. A linear model was also built so that the performance of the network could be tested against an alternative technique.

The pruned neural network produced a 61% improvement over the linear method and a 6% improvement over the unpruned network. The pruning method produced a network which contained only 22 weights. Chapter 3 presents a simple regularisation method along with some alternatives which may be used if your software does not support regularisation.

9.5   Speech recognition

In this section, we consider the specific pre-processing decisions which might be taken when building a neural network speech recognition system. The example is chosen to illustrate the point that knowledge of the system which produces a signal—in this case speech—may be used to great effect when encoding data for a network. Speech recognition is also an interesting example as we are able to base some of the pre-processing decisions on knowledge about a particularly good speech recognition system–the human ear and brain.

Sounds are caused by molecules (usually air) vibrating at a number of different frequencies. The air pressure just inside our ear consequently varies as it is compressed and rarefied. If we think of this pressure as a continuous variable, then we can express the task which the ear faces as that of extracting the constituent frequencies from the sound waves from a series of single values. These constituent frequencies are then used as input to the next stage of the brain's sound processing system. The vibrations caused by mechanical machinery are similarly transmitted through air or another medium. They can also be converted to a digital stream and transmitted or recorded. The job facing a computer analysis or recognition system is to transform this stream of numbers into a representation of the salient features of the system by which they were produced. Knowledge of these features and their physical effects on the environment is invaluable when selecting a data processing technique.

9.5.1 Choosing the bandwidths and centres

Human speech carries most of its information between 50 and 4000Hz with more information contained towards the lower end of the scale. The ear uses narrower band filters for low frequency sounds. A power spectrum which is calculated with unequally spaced filter banks is said to produce a *mel spectrum*. Combined with the cepstral analysis described below, such a transform produces a set of *mel–cepstral coefficients*, much used in speech recognition systems.

Cepstral coefficients

The vocal tract acts as a filter, convolving the waveform as it emerges from the vocal folds so it would be useful if we were able to separate out frequencies produced by the vocal folds from those added by the vocal tract. We know that convolving the waveform, $V(t)$ with the impulse response of the vocal tract filter, $S(t)$ has the same effect as multiplying the transform of $V(t)$ by the transform of $S(t)$. The magnitude of the transform of the final signal, ω, is

$$|F(\omega)| = |V(\omega)| \cdot |S(\omega)| \tag{9.1}$$

As $\ln(a \cdot b) = \ln(a) + \ln(b)$ we find

$$\ln|F(\omega)| = \ln|V(\omega)| + \ln|S(\omega)| \tag{9.2}$$

If we now take the inverse transforms, $\mathcal{F}$, we see that

$$\mathcal{F}(\ln|(\omega)|) = \mathcal{F}(\ln|V(\omega)|) + \mathcal{F}(\ln|S(\omega)|) \tag{9.3}$$

In other words, our new signal has additive components corresponding to the fundamental frequency produced by the vocal folds, and to the formants added by the vocal tract. This final inverse transform creates the *cepstrum* of the original signal (note the clever(?) letter reversal to reflect the process).

9.5.2 Formant analysis

Perhaps more important than considering the way in which the human ear recognises sounds is the consideration of how the human vocal system *produces* speech. Conceptually, its a fairly simple system: the lungs force air through the larynx, which contains a set of vocal folds. The folds open and close rapidly to regulate the flow of air into the vocal tract and so produce the fundamental frequencies on which an utterance is formed. Sounds produced by the vibration of the vocal folds are said to be *voiced*: say "Urr" and you'll feel them, as opposed to saying "sssss", in which case you won't. Needless to say, the folds can't vibrate very fast so although the sounds it produces do contain higher harmonics, they contain far more power in the lower frequency bands.

In the vocal tract, the sound is modified by a set of filters, one of the effects of which is to add resonances at certain frequencies. These frequencies, known as *formants* reflect the shape of the vocal tract and are so of great interest to us when building a speech recognition system. The formants are numbered from the lowest frequency up, F1, F2 and so on. The first two or three have often been found to be sufficient for good speech recognition. Lippmann [58] was able to split 10 different voiced vowel sounds into classifiable clusters using only the first and second formants, and Smith and Tang [92] successfully used a *vowel quadrilateral* which coded the coordinates of the first and second formants for speaker independent vowel recognition.

Formants are normally quite simple to find from the power spectrum of an utterance. The frequency bands with the greatest power represent the formants which are known to move smoothly, thus allowing themselves to be tracked from sample to sample within this smoothness constraint. A similar method can be applied to a filter bank. Tracking the first and second formants produces a much smaller data coding than many spectral methods and so makes an ideal choice when the training set is small or sparse. As we saw throughout part I, there are several constraints on network and training set size, and generalisation ability. When data is sparse, a compact coding scheme such as this will improve the generalisation ability of a network over the range on which it is trained.

9.5.3   Data collection

Now that we have made some of our pre-processing decisions, we are in a position to collect some data. The following facts will influence this process:

- The Nyquist limit tells us that we must sample data at twice the maximum frequency in which we are interested.

- The duration or unit measure of a signal must be chosen.

- If the system needs to generalise over speakers, it must be trained on examples from different speakers.

- Speech lives in a noisy, high dimensional space. The training set must consequently be large if good generalisation is to be achieved.

9.5.4   A review of neural network solutions

Time delay networks

By far the most prevalent method for neural speech recognition involves the use of time delay networks. Much of the pioneering work in this field is due to Waibel [112],[17],

[113] who has constructed large scale networks from smaller modules with the use of *connectionist glue*. In [112], a network with two hidden layers was built which used a set of 16 melscale filters to construct a window of three 10ms frames. The three frame window over the 16 filters produced 48 input units. The first hidden layer contained eight units but also had a window, this time of five frames, moving across it. This is an extension to the time delay method presented in part I which had delays only on the input layer. The second hidden layer contained three units, and fed into the three output units which represented the categories of spoken phones /b, d, or g/.

An utterance was spread over 15 frames in total, the subsequent outputs from the second hidden layer being integrated into the final three output units which are able to respond to features regardless of *where* in the total 150ms they fall. This network was able to recognise 98% of the data with which it was tested. The ability to recognise one of three different phones, it has to be said, has limited commercial applicability. Waibel showed that training a second network to recognise /p, t, k/ and then testing examples from /b, d, g, p, t, k/ on each network produced only 60% success and that training a larger network on all six took six times as long as the original network had. Clearly, neither of these approaches were satisfactory.

To solve the problem, Waibel introduced the concept of *connectionist glue*. He took the weights to the first hidden layer of each of the two separately trained networks and attached them to a common six unit input layer. The outputs from the new hidden layer were attached to a common second hidden layer by new, random, weights. New weights from the second hidden layer to a new output layer were also set at random. Finally an extra set of hidden units were inserted into the first hidden layer with random weights both from the inputs and to the second hidden layer. The resultant network was successfully trained with only a small time overhead as the task was simply to learn from the features already present in the first hidden layer. The network achieved a 96% recognition rate.

Chapter 6 presents a procedure for detecting whether the input to a network is within that network's experience. This may provide a different method for building modular networks which consist of small sub-networks built on a small number of the overall set of examples. Such an approach does however rely on features being common to the examples in each sub-network and independent of those in the others.

Many improvements to the basic time delay architecture have been suggested. Several authors [32], [22], [82] have combined a time delay neural network with a hidden Markov model (HMM)—the traditional state of the art speech recognition method— and achieved up to a 15% improvement over the individual methods. Hidden Markov models are based on posterior probabilities relating to state transitions, and the fact that MLPs are able to calculate such probabilities makes them ideal for inclusion in such a hybrid system.

Recurrent networks

Less work has been carried out into applying recurrent networks to speech recognition, despite the fact that the method has the potential for overcoming many of the problems associated with choosing a window size for a time delay network. There are obvious similarities between the states in an HMM and those in a recurrent network. Albesano et al. [5], for example, constructed a recurrent neural automaton based on an Elman style recurrent network. They used a small window of three steps of cepstral coefficients and a recurrent context layer and fed the probabilities generated at the output layer to a set of word models for decoding. The remarkable part of this research was that the network was tested across the public phone system. Despite the noise and lowband width inherent in such a system, they were able to achieve 88% correct recognition on connected words and 97% on isolated words.

Stévenin and Gallinari [96] used a similar recurrent network to build a model of the different concepts required for making enquiries to an automated airline ticket reservation system. The recurrent network was designed to learn the semantic structure between words in typical spoken queries to such a system in order to aid understanding. Concepts such as original city name, destination city name, and date of travel were identified by the recurrent network.

The fact that a neural network implementation may be stored in a very small area allowed British Telecom [120] to load a pre-trained network onto a Motorola 56001 DSP board for use in a prototype telephone number enquiry system. A wideband telephone handset was attached to the board which carried out the spectral feature extraction and neural network operation and fed the resultant numbers to a BT telephone number look-up database. From start to finish, the recognition time for a single spoken digit was less than 1ms.

9.6   Production quality control

In this example, we investigate the use of a neural network based system for quality control on a production line. A company making machinery carried out quality control by running the machines as they came off the production line and having human experts analyse the sounds they produced. A neural network was trained to classify machines to be accepted or rejected.

9.6.1   Data collection

A hundred example data points were collected from a number of machines which had already been classified as good or bad. An equal number from each category were collected, and each machine was further scored on a scale which reflected quality level. The data was collected using an accelerometer which converts vibration into an electrical signal. The signal was digitised and passed through a Fourier transform algorithm to produce 500 spectral coefficients. A single spectrum was calculated for each machine as the signal did not change over time.

9.6.2   Data preparation

Dimensionality reduction

With only one hundred training examples, thirty of which were set aside for testing, 500 dimensions are clearly too many. A set of nine power bands were chosen by a combination of knowledge about the frequencies which are important and a statistical analysis. The statistical analysis simply established, by means of a t-test, whether the values in each power band from the set of good examples were significantly different from their counterparts in the set of failed examples.

Data scaling and coding

The data from the selected columns must be scaled to a range between zero and one and at this point we have a choice. We can either compute a scaling function based on the range of values covered by a combination of every variable, or we can compute individual scaling functions for each individual variable. The former method has the advantage of conserving some information about the variance of each variable, whereas the latter method ensures that each input unit receives activation which encompasses its full operating range and consequently does not bias the network as it learns. Normally, when combining variables which inhabit different ranges, the latter method is the natural choice. In the example currently under discussion however, we must decide whether we should extenuate small changes by scaling some power bands by a smaller amount than others.

The decision made in this case was to scale each power band independently, thus filling each input range from zero to one. The decision was based on the following observations: we do not know *a priori* which power bands are more important and nor do we know whether the variance in each band is of equal importance to the discrimination task in hand; we may want to add noise to the input units to aid generalisation and this noise should be an equal proportion of each input unit; the input units of a neural network do not receive activation from a bias unit so there is no mechanism for scaling the values adaptively during learning; the weights from the input units to the hidden layer scale and combine the values from the input units and could consequently be forced artificially high if input values are kept artificially low. This final point becomes important if we wish to regularise the weights' sizes in order to control the generalisation ability of the network.

In order to verify that the above assumptions were, if not correct, at least practically optimal, both scaling schemes were used and the results of training a network on each were compared. The results are presented below, but suffice to say that our assumptions were borne out: the network trained on data which was scaled with respect to individual inputs performed far better than that which was scaled across all units.

The machiness which produced the training data had been rated on a quality scale from one to five, one being perfect. The examples were also scored as pass or fail, and those with a score of three sometimes fell into one category, and sometimes into the other. The category labels, rather than the scores were used as target outputs and were represented with two output units; one representing the probability of the machine passing, the other that of it failing. The target values were always one or zero. For testing purposes, the values were thresholded at 0.5 to produce a binary representation.

9.6.3   Building a network

Due to the small number of training examples available, a tightly constrained network was required to ensure good generalisation ability. A network with nine input units, two hidden units and two output units was built, producing a model with $9\times2+2\times2 = 22$ weights. The training set contained 64 examples, so the network was still over constrained. This was partly overcome by the addition of noise to the training data.

Training the networks

A series of training runs were conducted under a variety of conditions. The conditions which were varied included the number of hidden units, the amount of noise introduced to the training data and whether the input data was scaled on an individual unit by unit basis or with respect to the total power in the signal.

We shall address the latter issue first. As mentioned in section 9.6.2 above, scaling the values on each input power band individually rather than scaling every power band by the same amount produced better network performance. The training errors for each network were similar, averaging at 90%. The test errors however, differed widely. For the network trained on individually scaled data, a 77% success rate was achieved. For the network trained on data produced by uniform scaling, the best result was only a 56% success rate.

There were several effects, both to the training and test errors, of adding noise to the inputs. As the level of noise was increased, the error on the training set when the binary thresholded values were calculated only increased slightly. However, the network produced its answers with far less certainty the more noise we added. The average value of a correct output when no noise was present was 0.997, that is to say 99.7% certainty. This dropped to 0.785 when the input noise was increased to ±0.2. The percentage correct dropped from 92% to 88%. The percentage correct from the test set, given no noise in the training data, was 58%. This increased to 68% with noise of ±0.2.

The same experiments were carried out on a network with only one hidden unit, producing poor results. The training success dropped to 89% with noise of ±0.1 and 76% with noise of ±0.2. The test error dropped to 58% regardless of the noise level.

Finally, a network with four hidden layers was used, producing a success rate of 94% on the training data and 77% on the test data. These results were the same with noise set at ±0.1 and ±0.2. Using four hidden units but not adding noise increased the training success rate to 98% but reduced the test success rate to 67%. So, the surprise result is that the larger—and consequently the more at risk from overfitting—network produced the best generalisation score. This was only true in the case where noise was added to the training inputs as a regularisation measure. The point to note is that network size alone is not necessarily the most important factor when it comes to generalisation ability.

9.6.4 Error analysis

The errors and the outputs which were given with less certainty were analysed with reference to the original scale. Of the test errors made, only one was in response to a machine which had been awarded a score at either extreme of the scale. All of the test examples which produced uncertain outputs (i.e. output values between 0.4 and 0.6) were scored at an uncertain mid-scale point. This is an encouraging result as it confirms that the network is confused by the same examples as the human analyst from whom the data was taken.

9.7 An artistic style classifier

Finally, for a bit of fun, here is an example based on a story I recently saw in a newspaper. Japanese scientists have managed to train pigeons to distinguish between the works of Cubist painters such as Picasso and Braque and those of Impressionists such as Monet and Pissaro. Another great application of modern science. However, it struck me that the pigeons in question must be extracting some fairly simple cues from the pictures in order to carry out the discrimination and that the task facing the pigeons could provide a useful example of the process by which images can be processed.

9.7.1 Where is the useful information?

The example is applicable because it forces us to address the single most important issue in coding data for presentation to a neural network. That is, defining the exact nature of the task to be carried out. In chapter 8 we are told that a project must first be defined in terms of the task to be carried out. In this case the task is to distinguish Cubist paintings from Impressionist paintings. The next stage requires a definition of the exact input–output mapping required of the network. It is not sufficient to say that the input is a representation of the painting and the output is a category label, we must define the nature of the representation to be used.

Semantic features

We must decide which aspects of the paintings in question will help in making the discrimination and ensure that it is possible to code those features. The features from the paintings may be extracted and coded in one of two different ways. We might choose a set of semantic features which must be coded by hand. By a semantic feature,

I mean one which has meaning to a human. Perhaps the presence of a cutting from a French newspaper or a stringed instrument could be coded as an aid to spotting Cubist works. Such a technique cannot be automated but has the advantage of being able to include high level knowledge and of not requiring any image capturing and processing equipment.

Structural features

A second choice might be to use information in the form of the pictures. That is to say, the lines and shapes which make up the picture. Differentiating Cubism from Impressionism should be made simpler by the fact that paintings in the former style are made up of sharp edges and the latter display a smoother flow from one area of colour to another. The standard way of finding edges in a picture involves differentiating the picture in each direction. Edges or lines are characterised by high local derivatives (as there is a sudden change from one level to another). Passing a high frequency filter over the image before differentiating removes fine texture and details which we do not want to show up as lines. Therefore we can find edges in an image by filtering out the very high frequency components and then differentiating the resultant image.

Edge detection with filters

Figure 9.4 shows the result of taking a small part of each of a set of paintings and carrying out the following steps: a horizontal Gaussian filter with a length of 15 pixels and a width of five was passed over the entire image and the second derivative in the vertical direction of the resultant image was calculated. Starting with the original image again, a vertical filter of the same size and proportions was passed over the image and the resultant image was second differentiated in the horizontal direction. The two resultant images each contained the horizontal and vertical edges of the image respectively. These images were added together and normalised so that the intensity values fell within the same range as those in the original image.

Encoding different aspects of a picture

Our pre-processing has simplified the task of coding the pictures for input to a network but it has not yet provided a concise representation for us to use. Simple calculations such as the average length of the edges we have detected, or the average area of regions without any edges might provide a useful starting point. Another approach is to simplify the image further by setting thresholds on the grey level values on a filtered image in the same way as that employed on the simple bit map example above. Thresholds have the effect of grouping areas of similar brightness into uniform "blobs". These blobs may then be coded based on statistics such as length, area, circumference and so on. Figure 9.4 demonstrates the effect of setting a stepped threshold to the filtered images. A stepped threshold leaves no room for grey levels between the upper and lower threshold values, thus creating a purely black and white image. Note the long thin blobs in the two Cubist paintings, which indicate the

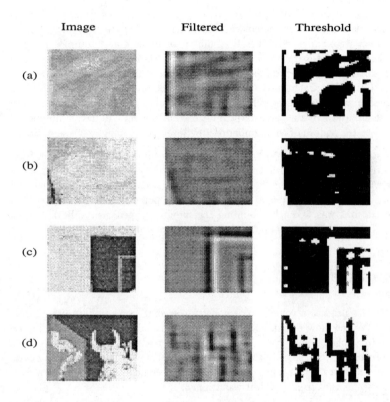

Figure 9.4: Grey level extracts from four paintings by different painters from the Cubist and Impressionist movements in art, a filtered differentiated version of the image, and the results of applying a threshold to the filtered image. All calculations are done on the grey level numeric representations. (a) Monet; (b) Pissaro; (c) Gris; (d) Picasso.

presence of lines, compared with the relatively evenly proportioned blobs in the two Impressionist pictures.

9.8   Fingerprint analysis

Mitra et al. [66] have used a neural network for classifying fingerprints. The finger prints were scanned in and digitised to create grey level images from which various statistical descriptors were calculated. In order to calculate the descriptors, a co-occurrence matrix which describes the number of times that pairs of cells with given grey levels, and separated by a given distance, coincide in the image is calculated. A single matrix is produced for each of a set of distances, δ and angles, $\Theta = 0°, 45°, 90°, 135°$. Each entry, $P(i,j;\delta,\Theta)$ in the co-occurrence matrix P is a count of the number of times a pixel with the grey level of i falls at a distance δ and an angle Θ from a unit with a grey level value of j. A matrix will have a number of entries equal to the square of the number of grey levels in an image representation.

The set of statistical measures to be used as input to the network were taken from the co-occurrence matrices and not from the images themselves. These included homogeneity which is simply the sum of the squared co-occurrence matrix values and entropy (randomness in the image) between pairs of points. A simple measure of directional features was taken by counting the number of peaks or valleys in each direction while traversing paths in the vertical, horizontal, and diagonal directions.

9.9   Summary

This chapter was used as a vehicle to demonstrate several issues in data preparation and coding. We saw how a task could be described in different ways depending on the data coding scheme employed. The fast Fourier transform was shown to be a useful pre-processing tool, as were traditional linear filters. We also saw how a neural network could learn to act as a non-linear filter which could be applied to data from the same source as that from which it was trained.

Chapter 10

Financial and Business Modelling

Si possis recte, si non, quocumque, modo rem.
If possible honestly, if not, somehow, make money.

Horace

10.1 Introduction

An engineer, a mathematician and an economist are shipwrecked on a desert island with nothing but a crate of tins of beans and some matches. They do not have a tin opener and so discuss various theories on how they might get at the beans. The engineer says "I happen to know that air—and beans—expand when heated. If we build a fire we can heat the tin and blow the beans out." The mathematician says "Fine, I will build a predictive model of the trajectory of each of the beans as they leave the tin so that we can catch them before they land." "You are all talking nonsense" says the economist, "Why don't we just *assume* that the tin is open and get straight down to eating the beans?"

This chapter investigates a number of attempts (successful, I am assured) at using neural networks for making money. The chapter discusses two different approaches to money making. The first is by operating in a free market; selling, buying, or manufacturing. The second is by speculating on the various markets for shares, foreign currencies, futures, options, and financial products.

10.2 Market modelling

One of the main tasks for a company's marketing department is to quantify the contribution to demand made by each factor in their marketing mix. Factors such as promotions, pricing, advertising, season, and competitors' prices all effect the level of demand. Simple models based on elasticity of price and demand are not sufficient to allow a company to choose the optimal marketing mix. Neural networks are able to build models which can accurately calculate the elasticities between any number of

221

variables. They can also allow for non-linear relationships in the data.

10.2.1   Accurate elasticity modelling

Traditionally, elasticity is calculated as a ratio. Price elasticity of demand, for example is calculated as the change in demand produced by a change in price divided by the change in price. Such ratios are clearly linear. As we saw in chapter 7, a neural network model is able to calculate the elasticity (i.e. the derivative) at any point in the system model. In other words, elasticity may change with other market factors, and the relationship which causes this change is captured by the neural network.

Hoptroff [49] used a simple feedforward MLP, coding the seasonal trend explicitly, to model the relationship between promotions, pricing, advertising, and season and demand for a client's product. Once the model had been built the effect of each variable was isolated by varying each in turn over its entire range whilst keeping all others constant. As we have seen in chapter 7 however, this practice is only valid when a linear relationship exists between the chosen variable and the output. Misleading results may be produced if great care is not taken with such a method. If we assume that, in the real world system, we are only going to change the one variable under consideration, keeping all others constant, then varying that one over its range is acceptable. For example, if we can change the price level but the level of all other variables is fixed in the short term, then we can investigate the effect of price changes in isolation. If we are free to alter advertising expenditure as well, then the resultant two dimensional space must be explored. Chapter 7 of this book concludes with a discussion on methods for optimising a set of input variables with respect to a given output value.

Similarly, Hoptroff showed how it was possible to forecast the number of advertisements which would be booked for a free distribution magazine. Forecasts were made based on economic indicators and a one year history of advertising revenue. The neural model displayed a marked improvement over the company's existing technique. Hoptroff also modelled performance of Britain's top 100 construction companies revealing a model of profitability and volatility against company size which showed the optimal size of company to invest in for maximal return. Tam and Kiang [104] showed how neural networks could be used classify banks in terms of their risk of bankruptcy. Such methods may be used as an aid to portfolio management.

10.2.2   Data mining

Neural networks have been successfully used in a field of data processing known as *data mining*. Data mining can be defined as the extraction of useful information or knowledge from a set of data. Effective data mining is of particular use in commercial applications as knowledge can often be converted into profit. Data mining sets out to answer questions on a level once removed from the data itself. Rather than asking what the output would be if the input was x, data mining asks what is the most important contributing factor to last year's profits. Here are some examples of how companies have used neural networks for data mining tasks.

Radio Rentals [3] have used neural network techniques to predict the likelihood of customers continuing a rental contract. A model based on customer profiles was able to spot customers who would be most likely to respond to a selective promotions campaign. In this way, Radio Rentals were able to increase customer loyalty and reduce the cost of mail shots. In a similar application, Thomas Cook [108] have employed a neural network to identify the type of customers most likely to respond to selective mail shot promotions. A major brewery [1] used a neural network to model the profitability of each of its pubs. The system was able to pinpoint the effect of a new information technology system which had been implemented, and was also able to reveal the factor which would most improve profitability in any given pub. As we saw in chapter 7, revealing such factors is possible with reference to the derivatives of the neural network.

10.2.3   Neural market simulators

Neural Edge [2] describes the use of a neural network based simulation of the retail book market in ascertaining the most probable effects of certain possible changes to that market. There is a chance that the Net Book Agreement (NBA), the device by which retail prices are controlled, may be suspended and there is also a threat of VAT on books. There is a consequent fear that a price war could follow the abolition of the NBA and a major book retailer was concerned about the results of such a war. Using a neural simulation of the market to run a "war game" between players representing publishers and retailers, the retailer investigated the possible outcomes of a price war. The results highlighted the danger of a price war and showed how it would have a destructive effect on the market as a whole.

The advantage of using a neural simulator of a market is clear. Strategies may be dry run and the results analysed before any real world commitments are made. A neural network can be thought of as reflecting a set of constraints which existed in the training data. These constraints put limits, or costs on different combinations of input variables. If those input variables are factors in a marketing mix or resources to be allocated, the network can be used to explore the effects of a series of different variable value combinations within the constraints the network has learned. By introducing optimisation methods, neural simulators may be used to choose the most profitable course of action available to a company, given the constraints the network has learned.

10.3   Financial time series prediction

10.3.1   The efficient markets hypothesis

There is a justifiable scepticism surrounding the idea that it is possible to make money by predicting price changes in a given market based only on its past behaviour and a number of publicly available indicators. Ignoring the cases involving insider information, this scepticism exists for a number of reasons, many of which are explained by the *efficient markets hypothesis*. In its strongest form, the hypothesis asserts that markets follow a random walk which cannot be predicted from past prices. Any chance of potential profits is utilised immediately, removing the opportunity almost as soon as it is created and certainly before the technical analyst has seen it in the data. This strong assertion assumes perfectly equal technology and—equally importantly—knowledge for all traders. The question of interest to us is, can we use a neural network to beat the efficient markets hypothesis? White [117] uses a neural network model to test the efficient markets hypothesis and finds no evidence against it. Similarly, Lowe and Webb [59] find no evidence to refute the hypothesis.

The issue central to this discussion is that of data quality: given that we possess sufficient data to describe the evolution of a market, the question that remains is "Does the data contain sufficient information to allow us to predict future values?". As we shall see, very few researchers concentrate on this question, choosing instead to assume that the information exists and investigate ways of modelling it.

There is a possible way around the weaker reality of a semi-efficient market because the hypothesis relies on the *equal public availability* of market information. If prices do not follow a random walk, but a non-linear one, then anybody who is able to model the price structure and make valid predictions using that model will have access to information which is not publicly available. The efficient markets hypothesis will no longer apply to the person with the model until everybody gains access to the same knowledge and things even out once more. Given that the efficient markets hypothesis relies on perfect knowledge, universal use of perfect prediction technology would only serve to enforce the conditions under which that technology is useless; as soon as a possible profit is predicted, it is acted on and expected profits return to the level of the risk free return plus a risk premium associated with a stock holding. Put another way, chances of superior profits occur when brokers set their prices incorrectly and investors are able to spot the discrepancy before it is corrected. Perfect prediction for all would remove these discrepancies and with them the opportunities for superior profit. The function of technology in the hands of a subset of all investors is to ensure that the market is not perfect and so this limiting hypothesis does not apply. Only when there is perfect knowledge for all will the strong efficient markets hypothesis hold.

Trading on a commodity because you know that its price is about to change in your favour is called arbitrage. Predictions of price changes are known to be probabilistic, and so create statistical arbitrage. Statistical arbitrage refers to the process of trading on price movements which are most probable, given the predictions made by a statistical model.

White [117] set out to test the simple efficient markets hypothesis (that part of it which states that prices follow a random walk) which is stated as

$$E(r_t|I_{t-1}) = r^* \tag{10.1}$$

where $E(r_t|I_{t-1})$ is the conditional expectation of return at day t given the publicly available information, I_{t-1}, and r^* is a constant consisting of the risk free return plus a risk premium. By stating that I_{t-1} represents information on past price values this asserts that price history information is of no use in forecasting r_t as r^* remains constant.

White first reproduces standard statistical findings by embedding this equation in a linear auto-regressive model and showing that the R^2 value is not statistically significant. This supports the simple efficient markets hypothesis. Perhaps the relationship is non-linear: White tested for this by training a network with one hidden layer and achieving good convergence on the training set. When tested on non-training data however, the system performed badly giving a correlation of only 0.0751.

White is not alone in doubting the efficacy of price predictions; others have cited unpredictable external events such as the Gulf war or a trading embargo which would undermine any system which did not take them into account. Tyree [109] used time delay networks to test the efficient markets hypothesis and found no evidence against it. The following examples show how researchers have reported more success. Stories of mathematicians implementing their systems and retiring to the Caymen Islands are rather thin on the ground and many still maintain that, as far as making a killing on the stock exchange with a neural network goes, there is just no future in it.

Brealey [18] spends the first half of his book *An Introduction to Risk and Return* telling the reader that technical analysis (i.e. prediction based solely on past values of stock prices and their relation to other indicators) benefits nobody but the brokers. He points out that apparent regularities in price **level** can be caused by totally random levels of price **change**. Only if the direction of the changes persist is it possible to make money; and this rarely happens.

A stronger version of the efficient markets hypothesis includes information from fundamental analysis (that involving information about the companies whose stocks we may wish to trade with). Proponents of technical analysis claim that their predictions are possible because all publicly available information is reflected in the current stock price: further information gathering is therefore unnecessary. We can now see why the direction of price changes do not persist. Pettit [73] showed that when a new piece of information—an increase in dividend for example—becomes publicly available, price change will make one large jump and then flatten out. By the time the information is reflected in the price, the technical analysts are too late and only a small number of fundamental analysts would have managed to act before the price change.

If we concede that we are not going to make our fortunes predicting price movements, then we must answer the question, *"How do people make money on the stock markets?"* Brokers charge a commission and quote both a buy price and a sell price and their profit is the difference. Some people get lucky. Large investment houses build portfolios which diversify across industries, risk types and even countries. The goal now is to build a portfolio with an optimal ratio of reward:risk. The current chapter introduces some attempts at technical analysis using neural networks and goes on to show how they have also been applied in fundamental analysis.

10.4   Review of published findings

As we saw in the chapter on time series analysis, there are four common types of time series prediction task. Those relevant to financial forecasting are discussed below.

10.4.1   Forecasting a single raw time series

In this context, forecasting a single raw time series corresponds to technical analysis.

Forecasting exchange rate prices

Refenes [81] used overlapping time windows to convert exchange rate series into spatial vectors. The data—hourly updates of 260 days worth of US dollar/DM exchange rate values—was coded into two moving windows with the intention of mapping the contents of the earlier window of size n onto those of the second, later, window of size m. The two windows move across the data series at a step of s. The task then is to predict the contents of window m from those of n. The authors show how important network design is; choosing the sizes of n, m and s carefully as well as considering the choice of activation function. One step ahead prediction was achieved by setting $m = 1$, i.e. setting the output vector to be a single value. Multi-step prediction was achieved by taking the single valued prediction and feeding it back as input rather than by extending the size of the output window, m.

Refenes notes the importance of correctly predicting turning points and evaluates the system in terms of its ability to identify *major turning points*. Based on a system of buying and selling in anticipation of predicted turning points, the Refenes network made at least 22% profit on the last 60 trading days of 1989. However, the unit of prediction used was the data point whilst the unit of interest was the turning point or even the percentage profit. In other words Refenes' system was not designed specifically to predict turning points, nor to maximise profit from the buying and selling criteria used, but simply to predict the next value in the series and leave the rest to you.

In a different paper, but using the same data set, Refenes [79] used a constructive architecture which added hidden units to the network each time the error term flattened out. Using the same data windowing, the constructive network made at least 25% profit on the last 60 trading days of 1989 as opposed to the 22% figure given for the same period in the earlier work. Using the same data, the same trading strategy, but traditional statistical forecasting methods, the following rates were achieved: exponential smoothing produced no usable prediction, it simply followed the current trend and missed the turning points, auto regression made 9%, and a non constructive (fixed number of hidden units) network made between 18% and 20%.

However, Swingler [99] takes a closer look at Refenes' findings and a few cautionary tales are revealed. His return of 22% is based on a prediction which takes 200 data points from a non-stationary, noisy, non-periodic time series and predicts the next 60 values. That is quite an achievement. Before we can be sure that a model is truly

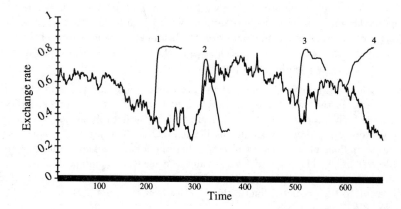

Figure 10.1: If we tested our network with prediction 2, we might think that we have a good system; predictions 1,3 and 4 however suggest otherwise.

robust, we must test it from many different start points. If it is able to make correct predictions every time, then our model is robust. If, however, it is only able to make correct predictions some of the time, we must come up with a method for knowing when a prediction is good and when it is not.

We trained a neural network with a moving window of 10 units and five hidden units over an 800 point series of US dollar/DM exchange rate values. Figure 10.1 shows the results of testing the network 60 days into the future by taking each output and feeding it back as input. This test is carried out from many different starting points, four of which are shown in figure 10.1. If we look at the prediction from starting point 2, we might think that our network has predicted the peak quite well. However, from predictions 1, 3 and 4 we can see that the network prediction always follows an initial path upwards and then either flattens out or falls back down; a prediction of a high turning point is consequently nothing more than a chance event.

A related issue to be aware of is the effect of trading costs. LeBaron [7] points out that it is not realistic to talk about the success or otherwise of a system unless trading costs are taken into account. This depends on the fact that if you are doing one step ahead prediction and the change at each step is small, then the profit at each step will be similarly small. This would not be a problem if you could automatically trade and make a profit every minute with zero costs, but brokers take a percentage of the *transaction value* so the percentage change must be greater than the commission before you really profit. A trading cost of between 0.01% and 0.1% should be accounted for. Making 0.1% a minute may seem to sum up to a tidy profit but, due to trading costs, does nothing more than pay your broker's mortgage.

Forecasting stock values

Jang et al. [50] extended the use of time windows in a *dual net* approach where two neural networks run in parallel: a short term network which looks at a 12 day period and a long term network processing data over the last quarter. The output of the two networks is fed into a decision making algorithm which makes decisions on whether to buy or sell each stock holding in a portfolio.

This approach looks more intelligently at the problem in hand and the kind of information inherent in the data. Network inputs consisted of a set of technical indices describing the highest price, lowest price, closing price, trading volume, and measures of moving averages, variance, bias and oscillation of the stock price. Network outputs were predictions of the *forward* $K\%(3)$ value, the forward highest price and the forward lowest price. The *forward* $K\%(3)$ value is a measure of the probability of a profitable trade; it represents the position of the closing price for the current trading day in relation to the predicted fluctuation in price over the coming three days. The formula for $K\%(3)$ is shown below:

$$forward\ K\%(3) = 100\frac{C_n - MIN_{i=n}^{n+3}(L_i)}{MAX_{i=n}^{n+3}(H_i) - MIN_{i=n}^{n+3}(L_i)} \tag{10.2}$$

where H_i is the highest price for three days, L_i is the lowest, and $C - n$ is the final closing price.

This is an example of a system which make predictions from the raw time series alone but carries out intelligent pre- and post-processing in order to transform both the data and the network task into a more useful domain. Although multiple linear regression performed as well as the neural system on short term predictions, the network performed significantly better on long term (72 days) prediction.

Coding schemes

Cullen [28] investigated the use of different types of coding scheme for performing financial prediction. In chapter 2, we discussed coding schemes for time delay neural networks such as the exponential trace model and the Gamma memory [111]. Cullen compared a simple delay window, an exponentially weighted window, and a Gamma memory for their ability to predict United States plant investment figures from 1982, testing both single and multiple steps ahead. Such investment data is believed to be the most important factor of GNP.

Cullen found that all three coding schemes produced similar training errors but that the exponential and Gamma models provided consistently better generalisation than the simple delay window. No differences were found in the ability of the different codings to facilitate multiple step prediction. This was due to the fact that none of the models was able to make any accurate long term predictions at all.

10.4.2   Network testing and analysis

Taking the set of Swiss franc/US dollar exchange rate values from the Santa Fe time series forecasting competition [115] and training a recurrent network on a one step ahead prediction task appears, at first glance, to give the key to a fortune. Figure 10.2(a) shows a plot of the output of a recurrent neural network predicting one hour ahead and then taking the actual value, rather than the predicted value, as input in order to predict the next step.

Looking at the graph and reasoning that an hour is sufficient time in which to make a trade, may give the impression that superior profits are possible. Clearly this is too good to be true: a closer inspection of the graph—as in figure 10.2(b)—shows that the network is simply predicting that the price level one hour from now will be the same as it is now. A commonly quoted effect of the efficient markets hypothesis is that such a policy is actually optimal. Figure 10.2(b) also illustrates the point that the new information is not reflected in the time series until it is too late: the drop in price drags the prediction down one step later but the price has already flattened out again and the chance of a profit has been lost. This result has been found to be consistent for a large number of seemingly random time series and also occurs when a network is trained on randomly generated sequences. That is to say that training a neural network on data produced by a random walk will produce a random walk model. Lowe and Webb [59] used a radial basis network to predict British Telecom stock values and state that a lower error on an evaluation test was achieved by following a random walk model.

As Burgess [21] and Weigend [9] point out, financial time series may consist of up to 80% noise. Therefore a good performance metric is essential if any confidence is to be placed in a predictive system. The question of noise introduces new doubts concerning the validity of financial prediction systems. It is accepted in physics, for example, that a level of noise above 10% introduces serious doubts into any analytical model. Claims have been made concerning the presence of chaotic structure in financial systems [8]. Many found evidence for non-linearities but few found evidence of chaos. As we saw in chapter 4, there is a difference between chaotic behaviour and non-linear behaviour. A system may be non-linear without being chaotic but becomes chaotic when the non-linearities are such that the system will diverge from two proximal states at an exponential rate. Chaos implies that a small perturbation of the system will lead to a large divergence of its behaviour, and any level of noise will introduce perturbations. The level of noise present in financial time series makes it very unlikely that a chaotic predictor could be built, but the findings of Yao and Tong [122][1] imply that such systems may be less chaotic under certain conditions and so strengthen further the need for performance metrics.

Portfolio management is based on risk minimisation and potential profit maximisation. Risk used to be measured as the historical volatility of the stock in question; a volatile stock carries a greater risk. Given perfect predictive ability, there is no risk, and given statistical arbitrage, the risk is related to the confidence we have in the prediction. In chapter 6 we presented methods for deriving errors measures from neural networks.

---

[1]These findings are discussed in chapter 4 on time series analysis.

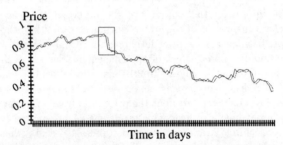

(a) Plotting the whole time series produces a graph which appears to indicate good predictive ability for the neural network.

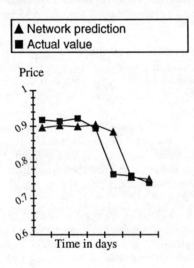

(b) A closer look at the area in the box in (a) shows how the network prediction lags behind the price movement by one step. If we were to move the network prediction one step forward (i.e. into the future) then we would be making the perfect predictions suggested by the chart in (a).

Figure 10.2: Predicting the hourly dollar/Swiss franc exchange rates.

Refenes [80] has presented a set of measures of particular use for determining the performance of a financial predictor. These measures are discussed below.

The first is the correlation coefficient. This is a standard statistical measure of linear predictability between two variables. The correlation between the actual output and the target output is an easily understood measure of network performance. The network must also be tested against methods known as *trivial predictors*: simple methods for predicting a given variable. In financial prediction—due to the random walk consequence of the efficient markets hypothesis—trivial predictors are of great importance. The random walk model is based on the fact that in an efficient market the current price is the best predictor of the subsequent price. The prediction then, is $x_t = x_{t-1}$. Network prediction, y, can be compared against the random walk model as a ratio of the error made by each:

$$T = \frac{\sqrt{\sum_{t=1}^{n}(y_t - x_t)^2}}{\sqrt{\sum_{t=1}^{n}(x_{t-1} - x_t)^2}} \qquad (10.3)$$

The value T, often referred to as Theil's coefficient of inequality, will be less than one if the network model is performing better than the random walk model. A value greater than one signals that predictions are worse than random walk and a value equal or close to one indicates that our model is equivalent to the random walk. A point worth noting here is that the random walk is a solution for time series with small step by step changes which lies in an easily reached local minimum. That is to say that, if a time series moves in very small steps, then a very low error can be achieved by predicting that the value at the next step will be equal to that of the last. This near—but clearly useless—solution may be a long way (in weight space) from the correct, predictive solution. Back propagation aims to reduce the error, not to carry out the specific task we have in mind.

An obvious way to avoid falling into such a local minimum is to design an error function which does not contain such points. Predicting the direction of the change is a simple example; a random walk model which predicts that the next value will equal the current value will settle on a large total error given such task. Several other methods for constructing a more useful cost function are discussed below.

A second trivial predictor asserts that the best prediction is the historical mean value. In this case, the T value will be

$$T = \frac{\sqrt{\sum_{t=1}^{n}(y_t - x_t)^2}}{\sqrt{\sum_{t=1}^{n}(\overline{x} - x_{t+1})^2}} \qquad (10.4)$$

The T value is interpreted exactly as in the previous case.

Other performance metrics include measuring the number of predictions for which the direction of the change is correct—which is useful for financial prediction tasks as the direction is often all that is required—and measuring the profitability of a trading strategy based on the network predictions. Profit based tests compare the profit made by the network against measures such as the profit which would be made if the stock in question was bought and held or against the ideal potential profit to be made if perfect prediction were possible.

Finally, performance may be measured on the basis of a portfolio of stocks which is managed with reference to the neural predictor. In this case, we are interested in the way in which profit accumulates over time; as described by the portfolio's *equity curve*. It is not sufficient simply to achieve an increasing equity curve; the curve must also be free from large drops—known as drawdown—and we must disregard large profits as uncharacteristic. The consequences of equity curve analysis are two fold: firstly strategies which involve large drawdowns from time to time are seen as being high risk and to be avoided. Similarly a system which relies on the occasional large profit from a single trade is seen as equally risky.

LeBaron and Weigend [9] use a method called bootstrapping, as discussed in chapter 2 on data preparation, to attach confidence limits to network prediction. The method requires a large ensemble of networks to be trained on different combinations of training and test data. This study aimed to predict New York stock exchange trading volumes: a particularly noisy series of data. Due to this noise, there was a large variation across the predictions made by the network models trained on different partitions of the data set. By measuring the distribution across these predictions, they were able to determine whether to treat the average prediction as a true value or as noise. It should also be noted that the authors used 2523 networks—which is time consuming to say the least—and found no improvement over linear predictive methods.

In summary, a good predictive trading system is one which out performs any trivial system, returns a superior profit, and reaches that profit without the risk of large drawdown or a reliance on a small number of highly profitable events. Methods for attaching error bars to predictions, such as those investigated in chapter 6, may provide useful tools for creating such a system.

10.4.3   A profit driven approach

The average error of a set of predictions is not the best measure of how well a financial system is doing, profit percentage is. It is better to build a system which learns to maximise profit rather than minimise mean squared error. The system should spot good trading opportunities and know when to trade and when to sit tight. An automated system which forces a trade at each time step would not only be inefficient but be disastrous for market stability if it were to become common practice.

A profit driven system would be based on the following steps:

- Design a system for profit maximisation on a training set assuming predictive ability.

- Code the target output to represent buy, sell, or hold. A binary representation with three units is ideal.

- Train the network.

- Train another to predict the errors of the first.

- Follow the first network's advice when the second network indicates that the market is in a predictable state.

We have seen in chapter 6 how it is possible to train a second network to indicate whether or not a given input vector is in a region of predictability. The obvious problem with applying this method to financial data is that there seem to be no periods of predictability. Further analysis is required in this area before any definite answers are known.

Trading strategies

LeBaron [7] describes a trading method called the reversal strategy by which the return on a transaction, r_t is calculated as

$$r_t = \log \frac{P_t}{P_{t-1}} \tag{10.5}$$

where P_t is the price at time t.

If the trend is upwards, then r_t is positive. If the trend is downwards, then r_t is negative.

Logged differences are used to allow for the non stationary nature of the series. The reversal strategy of trading works as follows. For some threshold, λ:

- **If $r_{t-1} > \lambda$ then** buy.

- **If $r_{t-1} < -\lambda$ then** sell.

- **If $\mid r_{t-1} \mid \leq \lambda$ then** continue the current position.

This translates as if the return moves above a given threshold then buy, if loss is greater than the threshold then sell, and if return does not move sufficiently then maintain the current strategy.

Burgess [20] describes a method for using neural networks to aid the process of choosing a trading strategy. Different trading strategies are required for different types of market behaviour. Whether the market is moving up, down, or simply stagnating, it is possible to make money on trading. The difficulty lies in identifying the current market behaviour. Burgess used neural networks to recognise changes in market conditions which would prompt a change in trading strategy.

Zhang and Hutchinson [123] set themselves the task of predicting the direction of the price movement in the Santa Fe [115] data rather than its absolute value. Samples were taken from the tickwise data ensuring that the gap between points never fell below a given value; this did not ensure equal spacing but reduced the number of zero change values. The change values were coded as 1 = increasing, 0 = unchanging, and minus 1 = decreasing. The input to the network consisted of the coded change values for the past seven data points along with a measure of the length of time between the first and last point. Output was the coded value of the next data point given the sampling restriction described above.

The data was fed into a 8–20–20–1 MLP with an output activation function capable of producing output in the range from minus 1 to 1 and trained with a very low learning rate. The network predicted the correct direction change for 52.4% of the cases compared to 41.4% by the random walk method.

10.4.4   Forecasting a single time series where other inputs are known at each time step

Forecasting currency exchange rates

De Groot and Würtz [42] report that univariate statistical analysis on IMM Swiss franc exchange values show the time series to be random walks. Having expressed grave doubt that a neural network could learn to model a time series from the series alone, they go on to describe a study in which external indicators such as the London Gold price, the US dollar index and the COMEX gold future are used to predict Swiss franc exchange rates. The authors point out the importance of rigorous pre-processing, only using the network when the task is properly defined and the data in a form well suited to that task.

Using standard statistical techniques such as Wilcoxen's two sample test and Spearman's ρ test, a set of indicators were chosen and a linear predictive model built. The model did not predict actual values, but simply the direction of the next move. Using a trading scheme of buying when the forecast says that the price is set to rise, and selling in the opposite case, the linear model returned $13.1 \pm 4.2\%$. A set of neural networks trained on the same indicators and combined in a number of different ways returned $16.5 \pm 4.0\%$. The methods of combining the results of the networks included taking the average output, the majority output, or only trading if the majority of the networks agreed on the stock movement.

Non-linear causality between stock index futures and cash markets

Abhyankar [4] points out that a lead–lag relationship has been known to exist between stock index futures and the cash market. Granger [41] provides a method for calculating incremental predictive ability between two time series. Baek and Brock [6] proposed a non-linear measure of Granger causality which was subsequently extended by Hiemstra and Jones [47]. Abhyankar investigated the presence of linear and non-linear Granger causality between the FT-SE 100 index futures and the cash index returns from 1992. He found unidirectional linear causality from the cash index futures to the cash returns but strong non-linear causality in both directions. These results suggest that a neural network based model may be able to improve on existing market models.

Forecasting moves in the UK economy

Hoptroff [49] uses a mixture of external factors and past values of those factors to make predictions of moves in the UK economy. Measures were taken of stock levels, factory spare capacity, business optimism, company turnover, new orders, expected stock levels, housing starts, capital investment, retail sales, new car registration, interest rates, unemployment, production levels, consumer credit, FT-A-500, and GDP(0) for five periods created 80 input values. A measure of each variable for the present time, from the last three quarters and from two years ago. Choosing past values is similar to data windowing in that it associates past values with those of the future.

A one-hidden-layer MLP with two hidden units was trained to predict the CSO coincident indicator (a smoothed measure of GDP) two years in advance using monthly data from 1963 to 1992. The period from 1987 to 1990 was used to independently test the system. The system predicted two years ahead as well as the leading indicator did for one year. It was also smoother. Obvious unforeseeable events such as the coal strike and deregulation were not forecast by either system.

10.5 Conclusion

The question addressed by this chapter is "Can a neural network help us to make money?" I think we have seen that the tentative answer is yes. Several companies have improved processes such as decision making, resource allocation, direct market targeting and price setting with neural models. The fact that neural networks may be differentiated and traversed, as laid out in chapter 7, makes them ideal economic modelling tools as they allow us to dry run and test different strategies.

We have also investigated the use of neural networks for predicting financial time series and found less encouraging results. These are, however, early days and as attention shifts from the dream of beating the efficient markets hypothesis to the reality of decision support for tasks such as portfolio management, it seems likely that neural networks will join the list of tools available to the financial analyst.

Chapter 11

Industrial process modelling

Gold is for the mistress—silver for the maid—
Copper for the craftsman cunning at his trade.
"Good!" said the Baron, sitting in his hall,
"But Iron—Cold Iron—is master of them all."

Rudyard Kipling

11.1   Introduction

This chapter is intended to serve as an illustration of how the techniques which were introduced in part I may be applied to a set of real world problems based on the monitoring and control of physical systems. It is not intended as an in depth explanation of the techniques required for process control, rather as large pool of examples with which to illustrate a series of problems and solutions. Detail is left intentionally scant; scope spread fairly wide. Many points are made along with references to sections in part I of the book. The chapter also introduces a small number of advanced techniques which are often applied to monitoring and control problems.

11.2   Modelling and controlling dynamic systems

There is a distinction between a neural network model of a system and a neural controller for a system. Often a neural controller will make use of a system model either for training or operation or both. In the case of one step ahead control, a neural model is used as control decisions may be made on the strength of the next predicted system state.

11.2.1   Back propagation through time and neural emulators

There are two techniques which appear frequently in the literature on neural networks in control. These are back propagation through time and neural emulators. Let us imagine cycling a neural network several times to produce a series of of control outputs which move a system to a particular goal state. If the goal state must be reached in a fixed number of steps, a single error measure is available after the network has been cycled that number of times. The problem now becomes clear: we have an error for the final cycle of the control network, but none for any of the other cycles. The error for the previous cycles may be calculated using a technique known as *back propagation through time.*

Back propagation through time works by feeding the error derivative from the controller network at one time slice through a model of the system being controlled and then through the same control network at the previous time slice. This is repeated until the error at the first step becomes available. This process requires that the model of the system being controlled is differentiable. Neural networks, as we saw in chapter 7, are differentiable and for this reason it is useful to build a *neural emulator* of the process which is to be controlled. Back propagation through time and neural emulators are discussed in detail below.

Batch distillation control

Cressy et al. [27] used a software emulator of a batch distillation process to train a neural emulator on the forward operation of the process. Controller errors were back propagated through the emulator and so converted from system output errors (i.e. incorrect mixture strength) to errors of control input which could be altered. This method was first suggested by Nguyen and Widrow [71] and is widely applied to many neural control problems.

The system

The real world system which Cressy et al. set out to control was a batch distiller which took the following inputs:

- Initial ingredients at time step 1

- Moles of liquid in reboiler: $S(1)$

- Moles of methanol in reboiler: $M(1)$

- Reflux ratio at time step n: $R(n)$

- Ambient temperature at time t: $T(t)$

The system gives an output estimating the number of moles of product collected, $P(n)$, and product quality, $K(n)$, at step n. The system state at step n is defined by the vector $\{S(n), M(n), P(n), K(n)\}$. The system is temporal in nature; it moves through a set of states from an initial condition to a desired product. The target product, $K(N)_{des}$ is only known for the final system state.

The system model

A software simulator of the distillation process was built, the output of which was used to train a neural emulator with the same inputs and outputs and the same forward dynamics. The simulator allowed the training to be done off-line. As the state of the distillation process at any time depends only on the state of the system at the previous time step, a simple feedforward one step ahead model was built. The advantage of using a neural emulator is that it is simple to differentiate for use in the back propagation algorithm.

The controller

The controller can be defined as follows:

- Input: $S(n)$, $M(n)$, $T(n)$, $K(n) - K(N)_{des}$ (fed back error).

- Target: $K(N)_{des}$. The target represents the state of the system at the final step.

- Error: $K(n) - K(N)_{des}$. The error represents the difference between the current output and the final target output. The error is converted from one of system output to one of system input by back propagation through the neural emulator. It is converted from an error at step N to and error at step n using the back propagation through time algorithm.

- Output: $R(n)$: This is the new setting for the reflux ratio.

The problem for the controller was to set the reflux ratio at each time step n to guide the system to the desired product quality $K(N)_{des}$ at the final step: N.

Training the controller

Back propagation through time was used to train the controller. The back propagation through time algorithm has two phases: the forward pass during which the forward dynamics of the system, guided by the neural controller, are emulated, and the reverse pass during which the error $K(n) - K(N)_{des}$ is propagated back from time N to time 0. The two neural networks used in this process—the emulator and the controller—are duplicated at each time step and the errors used to update the controller are averaged once the reverse pass has reached step 0.

Once the forward pass is complete, the errors are propagated back through time as follows:

1. The final error $(K(N) - K(N)_{des})$ describes the error in terms of the output of the emulator, but in order to alter the controller that error is required in terms of input to the emulator (i.e. $R(n)$). The error is passed back through the emulator in precisely the same way as it is during the emulator training stage. The error is calculated on the input to the networks as a Jacobian matrix, as discussed in chapter 7 (as there is only one output variable in this case, the matrix will simply be a vector).

2. The error is now expressed in terms of the control signal from the time step before, i.e. the error on the output of the neural controller, so it can be passed back through the controller.

3. The previous three steps are repeated, passing the error back through each copy of the networks, until step 0 is reached. The errors are averaged and the weights in the controller are then updated accordingly.

It is essential for the above training scheme that we know how many time steps the process is required to take. A training set is not generated explicitly; rather the controller learns by its attempts at controlling the emulator.

Direct weights from the input units to the output were used in this example to reduce attenuation of the error as it passes through so many network copies.

Using the Controller

During use, the controller looks at the current system state, $\{S(n), M(n), P(n), T(t)\}$ and the error $(K(n) - K(N)_{des})$ and gives the required reflux ratio as output. No forward prediction of the process nor reverse propagation of the error is required; the controller has been trained to move from one state to the next based on current state alone. The training stage has already translated errors at the final step: firstly into errors at step n by back propagation through time, and then into control signals by adjusting the weights in the neural controller.

11.2.2   Using state-space equations in place of a neural emulator

Beaufays et al. [14] demonstrated the use of several techniques in applying an MLP to the task of controlling a power generator which feeds a power line to several users. The generator is of the steam driven turbine type. As more power is demanded, the system controller must open the steam valve sufficiently to cover the increased load. As the load varies, the frequency of the system varies and must be brought back to its nominal state as quickly as possible. Such systems are known to posses non-linear dynamics, but traditional approaches to control have been based on linear models for each operating point in the system. It is known that such systems will return the generator to its nominal output value, but at a speed considerably slower than is possible. Clearly a neural network controller should be able to improve on the linear method.

In chapter 7 we discussed the use of network derivatives for extracting explanations of a network's behaviour. To facilitate this, the Jacobian matrix of partial derivatives of each output unit with respect to each input unit was calculated. Beaufays et al. were able to use the state-space equations of the plant, which were differentiable, so did not need to train a neural emulator in the way that Cressy [27] did. The error vector at the output of the generator is differentiated with respect to the input control vector to produce the required Jacobian. The resultant errors are passed through the back propagation algorithm in the standard manner. Using the system state-space equations saves time and improves accuracy but removes the possibility of using the neural emulator for monitoring the system in case of malfunction.

If a single control operation was sufficient to return the system to a steady state then the system just described would be sufficient. However, several control actions are required to remove all the transients caused by a perturbation to the load. Furthermore, the target state of the system is not known at each of the steps. Only the final goal state is known. Once again, back propagation through time may be used. The number of time steps to be back propagated over is defined at the start. The number is chosen to be sufficient for the controller to return the system to a steady state. This is a somewhat arbitrary parameter and will be easier to choose in some applications that others. It is of course possible to iteratively reduce the number of steps until the network is no longer able to perform the task. Similarly, there is no reason why the network should not arrive at the goal state in less than the chosen number of steps. The resolution of the steps is chosen with reference to the particular task at hand.

The neural controller was not only able to return the system to a steady state in less time than that required by a traditional controller but was also able to limit the transients caused by overshooting the target state.

11.2.3 Representing time with a input window

Rather than using back propagation through time, Sheppard et al. [89] used a feedforward network with a time window to represent the past history of control signals to implement a predictive controller for a gas furnace. The network performed a prediction of the subsequent temperature of the furnace, working on a "what if" basis. The difference between the predicted temperature and the actual temperature are used to alter a hypothetical future control signal. This control signal is fed back into the predictive emulator along with the temperature history vector in order to predict the next temperature. As the control signal was based on the difference between the predicted and actual temperature, a measure of the accuracy of the network prediction was required at each step. This was achieved by the use of spread encoding for the temperature output representation.

Sigüenza et al. [90] explain how using a time window relates to Takens' [103] theorem on state-space reconstruction in order to build a predictive model of a paraffin de-waxing unit. The importance of Takens' theorem is that it states that the dynamics of any system may be modelled without access to all of the internal state measurements of that system. It is possible to build a model from the observable behaviour—in the present case, the temperature—given a sufficiently sized vector of previous outputs. Similarly, Maund et al. [63] showed how vibration in a spacecraft simulator could be damped using a neural controller trained only on measurements of displacement and velocity.

11.2.4   Representing time with a recurrent neural network

Karjala et al. [53] simulated the dynamics of a drainage tank in software, producing a set of noisy measurements of the flow rate from the tank. A recurrent network of the type discussed in chapter 4 was trained on noisy measurements of output flow rate, input flow rate, and liquid height, and was asked to predict the subsequent value of each. In this way it was hoped that the network would smooth the data and predict a noiseless output value for each of the inputs. For the output flow and tank height, the network was able to remove the noise from a set of test data, giving clear readings from simulated noisy sensors. The network was not able to smooth the input flow rate: hardly surprising as it depends on no other variable in the system and is discontinuous.

Goudreau and Giles [40] showed how a recurrent network could be used to learn to route messages through a parallel computing system. In such a system, a set of switches receive messages and decide whether to give the message to the processor associated with that switch or to pass it on. There is no external control: the switches use the information in the message to decide how it should be processed. The process by which a recurrent network learns the routing problem is very similar to that discussed in chapter 4 in relation to learning finite state grammars. Rather than building a look-up table for every possible routing, a partial table is built which contains many missing entries. The network is then required to learn a general representation from the partial look-up table. The ability to build a generalisable model of an incomplete look-up table is a very useful quality which may be applied to many inference tasks.

11.2.5   Production control

Madey et al. [60] used a neural network simulator to control a production system which took inputs relating to raw material density, machine feed rate and machine feed pressure and produced outputs relating to the probability of a machine breakdown, the production rate, and the number of defective units produced. These outputs also provide a measure of profit. As a measure of material density is not available during run time a controller must learn to reset the machine by observing four variables: feed speed, feed pressure, production rate and number of defective units produced.

A training set for the neural controller was generated using a software simulator of the system and deriving—by trial and error—optimal answers to random scenarios.

The scenarios described the system state in terms of the four variables just described and asked what change in the pressure and feed settings would maximise profit. Different possibilities were fed through the simulator until profit was deemed to be at a maximum.

The task for the controller was to predict the required settings which produced the maximal profit given the current settings and production rates. A feedforward MLP was trained to map an input describing the four variables onto an output which gives the settings chosen by the trial-and-error optimisation process. At run time the controller receives input from the system and changes the system settings accordingly in a feedback loop.

11.2.6   Control of a microwave oven

The Sharp R-4N76 is a one touch controlled microwave oven which has been trained to recognise the "signatures" which the humidity generated by different types of food describe as they cook. Using a single humidity sensor, and with the requirement that the user states only whether the item to be cooked is food or drink, the oven is able to not only stop when the food is ready, but stop at correct intermediate points to allow the user to stir the food. The training process consisted of cooking hundreds of examples in an oven with a set of sensors, collecting data from each, and selecting the most useful single sensor. Data from this sensor was then used to train the the network to spot the trajectory produced by the change in humidity over time. In this way, stop points, and stop-and-stir points could be identified. Further technical details are understandably sparse.

11.2.7   Process monitoring

Many of the methods discussed in chapter 6 on error analysis are relevant to the task of process monitoring. Whether the process involves an industrial machine, a helicopter or a human patient, the methods are the same. The most useful tool available to the condition monitor is the novelty detection network presented in section 6.9. Such a network may be trained to model the normal operation of a system and to flag any deviation from that mode. Whilst it may not be possible to learn the nature of the error from such a system, it is possible to train a network without having to collect data from a malfunctioning system.

Many standard system monitoring techniques are based on principal components analysis (PCA). The first two or three principal components of a system's output variables may be plotted against one another as the system evolves over time. Deviation from normal operation is easy to spot on such a plot as there are only a small number of dimensions to monitor. Using an auto-associative network in the same way as the traditional PCA allows us to build a non-linear representation of a system's normal behaviour rather than the linear representation provided by PCA. What does that mean? A principal component is a single variable which describes as much of a multi-dimensional set of data as is possible with a single straight line. A single variable in an auto-associative network describes as much of the data set as is possible with a curved line. Under the right circumstances, such a representation is able to convey more information about a system in a smaller number of variables. The job of human operator who must monitor a system's operation may be reduced considerably if the number of variables being monitored may be reduced; auto-associative networks offer a method for non-linear variable reduction.

If a system may be safely "seeded" to produce certain types of abnormal behaviour, or if such data already exists, then a straightforward categorisation network may be used to spot each different type of malfunction. As the outputs from such a network approximate probabilities, it is likely that a set of rules by which the network output is translated into a warning or alarm will be required. The use of thresholds was discussed in chapter 6 where we saw how a trade-off between missed errors and false alarms could be balanced. Thresholds may be set on each independent output unit so that errors with different degrees of seriousness may be dealt with in different ways. As thresholds do not need to be learned from the training data, they may be tuned at run time either by hand or by an optimisation algorithm.

Patient monitoring

Dodd [30] describes a neural based system for decreasing the number of false alarms made by a medical monitoring system. The existing system monitored respiration, heart rate, blood pressure, saturation of oxygen and other vital signs. It did not combine (or *fuse*) the measures, and so sounded an alarm if any one reached a dangerous level. As a neural network is able to map several variables onto a single output, the measures could be fused and an alarm only sounded when a critical combination was displayed. The difficulty with training such a system was that data from patients in a critical condition was sparse and could not be artificially induced (for obvious reasons!). The solution employed by Dodd is subject to a UK patent and described as a method for synthesising an alarm condition by a statistical technique. In chapter 6 I discussed several such techniques which are able to perform the same function.

A similar system [94] has been developed at St. James's hospital for monitoring the progress of premature babies in ventilators. The ventilator settings must be adjusted with respect to the condition of the baby. As there are several settings and the relationship between each is complex, an expert system is used to choose the correct level for each. The expert system is limited by an inability to adapt its recommendations as the state of the baby changes. A neural network model based on the expert system was implemented and then extended to be able to take the response of each baby into account when updating the recommended settings.

11.3 Case study: predicting driver alertness

This section discusses the application of some of the methods discussed in this book to the task of building a neural network based system for predicting driver alertness from steering behaviour. This work is discussed fully in Swingler [100], [101].

There is a limit to the accuracy with which we can predict a person's state of alertness from some aspect of their behaviour. Driver behaviour and alertness are, however, clearly related and this should allow us to build model which can predict one from the other. For such a model to be of use it must be very general in its ability. Such generality is available at the expense of accuracy and a trade-off must consequently be made. The trade-off may be in terms of overall error rate or in terms of quantity of usable predictions. We show how an acceptable level of generality was achieved and how the trade-off between error rate and quantity of usable predictions was managed.

The basic idea is that we select the parts of the training set that we consider learnable and train a neural network. We then take the network, discover all the situations in which it fails, and build a system which allows the network to operate only under the correct circumstances. All other situations must be dealt with by a filtering process and exception handling routines. In this way we achieve a level of complexity which matches the level of information available to us. A working prototype system has been produced.

11.3.1 Task definition

Our task is to build a neural network model of driver alertness based on the driver's physical actions in controlling the vehicle; a task which is inherently noisy and full of contradictory examples. In order to build a model which is trained on a small number of drivers and yet is able to generalise well to many, we clearly need to aim for the most general and robust model possible. Many of the decisions discussed below were taken with that specific goal in mind.

11.3.2 Data collection

Recording a reliable measure of driver state

In order to train a supervised neural network, a reliable measure of a driver's state was required. This measure could be intrusive as it was only needed for collecting training data for network development. The network will learn to predict this reliable measure from some other less accurate but non-intrusive measurements of driver actions.

Electrophysiological recordings were taken from drivers using scalp based electrodes and a portable recorder. Measurements included the electroencephalogram (EEG) which measures brain activity; the electrooculogram (EOG) which measures eye movements, and the electromyogram (EMG) which measures muscle activity. A method has been developed by which a seven stage categorisation may be carried out based on these measures. The scale is arranged so that a score of one indicates that the subject is active. Stages two and three are classed as quiet waking stages with decreasing muscular and ocular activity. Stage four is characterised by intermittent alpha activity in the EEG measure and stage five by constant alpha activity and some eye closure. Stage six is identified by the presence of theta (low frequency) waves in the EEG measure and characterised by occasional microsleeps. Stage seven is the first stage of sleep. No driver reached stage seven at any point during the road trials. The scores derived by this system were validated, to a degree, by the inclusion of a sleep latency test where subjects are given the opportunity to sleep in a dark room at the conclusion of a trial.

Other measures of alertness

All subjects were recorded on video tape for use in an eye blink analysis and the supervisor for each run made regular notes on the driver's apparent state, asking questions when appropriate. Additional data from other vehicle controls were also used to build an accurate measure of each driver's state.

Recording a driver's control actions

The following recordings were taken from the car and driver: throttle angle, two measures of steering pressure, road speed, brake pedal pressure, direction indicators activated, a set of strain gauge measurements taken across the back and seat of the driver's chair, and in car temperature. The measurements were all time stamped.

11.3.3   Data pre-processing

The goal of the data pre-processing stage of a neural network based project is to manipulate the raw collected data into a form with which a neural network can be trained. This involves choosing the best variables to use as predictors and an appropriate output resolution or target accuracy. These decisions are based partly on the structure of the data and partly on the limitations imposed by the methods of neural network development. These decisions also affect the complexity of the final neural model.

Pre-processing the steering data

The steering movements were produced as single bytes at a rate of 20Hz. This produced a vast amount of data which needed to be reduced in size for input to a neural network. The reduction in size is required for two reasons. Firstly, drivers do not fall asleep in a twentieth of a second, so data must be combined and reduced over time. Secondly, there is far more apparent accuracy in the steering data than we can expect from a final predictive system; far more information is reflected than we can sensibly use. There are several different ways in which a constant stream of data can be encoded for use in a neural network.

Treating the data as a continuous stream

Recurrent networks such as those proposed by Elman [33], Williams and Zipser [119], and Swingler [102] have been used extensively to extract time varying structure for a range of signal processing applications. Using such a network for the present study would have proved difficult as there was such a large amount of data. Time delay neural networks, as used by Waibel [112], Refenes [81], Weigend et al. [116], and Mozer [69] operate on a lagged vector of the data stream, transposing the temporal element into a spatial one. The vector can be input to the network in a raw form or processed further. In the case of steering wheel movements, it is clear that some pre-processing will be required if we are to extract the correct information from the data. A lagged vector of 20 elements will still only represent a second's worth of data, and a single second will not contain sufficient information for a measure of alertness to be predicted. Taking larger lagged windows would produce an input vector which contained so many parameters that we would be forced to build a neural network with far more weights than we should. For our model to be simple, our input representation must also be simple.

Fourier analysis

Past studies such as that carried out by Tarriere et al. [105] have based the analysis on the area between zero crossings of the raw steering measure, which extracts some information about the frequencies and associated power of the steering wheel reversals. The most explicit way to derive such information is to take a Fourier transform of the signal, thus producing a spectral vector which describes the power at each of a range of frequencies across the sample.

The steering data was sampled at 20Hz, and the EEG measures taken over a 16 second window. Matching the steering data to the EEG measure leaves 320 data points per EEG measure. As the fast Fourier transform algorithm requires an input vector of size 2^n where n is any whole value, the mid 256 points were taken for each analysis. A Fourier transform produces a vector of frequencies up to the Nyquist limit of the input data, which is equal to half of the original sampling frequency. A window of 256 points, sampled at 20Hz accounts for 12.8s and produces a spectrum of frequencies up to 10Hz.

Data was processed using a Parzen window to remove the effects of chopping the data into a window which is smaller than the original sample. Analysis of variance between the data at different frequencies was used to extract the range of frequencies which contained around 95% of the information which could be used to separate sleepy and alert drivers. This range was found to span 0.78Hz to 8Hz. Once the bandwidths for the steering analysis had been chosen, the steering data was downsampled and grouped so that a single spectral vector matched a single original EEG measure representing 16s worth of driving.

By choosing an appropriate spectral resolution for the Fourier transform, we were able to control the dimensionality of the vector which forms the input layer of the network. In order to build a model of the correct complexity, we must juggle several constraints on the task in hand. Input dimensionality is one such constraint, and one which, in this case, we have some control over. As each input unit has a set of weights associated with it, adding input units to a network increases the number of degrees of freedom of the model. The spectral resolution of a power spectrum is related to the bandwidth of each measurement. By averaging across larger bandwidths we can reduce the size of the input layer to a point where the network is of realistic size. Further constraints on network size are discussed below.

Re-scaling the steering data

Because most of the power values in the Fourier spectrum were clustered at the lower end of the overall range, and there were a small number of high power values, the spectral inputs were scaled down by taking the logarithm of each value. Such non-linear scaling ensures that the area which contains the majority of the input data is spread across as much of the input range as possible. Logarithmic scaling was suitable in this case as the data distribution was bottom heavy.

The results of the logarithmic operation were then divided by the maximum thus produced to ensure that values fell into the range between zero and one. Scaling the training data by dividing each value by the maximum from the training set introduces the risk of test data values being greater than one. There are several points worth making in relation to this. The first is that the squashing functions in the network will rescale any value, so it is not too important to spot such cases. The second is that such cases will fall outside the experience of the network and so require extrapolation from the network's model. This may not be a valid exercise as it involves making predictions about part of the real world that the network has never experienced. Contingencies should be included for assessing the outputs of a network under such conditions.

11.3.4   Choosing an output range and resolution

The alertness scores to be used during network training were based on recordings of EEG, EOG and EMG taken from the drivers. A visual analysis technique was applied to the raw codings in order to produce a seven point scale ranging from 1=*alert* to 7=*stage one sleep*. Because this scale is based on exact electrophysiological readings, it is intuitively obvious that we would not be able to accurately predict its full range based on a simple measure such as steering action. The resolution of the output range must be reduced so that it reflects the amount of information available from the input measure.

By using conditional entropy based analysis, the two states which were easiest to distinguish were identified. Conditional entropy analysis provides a measure of how well an event may be predicted by the occurrence of another related event. It is measured by calculating how well the event of interest might be predicted given no prior information, and subtracting a measure of the predictive power given by the knowledge of a related event. Entropy measures uncertainty and can be represented as a percentage score where 100% indicates no predictive ability. An average of this measure taken over all the examples of steering vectors and their corresponding EEG scores produced entropy values of 10% and 13% for stages two and six. Stages one and four scored 76% and 44% respectively. These scores indicate that stages two and six are the easiest to predict from the steering data.

The predictive ability we have of stage two and stage two events occurring without reference to the steering data is very low, having entropy values of 97% and 85% respectively. That is to say that each event occurs with fairly equal probability and so we cannot achieve much better than a 50% success rate by simply guessing. This is important for neural network training and assessment as if one event occurred 90% of the time, we could achieve a 90% success rate by always predicting that event.

Balancing the training data

The training data was balanced so that the split in training examples from each class was exactly half and half. This was done by splitting the training data into two files: one containing examples of stage six driving, the other containing examples of drivers in stage two. During training, at every cycle of the network, the next example was taken from one of the two files, chosen at random. When the end of a file is reached, the program returns to the start. The files are processed in parallel. In this way, not only does the network see a randomly ordered selection of examples from each of the two classes, it also receives a even split of examples. Each example from the smaller of the two classes is consequently seen more often, but the random nature of the process ensures that no single example is duplicated out of proportion.

The process was extended as data sets grew so that several files, each containing data from a different driver, were open in parallel, and examples were chosen at random from each. This ensured that the network did not move towards a representation of any particular driver and that examples were never seen in the same order. The computational overhead of this approach is considerably less than that required to search a single file for different examples at each step.

Deriving a target level of complexity

The conditional entropy analysis revealed that the predictive ability of the steering measure was far from perfect. This is due to the existence of many contradictory examples in the training data. For this reason, the score of driver alertness at the output layer was spread across two units with a binary coding rather than using a single unit to represent alertness along a scale. In this way, the network can be trained so that each unit will display a value relating to the probability of the driver being in either of the two alertness states chosen. Because of the contradictory nature of some of the training examples, it is clear that we can expect the network to produce an output indicating that the driver is fully in one state when the training data claims that he is not. The largest error we can expect from any unit at any time is consequently one. Furthermore, we know that the data set contains contradictory examples and so we must expect such errors to occur. The data balancing process ensures that the outputs always sum to one.

Filtering the training data for good examples

Once a set of examples from the relevant EEG stages had been extracted, the data from other sensors was scanned and any sections which contained sharp turns, low speed or any use of the indicators were removed. This was to ensure that steering behaviour which was obviously a result of non-cruising conditions was not used during training. The goal of the network is to take sections of smooth steady driving and determine a measure of the driver's state. All other situations, low speed driving or particular manoeuvres for example, may be accounted for elsewhere when removing errors.

The final training set

The final input vectors consisted of the mean and variance of the steering pressure along with twenty two elements of the power spectrum. There were two output units, one to indicate a drowsy driver and the other to indicate alertness. The target values for each were set to be one for a driver in each respective category and zero otherwise. The actual network outputs will be continuous valued representations of the probability of the driver being in each of the two states.

Selecting drivers

Although electrophysiological measures are a very good indicator of a person's state of alertness, they are not perfect. Some people never display alpha or theta waves while in a waking state, others produce theta almost continuously. Data was consequently only taken from drivers who displayed a normal range of EEG activity. This fact does not mean that it is not possible to monitor the state of drivers with abnormal EEG activity via another measure, it simply means that they do not provide a usable set of training data.

Data has also to be set aside for testing the network once it has learned the task. Two types of data were set aside in this case. Firstly, a proportion of the data from each driver in the training set was removed, and secondly some drivers were excluded completely from the training set.

A final set of 18 different runs were selected for building the training set. Once the examples of states two and six had been extracted, the data set contained around 4000 data points. This was built from a potential set of 24,000 data points. Clearly, under such noisy and ill matched conditions, far more data must be collected than would be required to train a simple, consistent mapping task.

11.4   Training the neural networks

Having built a representation to reflect the level of accuracy we can expect from the training data, we must now build a neural network which is capable of operating at that level.

Choosing network size

Hecht-Neilson [45] used Kolmogorov's theorem to derive the upper bound for the required number of hidden units as $H \leq 2I + 1$ where I is the number of inputs units. In this case we can set the upper limit at 48 hidden units.

Upadhyaya and Eryurek [110] have applied the fact that the number of parameters required to code P binary patterns is $\log_2 P$, and show that the number of weights required to code P patterns made up of I input units is $W = I\log_2 P$. This theory is not applicable in this case, however, as it assumes binary representations are used. There is the additional problem that it is not easy to identify how many different patterns we are trying to code. It predicts the use of 264 hidden units to build such a model for the drivers' state data. Clearly this is not what we need!

A network which contains fewer hidden units than input units must extract features from the input vector which reliably map to the output classes of interest. The input to the driver alertness network contains a vector of 24 spectral coefficients from which certain features relating to alert and drowsy driving must be extracted. Consequently the network will require fewer hidden units than input units. Clearly neither of the measures mentioned above fulfils this requirement.

Baum and Haussler [13] showed perhaps the easiest estimate to put into practical use. Assume an error limit such that $0 < \epsilon \leq 1/8$. They state that a network which learns to classify the training set to an error of at most $\epsilon/2$ from a data set which satisfies the size constraint $W \approx \epsilon N$ will reach the error limit of ϵ for the test set.

The training set contained 4000 data points. Using the Baum and Haussler rule, the maximum number of weights which a network could contain if it were to learn the data to within an error of 0.1 must be 400. Given 24 input units, a bias unit, and two output units, we see that

$$(24 + 1)H + 2(H + 1) < 400 \text{ so}$$
$$H < 398/27 \text{ so}$$
$$H < 14.7$$

so we cannot use more than 14 hidden units. This is clearly the most useful of the current estimates, and the one which we will use.

Relating to the degree of noise in the training set

Weigend [116] points out that the more noise there is in a data set, the larger the risk of fitting that noise with a neural network model will be. As the ratio of data to noise becomes smaller, the number of hidden units required to avoid overfitting also decreases. It is clear that the task of extracting a measure of alertness from steering pressure will suffer from a large amount of noise. The exact degree of that noise is unknown so three different sized networks were built, with 15, eight and four hidden units respectively.

11.4.1   Training each network

Several versions of each network were trained from different random start positions. The networks with only four hidden units failed to learn any useful representation, settling on an average error of 0.5 on each output unit by producing an output of around 0.5 to every input vector. The other two networks both reached an acceptable error rate although the 15 unit network did not perform significantly better than the eight unit network. Independent validation data from unseen drivers was used, in conjunction with the measures gained from entropy analysis and the level of noise in the data, in order to decide when to stop training.

11.4.2   Testing the networks

Testing was carried out in two stages. Firstly, the ability of the networks to perform the binary alert/drowsy discrimination task on which they were trained was tested. Secondly, a single network was selected to be embedded in a system designed to produce a running alertness score based on network output and several additional factors. In order to test the system in which the network is embedded, a prototype driver alertness monitor was built and a simulation program written which fed steering data to the monitor and converted the output of the system to a set of warning lights or an alarm. It does not make sense to test the network in isolation on a full test set as the assumptions under which the network was trained become violated. Certain types of data were intentionally removed during training and such data must be accounted for in the same manner during testing. It is for this reason that testing was carried out on a wider system rather than purely on the neural network itself.

Initial testing of each network

Once a number of examples of each network had been trained, they were tested on the two types of validation data which had been set aside. The four unit network was discarded and only the larger two networks were tested. As one would expect, initial testing on validation data showed that the smaller of the two networks was better able to generalise to unseen drivers and conditions than the larger of the two. Testing at this stage was designed not only to establish whether the networks were able to carry out their task, but also to uncover different types of error which the networks make.

Testing over the entire driving range

The networks were trained only on data from drivers in one of two states. They must operate correctly in all situations however, so it is very important to test the response of the network to drivers who are in the states which were not used during training. Examples of "alert" driving were actually taken from drivers in stage two of the EEG scale as stage one includes the type of muscle activity associated with major control operations such as braking or turning a corner. It is important that the actions of a driver in stage one do not trigger a false alarm.

Testing on unseen drivers

If the system is to be general enough to be fitted into production cars, then it must reliably generalise to all drivers. A number of the test drives were put aside so that the ability of the model to generalise could be assessed.

11.4.3 A general driver network

The eight unit network was found to be able to generalise best both to unseen data from training drivers and to data from new drivers. This network was embedded in a system which took account of the driver's recent states of alertness in order to smooth its operation. This also allowed for periods of doubt to be discarded.

11.4.4 Spotting false alarms

The penalty associated with a very general model is a high rate of uncertainty in the outputs. As the training data was properly balanced, the two output unit values always summed to one. Rarely did they show a perfect binary split however. To achieve such a split would require a far more accurate, and consequently brittle, model. In order to minimise the ill effects of this uncertainty, we must set thresholds which determine whether a data point should be used or deemed to be in a region of doubt. We must also look for other methods for reducing the error rate.

Investigating the response range of the network

The driver alertness monitor was trained on data from motorway runs where speed was high and steering pressure consequently quite low. Not only does it require less pressure to turn a car at high speed, but there is less need for sudden turns on a stretch of motorway. It is important, however, that we investigate the response of the network to a wide range of driving conditions to ensure that the alarm is not sounded every time the driver reverses out of the garage. This was done by specifically testing the network on the examples which were removed from the training data as being non-representative. The same algorithm which was used to remove these examples from the training data was used to remove their effect on the system output.

The effect of steering power

A test data set was built by setting input values at random and ordering the new set by total power. By plotting the output of the alertness measure of the network against total power, we were able to see the average response of the network as total power changes. This response was compared with the distribution of the training set to determine the type of behaviour we might expect from the network when it receives abnormal inputs. The network output drops to (or near) zero given inputs of greater power than those covered by the training data—indicating that false alarms are not likely to be caused by steering movements of abnormally high power. However, the output of the network to lower powered inputs is consistently high, suggesting that steering actions of lower than normal power could be a cause of certain false alarms.

Such a procedure must be used with care however. The analysis suggested that, on average, network output dropped as steering power increased. It would not be valid to draw any conclusions from this, however, as the values are simply averages about which the network output exhibits a large variance. The analysis suggests an average output of 0.5 around the point where most of the data falls. It is clearly erroneous to conclude much from the fact that drivers are, on average, half alert and half asleep. It is similarly erroneous to draw any other conclusions from such averages. Only at the extremes of the network operating space, where the variance on network output is low, can we draw valid conclusions from such a synthetic data set.

11.4.5   Building a prototype system

Once the neural network system had been developed, it was embedded in a system which drew on other indicators such as time at the wheel and a moving window of driver states to convert the network output into a dashboard scale. The false alarm removal system was also incorporated into the prototype along with allowances for spotting occasions when the network was operating on data from outside its operating range. A system was also developed which had a facility for being tuned in the car without further training. The tuning was simply based on thresholds and guided by the error-reject curve as described in section 6.3.1.

Given that we do not want the system to discard too many samples as unusable, and that we have a set of methods for removing false alarms, we clearly want to set the thresholds on the output units at a position along the error-reject curve which produces an over cautious output. As the curve is not linear, we must choose the optimal point with careful experimentation. Final testing was carried out on each different system rather than on the network in isolation. In this way different error reduction techniques and threshold settings could be tested.

11.4.6   Results

Choosing a fair performance metric for the final system was not an easy task as there are several different, and fairly arbitrary, methods for deciding how correct the system is at any given time. As the system could produce either a warning scale or an alarm, a performance metric was defined which counted correct alarms, false alarms and missed alarms. Periods in each test drive were labelled as requiring an alarm or high output from the alertness scale. A correct alarm was defined as any alarm falling within such a period. Drivers were tested in two hour runs, each typically containing four periods which required an alarm. The system sounded 1.3 false alarms on average for a two hour run, and missed on average 0.6 required alarms. If the system missed more than one period which required an alarm, or produced more than two false alarms for a particular driver, then it was deemed unsatisfactory for that driver. By this method, the system was found to work for 75% of the drivers. Figure 11.1 shows an example of the neural network output and the alarm system before and after false alarm removal.

It is worth noting that the data used to test the system suffered from a lot of the problems which were removed from the training set. For example, one driver spent the entire two hour drive in stage six, whilst the network only signalled two periods of danger. The driver's log, however did not suggest that he was practically asleep for the entire journey. It is consequently not possible to tell whether the network is performing correctly on this data. Such examples contributed to the 25% of drivers for whom the system was deemed to be unsatisfactory.

11.5   Robot control by reinforcement learning

Back propagation through time is one method for guiding a system through a series of unknown states to a final goal without the need for intermediate goals. Unfortunately, we need to know the number of steps in which the system may reach the goal state, and we must have a way of deriving an error measure when the goal is not reached. In cases where we do not know where the goal is, we do not know how long it might take to get there, or there is no measure of success other than whether the goal was reached or not, the approach breaks down. The following set of examples describe a method for implementing a learning process under such conditions. The examples are based on robot navigation as the scenario is easy to imagine.

We have a robot, in an environment, a goal and some obstacles. The robot must learn to find the goal and avoid the obstacles and it must be able to go around obstacles if it knows the goal is behind them. The environment is split into a number of discrete locations and the robot moves from one to the next, guided by what it has learned.

If we assume that data collection is not possible, and the robot must learn as it interacts with the environment, then we must also assume that the robot cannot cause any damage as it learns. In reality in such cases, a simulator would be used. In cases where no damage is possible, these methods allow for continuous on-line learning and improvement.

The robot can move based on one of two types of possible input information:

1. Input from sensors.

2. Positional information.

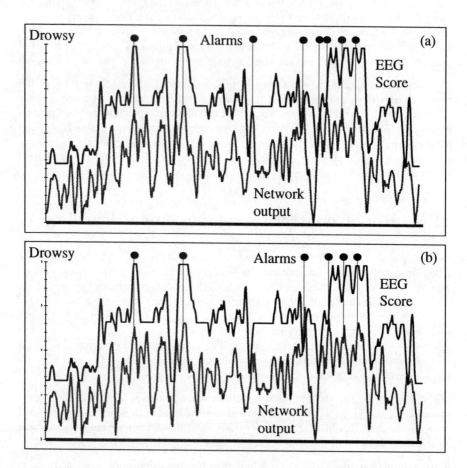

Figure 11.1: An example two hour run before (a) and after (b) false alarm removal has been carried out. The circles indicate where an alarm would be sounded.

The robot also has an internal state to help in its decision making process and the robot's output dictates the direction (N,S,E,W) of the next discrete one-step move it will make.

The robot's task can be one of several types:

1. Learn how to get from a fixed point to a fixed point around fixed objects

2. Learn how to get from a variable point to a fixed point around fixed objects.

3. Learn how to get from a variable point to a variable point around variable objects.

We can model either the *environment* in which the robot lives or the robot's *behaviour* given certain stimuli. Our choice will be determined by the nature of the task and the abilities of the robot. If the objects or the goal are to be variable, then the robot must have external sensors and we must model the robot's behaviour with respect to the sensations it receives.

11.5.1   Reinforcement learning

Reinforcement learning is a technique for assigning credit to some actions over others [11]. A system acts, receives reinforcement (which may be positive, negative or zero), and alters its behaviour accordingly. Reinforcement learning over time makes use of a technique called temporal difference learning (TD) which combines dynamic programming, parameter estimation which—in this case—involves discovering the correct weight strengths for the neural network, and sequential decision making. TD attempts to consider the long term effects of each decision step based only on a local measure.

11.5.2   Dynamic programming

Dynamic programming (DP) calculates, for each system state, the probable payoff attached to each adjoining state. It is then possible to build a model which knows the optimal next step at any time. We can imagine, in the case of robot navigation, that a set of signposts are erected in the model to point to the best state at each step.

The problem is that it needs to work backwards from the goal state through each of the preceding states in order to calculate the utility of each location. In a natural real time learning task however, this is not possible. TD learning provides a method for approximating the results of DP by repeated forward runs through a system. In other words, the neural network learns to approximate or fit a function to the data describing the complete task or environment model.

Simple route-finding tasks

Let us forget for a moment that we have to learn the task and assume we can build look-up tables indicating all we need to know in order to find the goal. Imagine four signposts—one for each direction the robot could take—of variable "strength" at each junction, which effect the random direction the robot will choose. Our robot must wander from a random start position, guided by the signposts, until it reaches the goal. Dynamic programming involves changing the strength of each signpost so that a good position will have a strong signpost pointing to it.

The signposts can be thought of as indicating the payoff which the next state will yield. Each state will also have an actual payoff value which, at the start of training, will bear no relationship to the signposts. The payoff associated with each state describes how good that state is in terms of how easily the goal state may be reached from there. Our task now becomes that of calculating the payoff values in the locations and then moving the signposts so that they match up properly with those values. The signposts cannot be moved without knowing the values in the locations which, in turn, cannot be seen from adjoining locations; hence the need for signposts.

In quick summary, we will be using three different measures during the learning process:

- The **reinforcement** associated with a state is a measure of success which is imposed externally by a teacher.

- The **payoff** associated with a state is the value which the model has assigned to a state from its experience of getting from that state to a goal state.

- The **policy** associated with a model describes the best direction to take from any given state.

The whole process can be described as follows:

1. Set all the payoff values to zero and the signposts at random.

2. Repeat: from the current location:

3. Choose a random direction, biased by the direction of the signposts.

4. Look at the value of the new state which you have chosen, and look at the reinforcement given when you get there (which will equal one for the goal state, and zero for all others):

5. **Changing the values**: change the value of the location which you just came from so that it better describes the value of that location in terms of the fact that it can get you to the current location; i.e. the error for state $t - 1$ is $r_t + \lambda V(t) - V(t - 1)$ where r_t is the reinforcement actually given at the next time step, λ is a discount term, and $V(t-1)$ is the value in state x at time $t-1$.

6. **Changing the policy**: if the reinforcement received is greater than the previous signpost suggested, then reach back and pull the signpost so that it points a little more towards this state.

7. Until learning is complete.

So you look back in time to the last step only and update the previous state value. The goal state is a slightly special case. As the algorithm updates the box from which it came and never leaves the goal state, this final state must have its value calculated strictly in terms of the original definition of the value of each box. Remember that the value given to a box measures the (discounted) sum of future reinforcement which could be gained from moving to that box under the current navigation policy. The goal state must have a value which reflects the external reinforcement given on arrival—in this case, one.

Reinforcement is consequently propagated back from the goal state to all other states in varying degrees. The update rule for each step is based on states which it is possible to reach from the current state. States which are next to the goal state will have their scores increased when the goal state is reached. On the next pass, the states next to those which are next to the goal state will have their scores increased a little too. As you might have guessed, it is a slow and long winded process. It is worth noting, however, that this technique has been used by Tesauro [106] to teach a neural network to play backgammon. The TD-gammon (TD stands for temporal difference, not, as you might think with reference to the training procedure which reportedly lasted a month, TDious) network has beaten many of the world's backgammon masters.

The whole process works for rather the same reason that a bubble sort works; a bubble sort is a method for sorting a sequence by comparing adjacent elements in a list and swapping their contents if they are in the wrong order. In this way a whole list can be sorted with each element "seeing" only its nearest neighbour. Dynamic programming works despite the robot only being able to "see" the next square into which it moves because it alters the relationship between the two units involved until the whole space is correctly "ordered". This is, as you might imagine, a time consuming process.

When the dynamic programming algorithm has finished, the goal state will return a value of one and the other states will return diminishing values the farther away from the goal state (in terms of ease of access) they lie. By plotting state values as heights in a three dimensional map, we would see a peak at the goal state, with sides sloping away in all directions. Any obstacles would have valleys in the shadow cast by them in relation to the goal state.

11.5.3 Learning an approximation to the solution

Setting all of the state values involves building a large look-up table of points. It may well be the case that the search space is so large that a look-up table approach is unfeasible. Firstly, the memory requirement may be prohibitive, but more seriously, a look up table must be complete. Missing values are not interpolated and we may need to wait a very long time before every entry is filled. What we need to do then, is to train a neural network to learn a representation of the table's contents based on a subset of its entries and then allow the neural network's generalisation abilities to fill in the rest.

In contrast to most applications discussed here, reinforcement learning uses on-line learning; i.e. it learns as it explores and does not require a data set. Lin and Mitchell [57] used a method they called Experience Replay to speed up training time. This involved storing previous exploration runs to be played back repeatedly off-line, just as any off-line procedure requires many passes through the training set. Barto et al. [11] have used a stimulus trace method to the same effect.

11.5.4   Learning an evaluation function

To learn a valuation function (the location values) for a fixed policy, the robot must find the best route via stochastic exploration. This involves mapping the state vector X_t which describes the robot's location at time t, onto the value $V(X_t)$ for that location. The error for state X_t is

$$error(X_t) = r(X_t) + \lambda V(X_t) - V(X_{t-1}) \qquad (11.1)$$

where $r(X_t)$ is the reinforcement actually given at the next time step, λ is a discount term and $V(X_{t-1})$ is the value in state X at time $t-1$.

11.5.5   Learning a decision policy

The task of learning a decision policy is similar to that of learning the evaluation function. Indeed, if you have an optimal evaluation function then the optimal decision policy is to simply follow the path which yields the best return at each step. There is, however, a complication, as in order to learn a good evaluation function, one must use a stochastic decision process which encourages exploration. The evaluation function is estimated *based on a given decision policy* so there is a trade-off between using a policy which promotes exploration and one which is optimal.

Fortunately, it is not as constraining as it might appear. An algorithm which concurrently updates the values in the boxes and the direction of the signposts can be consistent as it will converge on the same solution. At first the robot will wander randomly as the signposts will point, effectively, straight up in the air. As the signposts are moved, the robot will follow a more deterministic path because the signs will have more effect than the random exploration term.

In this way we can train the behaviour of the robot by mapping each state vector onto a chosen action. Whilst the values are required to train this policy, they are not needed for its operation; the robot can simply follow the signposts. Is it strictly necessary to learn the behaviour though? Why do we not simply learn the evaluation function and follow the optimal route? Firstly, from an ecological viewpoint, we know that animals learn behavioural patterns based on internal evaluation functions of some sort. This is clearly more efficient. From an implementational viewpoint it is easy to see why: in order to choose which action to carry out next based purely on evaluation functions, one must try each action in turn, remember and compare the reinforcement received (both external and evaluated) and then make the choice of which action should be followed. The need for a policy model is obvious, especially if the result of trying one of the choices is that the animal is eaten or the robot runs over the plant manager.

11.6   Summary

Many of the techniques from part I were demonstrated in this chapter along with several new methods. These are summarised below.

- Back propagation through time was introduced as a method for steering a system through a set of intermediate steps towards a final target state. Only the target at the final step needs to be known; errors at intermediate steps are propagated back through time. As this method requires a differentiable model of the system to be controlled, methods for using a neural network model and the state space equations of the system were presented.

- Auto-associative networks were demonstrated to be useful when monitoring systems for which no data describing faults was available. Such a network is able to detect when a system has deviated from the states it occupied during the normal operation on which the network was trained.

- Reinforcement learning was introduced as a method for discounting the error made at a certain time so that errors made at an earlier time may be quantified. This method differs from back propagation through time as we do not need to know the number of steps between each point and the final goal.

Chapter 12

Conclusions

> *An expert is someone who knows some of the worse mistakes that can be made in his subject, and how to avoid them.*
> Heisenberg

12.1 Summary

In this book, I have tried to remove some of the mystique which seems to surround the application of neural networks in non-academic settings by presenting a structured set of techniques, each aimed at a common goal. That goal is to produce a neural network solution which is able to generalise to examples on which it was not trained whilst maintaining an optimal level of accuracy for those on which it was.

The balance between accuracy and generality may be controlled via data quality, quantity and preparation, network architecture, and training regime. Having built a model, it is possible to discover how much confidence to place in each answer it gives and to derive clues as to why that answer was produced.

Part II presented a set of examples which were chosen to illustrate the techniques introduced in part I. Chapter 9 illustrated data preparation techniques, chapter 10 addressed the issues of data quality and network analysis and chapter 11 investigated the use of more advanced techniques such as back propagation through time and reinforcement learning.

12.2 A few typical mistakes worth remembering

12.2.1 Tank finding

A famous defence research programme used a neural network to decide whether or not a scene contained a tank. The team went out and took lots of pictures of tanks and, the following day, took the same pictures without the tank present. They trained a neural network on the grey scale values of each pixel in the images and achieved a very low error score. However, when it came to testing the network in the field, it performed worse than chance. Only then did somebody notice that the training pictures which contained tanks were all taken on a sunny day whereas the empty scenes were taken on a cloudy day. What they had built was a sunny day detector.

The main mistake made in this example was obviously lack of pre-processing. If they had worked out a coding system which made explicit the things they already knew would help in identifying tanks, their input codings would not have been the grey level scores over the whole image, but descriptors of areas in a pre-segmented image. The lesson to learn is that a network does not know what it is you are trying to do. If it finds something easier, it will do it.

12.2.2   Road following

Another vision based example: a robot was trained to drive a car along roads. The data set was obtained by driving a car with a camera attached and allowing the network to associate the incoming scene with the driver's steering movements. When the network was given the car to drive, it showed a remarkable ability for driving into trees. Trees and roads, it seems, share the common property of showing up as converging vertical lines in the field of view.

The network in this example had been well trained on one aspect of the task it was designed to perform: that of following a road, but had not been trained at all on another: that of avoiding trees. Neural networks are very good at generalising and the tree obviously looked far more likely than not to be a road. It is not enough to train a model to behave within the confines of normal operation, it must also be trained on what to do outside those limits.

12.2.3   Obstacle avoidance

In a similar problem, a small robot was trained to drive around a room avoiding objects. This was done by having different operators drive the robot by remote control and allowing the robot to associate range finder readings with steering actions. However, when it was set off to drive on its own it would drive straight into objects as if they were not there. This time the problem was as follows:

- The robot network had one output unit coded so that 1=left and 0=right.

- The closer to 1 or 0 the continuous valued output was, the further the steering wheel would turn. When there was an object directly in front of the robot, it had the choice of going either left or right, as represented by a score of 0.5 on each, but had no facility for choosing and so went straight on (the action usually associated with even scores on the direction units).

In this case, the designers had not properly considered the output coding. The categorisation task (left or right) contained a doubt region which should have been processed in two distinct ways under two distinct conditions. Condition one concerned there being no object, and so there being no decision. Condition two concerned there being an object dead ahead and required a forced decision one way or the other. A simple solution would have been an extra output class which determined whether the robot should move ahead or turn.

We have reached the end of this book. All that remains is for me to wish you luck with your neural network project.

Chapter 13

Using the accompanying software

13.1 Introduction

You will find a disk included with this book which contains source code for many of the techniques it presents. The routines are written in both C and C++ but the mixture of languages has been designed to allow the easiest possible interface between your own code and that included here. To that end there are two types of source file on the disk: a set of basic C routines and a set of C++ objects and programs. The C routines cover functions such as activation, error, and data scaling whereas the C++ programs are designed to bring the C routines together to form a useful program. The programs are further divided onto two sets: neural network code and data processing code.

Many C++ compilers insist that every file in a program must be compiled as C++ so you may need to rename the .C files as .CPP to force the C code to be treated as C++. Programs written in C are included here as .C files to indicate the type of code contained therein. The programs have been kept intentionally simple so that you may include them in your own code. The price to be paid for this is the fact that, as they stand, the programs are rather limited in their power and scope. The disk does not contain a neural network development environment; it simply contains source code designed to ease the burden of programming if you plan to write your own neural network code.

All of the source code is copiously commented so the best way to find out how something works is to look at the program. Sample make files are included on the disk.

The source code on the disk is covered under the same copyright as the rest of the book and may not be sold on to a third party without permission.

13.2   Neural network code

13.2.1   Basic routines written in C

Activation functions

The file **ACTIV.C** holds the following routines for calculating the activation of a given unit:

```
float tanh_act(float val, float lambda)
float tanh_derv(float val, float lambda)
float logistic_act(float val, float lambda)
float logistic_derv(float val, float lambda)
float linear_act(float val, float lambda)
float linear_derv(float val, float lambda)
float add_noise(float val, float noise)
int threshold(float val, float upper, float lower)
```

Each of the _act and _derv functions return the result of passing a value through the given activation function or its derivative. add_noise adds a random number between ±noise to the value it is given and threshold takes a value and two thresholds, returning 1 if the value is greater than the upper threshold, minus 1 if the value is less than the lower threshold and 0 if the value falls between the two.

Spread encoding

The file **SPREAD.C** contains a procedures for spreading a value across a spread encoded array and for calculating the expected mean, mode and variance of a spread encoded output. The following routines are included:

```
encode(double *bin_array, int bins, float val)
double decode_mean(double *bin_array, int bins)
double decode_mode(double *bin_array, int bins)
double out_var(double *bin_array, int bins)
```

The array bin_array holds activation values and bins is the number of bins you wish to spread across. The functions take a pointer to bin_array and changes its contents when required. double precision is used to ensure that rounding errors do not cause the values to fall into the wrong bins; you will know if this happens as the outputs will not sum to one.

Note that these routines only work on numbers within the range from zero to one.

Error functions

The file **ERRORS.CPP** holds the following routines for calculating the error of a given unit:

```
float diff_error(float target, float val)
float w_error(float weight, float val, float target)
float weight_change(float eta, float error, float output)
float momentum(float alpha, float delta_w)
```

dif_error calculates the simple difference target - val and w_error allows an extra parameter to add an importance weighting to the given example. weight_change calculates the required change to be made to a weight given the learning rate, the error above and the activation below. momentum simply returns the product of the weight change and the momentum term.

Calculating output probabilities

Output *a posteriori* probabilities, such as those discussed in section 6.3.2 may be calculated using the function float apost(float train_prob, float actual_prob, float net_out) in the file **APOST.C**.

Choosing network size

The following functions for choosing the size of a network are provided in the file **NETSIZE.C**.

```
int hid_to_ins(int inputs)
int hid_to_patterns(int patterns)
int hid_to_train(float error, int train, int ins, int outs)
```

The functions simply apply the rules discussed in section 3.2.2. It is important to remember, however, that the results are only estimates.

13.2.2   Neural network C++ objects

The file NET.HPP contains definitions for networks, units, and weight sets as described below.

13.2.3   Data hiding

The C++ object variables are all accessed through a process known as *data hiding*. Data hiding is a C++ concept which allows (actually positively encourages) the programmer not to access object variables directly but to go through a function. To see the value of a weight between unit i in the input layer and unit h in the hidden layer, for example, one would use the function get_in_wt(i,h) and similarly, to set that weight to the value x, one would use set_in_wt(i,h,x). An additional advantage of data hiding is that it allows one to check that an index is within the valid range before accessing an array. The network variable access routines carry out such a check and return the value minus 99 if you are attempting to access a memory location outside the bounds of the array. Enumerated types have their own error values when it is not possible to return minus 99.

Note that both the network objects and the data_set objects access array variables from a level higher than the object in which the variable is defined. Access is done at the array level. For example, the network object contains an array of unit objects for each network layer. The values in the unit objects (such as activation for example) are accessed from the network object via the array. For this reason, the first parameter in a data access function call must be the index in the array of the object to be used. To set the activation value of the third unit in the hidden layer array of a network called net1 to 0, for example, we would use net1.set_act(2,0). Remember that arrays are indexed from 0.

Network object members

The network class defines a multi layer perceptron with three layers of units: the input layer, the hidden layer, and the output layer. A layer of units is defined as an array of unit objects. Three counters (ins, hids, outs) keep a record of the size of each layer.

A network with three layers of units contains two layers of weights: those from the input layer to the hidden layer, defined herein as in_layer_weights and those from the hidden layer to the output layer, defined as hid_layer_weights. Each layer of weights is defined as an array of weight_set objects. A weight_set contains an array of floating point values, one for each weight coming out of a unit. The first weight_set in the array in_layer_weights contains the weights from the first input unit to each of the hidden units and so on. There is also a single weight_set for the bias weights in each of the two layers and an array of floating point numbers which stores the target values for each input example during training.

The data hiding routines for the network objects are in the file **NET_AC.CPP** and cover every member of the classes network, weight_set, and unit. Note that the weight access routines take parameters in the order in which activation flows, that is the first parameter indexes the unit from which the weight takes activation and the second parameter indexes its destination unit in the layer above.

```
class network
// A neural network class

  {

    int ins;        // Number of inputs
    int hids;       // Number of hidden units
    int outs;       // Number of outputs
    int recurrent;  // 1=recurrent network, 0=not
    // Input layer is extended to hold recurrent values.
    // size=ins+hids
    unit *input_layer;   // Array holding input layer
    unit *hidden_layer;  // Array holding hidden layer
    unit *output_layer;  // Array holding output layer
    float *targets;  // Holds target output vector
    weight_set *in_layer_weights;   // weights from input layer
    weight_set *hid_layer_weights;  // weights from hidden layer
    //  Access weights by
    //  in_layer_weights[i].weights[j]
    weight_set in_bias;
    weight_set hid_bias;

    // functions
    public:
    network(int nins, int nhids, int nouts, int rec);
    // Constructor
    ~network();// Destructor

    float get_in_wt(int i, int j);
    float get_hid_wt(int i, int j);
    int set_in_wt(int i, int j, float val);
    int set_hid_wt(int i, int j, float val);
    float get_in_dw(int i, int j);
    float get_hid_dw(int i, int j);
    int set_in_dw(int i, int j, float val);
    int set_hid_dw(int i, int j, float val);
    void forward_pass();
    void calc_out();
    void calc_hid();
    void out_errors();
    void hid_errors();
    void calc_errors();
    void update_hidden_weights();
    void update_input_weights();
    void update_weights();
    int save_weights(char *name);
    void randomise();
```

```
void hid_to_rec();
void load_inputs(ifstream &f);
void load_targets(ifstream &f);
void show_outputs();
void show_outputs(ofstream &f);
void learn_cycle(ifstream &f);
float get_in_act(int i);
float get_hid_act(int i);
float get_out_act(int i);
int set_in_act(int i, float val);
int set_hid_act(int i, float val);
int set_out_act(int i, float val);
float get_in_er(int i);
float get_hid_er(int i);
float get_out_er(int i);
int set_in_er(int i, float val);
int set_hid_er(int i, float val);
int set_out_er(int i, float val);
float get_in_derv(int i);
float get_hid_derv(int i);
float get_out_derv(int i);
int set_in_derv(int i, float val);
int set_hid_derv(int i, float val);
int set_out_derv(int i, float val);
float get_in_bias_wt(int i);
float get_hid_bias_wt(int i);
float get_in_bias_dw(int i);
float get_hid_bias_dw(int i);
int set_in_bias_wt(int i,float val);
int set_hid_bias_wt(int i,float val);
int set_in_bias_dw(int i,float val);
int set_hid_bias_dw(int i,float val);
};
```

A weight set is defined as follows:

```
class weight_set
  {
  public:
  int size;   // Number of weights from this unit
  float *weights;
  float *delta_w;
  weight_set();   // Constructor
  ~weight_set();  // Destructor
  };
```

`size` stores a count of the number of weights in the set, `weights` is an array of floating point numbers which holds the weights' values and `delta_w` is an array which holds the change made to the weights for adding momentum.

A unit is defined as

```
// The neural unit class
class unit
  {
  public:
  float activation;
  float error;
  float error_derv;


  // functions

  unit();   // Constructor
  ~unit();  // Destructor
  };
```

A `unit` object simply stores the activation, error, and error derivative for a unit.

The program code in the file **NET.CPP** shows how the back propagation algorithm may be implemented using the `network`, `weight_set`, and `unit` objects along with the C routines discussed above. Note that full use is made of data hiding; the program lines do nothing but call other functions to calculate the required values and set the appropriate units and weights. Here is an example piece of code from the `update_hidden_weights()` function:

```
set_hid_dw(h,o, momentum(get_hid_dw(h,o), ALPHA)
        + weight_change(ETA, get_out_derv(o), get_hid_act(h)));
set_hid_wt(h,o, (get_hid_wt(h,o) + get_hid_dw(h,o)));
```

This sets the required hidden layer weight change with reference to the previous weight change and the momentum parameter, `ALPHA`, plus the required weight change from `ETA`, the error derivative on the output unit above and the activation of the hidden unit below. This change is then added onto the current weight value. The functions `momentum` and `weight_change` are defined in the file **ACTIV.C**.

Creating recurrent networks

A simple recurrent network may be built by increasing the size of the input layer to allow room for a copy of the hidden layer. The recurrent section of the input layer (which starts *after* the final input unit) is activated using the `network` function `hid_to_rec()` which copies the hidden unit values back. The input layer is then treated in exactly the same way as a purely feedforward network. Multiple context layers may be added simply by including an array of unit objects for each sequence to be learned.

Adding a regularisation term

The function reg_error(int p) returns a regularisation term to be added to the error measure during learning. The parameter, p is a count of the number of patterns in your training file. reg_error(int p) is a member of the network class as it must know about the weights' values.

Calculating derivatives for explanations

The function calc_in_dervs(i,o) shows how the input derivatives may be calculated for gaining insight into the network's structure, as discussed in chapter 7. The only point to note is that the derivatives are calculated without reference to the errors. calc_in_dervs(i,o) calculates the partial derivative of the output unit o with respect to the input unit i. The result is stored in the error_derv variable of the input unit (but, as we have just seen, is not an error at all!). The function could just as easily return the derivative value.

13.2.4   Header files

The file **NET.HPP** contains the class definitions for the network, weights and unit. The file **NET_DECS.H** contains type and constant declarations. The main constants are the learning rate, ETA the momentum rate, ALPHA, the regularisation (or degree of noise) parameter, LAMBDA, and the squashing function slope, GAMMA.

There is also a **.H** file which belongs to each **.C** file and includes forward definitions of the functions contained therein. The C++ routines do not require such forward declarations as the class definitions contain that code.

13.3   Data preparation routines

The data preparation routines, like those for the neural networks, have been split into two distinct parts: the standard routines are written in C and an example C++ program is included to carry out the more involved procedures. The files **DATA.CPP** and **DATA.HPP** contain C++ objects and functions designed to produce a training file from a file of raw data. These functions call on a set of standard C routines, described below, which check, scale, and manipulate data.

13.3.1   Basic routines written in C

Scaling functions

The following data scaling functions are included in the file **SCALES.C**:

```
int check_linear(float average, float stdev,
        float max, float min, float scope)
int check_log(float max, float mean)
float linear_rescale(float val, float max, float min)
float log_scale(float val, float max, float min)
float log_rescale(float val, float max, float min)
float softmax_scale(float val, float average,
        float stdev, float scope)
float softmax_rescale(float val, float average,
        float stdev, float scope)
float normalise(float val, float average, float stdev)
float re_normalise(float val, float average, float stdev)
enum scale_functs choose_scaler(float average, float stdev,
        float max, float)
```

Each `scale` function scales a given value to between zero and one. Each `rescale` function restores a value to its original scale. `normalise` scales a value so that the data set from which it comes, when similarly scaled, will have a mean of zero and a standard deviation of one. `re_normalise` reverses the procedure.

Other data manipulation code

The file **MANIP.C** contains the following data manipulation routines:

```
double camax(double a, double max);
// Calculate maximum
double camin(double a, double min);
 // Calculate minimum
int is_out(double val, double mean, double stdev);
// Return true if val is an outlier
float stan_dev(float tot, float totsq, int n);
// Standard deviation from total, total squared, number.
```

Further statistical routines are included in **DATA.CPP**.

Entropy analysis

The program **INFO.C** may be used to calculate entropy values for a data set. To run the program, type

info *filename num_ins num_outs num_bins*

where *filename* is the name of the file in which your data is stored, *num_ins* is the number of input variables in the file, *num_outs* is the number of output variables in the file, and *num_bins* is the number of bins you wish floating point values to be spread across. The parameter *num_bins* determines the resolution with which floating point variables are analysed. A value of between ten and thirty is recommended. Note also that the program only works with numeric data. You cannot use character string variables. If you do wish to use such variables you must either encode them as numbers (as you would for a neural network) or re-write the program so that it is able to cope with strings. The data file must contain the inputs followed by the outputs, in columns which must be white space delimeted.

The program displays each of the input and output events it has found in the data, followed by the probability of each occuring. A single event is built by concatenating the binned values into a single string. Using ten bins, the input pattern {0.5 0.7 0.9}, for example, would produce the event "579". The program also displays the probabilities of each input event being followed by each output event. Having calculated each probability score, the program displays the entropy of the input variables and the entropy of the output variables along with the maximum possible entropy of each. Finally, the conditional entropy of the outputs, given the inputs and the conditional entropy of the inputs given the outputs are displayed.

13.3.2 Data preparation C++ objects

Data set objects

A data_set object represents a single file of data. It stores information relating to the file and its contents and is defined below:

```cpp
// The neural data set class
// Refers to a single variable, be it input or output.
// A single variable is assumed to come from a single
// column in a file
class data
    {
    public:
    enum pos_types data_type;
    enum scale_functs scaler;
    double average;
    double stdev;
    double temp_av;
    double temp_st;   // Temp variables for outlier removal
    double max;
    double min;       // Above only for numbers
    int no_of_cats;
    categ_ptr *cat_list;  // List of category names
    double value;  // Holds current value if a number
    char name[20];    // Holds current value if text

    // functions

    data();
    ~data();

    void assign_cat();
    void calc_type();
    int get_cat_num();
    void show_stats();
    void write_cat(ofstream &t_file);
    void show_cats();
    };
```

Data objects

A data_set is made up of a number of columns of data, each described by a data object:

```
class data_set
// Stores information for whole data set
// Based on data being in a single file
    {
    public:
    char *file_name;    // Name of file
    ifstream data_file; // File pointer
    int file_len; // Length of file
    int no_columns; // Number of columns in file
    data *data_col; // Array of data columns

    // functions


    data_set(char *nme, int cols);
    ~data_set();
    int outliers();
    void remove_outliers();
    void calc_stats();
    void final_stats();
    void row_stats();
    void show_stats();
    int read_row();
    void write_row(ofstream &f);
    void build_training_file(ofstream &t_file);
    void write_training_row(ofstream &t_file);
    void scale_row();

    int set_av(int i, float val);
    int set_st(int i, float val);
    int set_tmp_av(int i, float val);
    int set_tmp_st(int i, float val);
    int set_max(int i, float val);
    int set_min(int i, float val);
    int set_val(int i, float val);
    int set_type(int i, enum pos_types val);
    int set_scaler(int i, enum scale_functs val);
    int set_no_cats(int i, int val);
    float get_av(int i);
    float get_st(int i);
    float get_tmp_av(int i);
    float get_tmp_st(int i);
```

```
float get_max(int i);
float get_min(int i);
float get_val(int i);
int get_no_cats(int i);
enum pos_types get_type(int i);
enum scale_functs get_scaler(int i);
void assign_types();
};
```

The routines in **DATA.CPP** calculate global statistics about a data_set and carry out outlier removal, scaling, and category list building. There are also routines for building a training file. You may process data which is either numeric or categorical (i.e. text). Text is treated as a list of possible category values that a variable might take and represented using a local coding. The category values are held in the linked list cat_list in the data object. The variable no_of_cats in the same object records the number of different values a single category variable may take.

The data hiding routines for the data_set objects are in the file **DATA_AC.CPP**. As a data_set object is made up of an array of data objects, the data objects are accessed indirectly through the data_set array. For example, mydata.get_av(1) returns the average value in column 1 of the file pointed to by the data_set object myfile by accessing the array of data objects in myfile.

Glossary of terms

Activation function
A mathematical function which takes the weighted activation values coming into a unit, sums them, and translates the result to a position along a given scale. The activation function will often squash the summed value to within a given range and is consequently also known as the **squashing function** and **sigmoidal squashing function**.

Activation value
The value which is produced by a unit's activation function, also known as the unit's **output**.

Alpha (α)
A parameter referred to as **momentum** which dictates the proportion of the size of the previous change made to a weight to be included in the current weight change during back propagation learning. Falls between zero (no momentum) and one.

Analogue data
Physical signals such as vibrations from objects in the real world. Such data must be recorded and digitised for use with a neural network.

Architecture
Refers to the design of a neural network: the number of units and their pattern of connection. Architecture is sometimes used to refer to *types* of neural network such as multi-layer perceptrons (MLPs) or Kohonen networks, but in this book its meaning is restricted to the specific design of an MLP.

Auto-associative neural networks
A network which aims to reproduce, at the output layer, the pattern given as input. This must be done through a hidden layer which contains fewer units than the input layer. Auto-associative neural networks are often used to compress data or characterise data so that novelty detection may be carried out.

Back propagation of error
The act of calculating the error on a network hidden unit, based on the error derivatives on the units above and the strengths of the weights connected to them.

Back propagation through time
A method for calculating the error a temporal system is making at an earlier time step, based on the error after a fixed number of such steps.

Batch training
A variation of the back propagation learning algorithm in which the weights are updated with respect to the average error on each output unit after the entire training set has been presented to the network once. Batch training removes the need to randomly mix the order in which training examples are presented to the network but increases the risk of the network becoming trapped in a local minimum.

Bayesian statistics
A set of statistical methods based on the probabilities with which certain events occur.

Categorical encoding scheme
Any method which represents categorical variables for use with a neural network.

Categorical values
Categorical variables may take any one of a number of categorical values. For example the categorical variable *animals* may take categorical values such as *fish, dog, mouse*.

Categorical variables
Variables whose values may not be arranged along a sensible ordered continuum are known as categorical variables. Note that a categorical variable name (such as *animals*) is not a category in its own right, a category of animals might be *fish*; so *fish* is the category value.

Connections
See **Weights**.

Conventional techniques
The term used in this book to refer to non-neural techniques.

Convergence
The back propagation algorithm is said to have converged when no training example necessitates a weight change. This is very rarely achieved, however, and convergence is often used to indicate arrival at a good solution.

Convolution
Applying a function to a signal in order to smooth that signal by taking a weighted moving average. Equivalent to multiplying the Fourier transform of the signal with that of the convolution function.

Cost function
See **Error function**.

Cross-validation
Testing a network during training on a data set which is not used to change the weights. Used to control a network's generalisation ability. See **Independent validation set**.

Data compression
Re-expressing a data set using fewer variables. It may be lossy or unlossy compression; the former throws away information while the latter must allow the original signal to be reconstructed perfectly.

Data fusion
Combining data from several sources. An inherent quality of a multi-layer perceptron.

Data validation
Ensuring that training data contains the information required to perform a certain task.

Digital data
Any measurement which has been converted into a numeric representation for storage in a computer readable form.

Distance metric
Any method for measuring the distance between two data points.

Early stopping
Stopping the learning algorithm before it has reached the lowest possible training error in order to avoid overfitting. Often done in conjunction with an **independent validation set**.

Embedding dimension
The number of steps required from a time series to perform a state-space reconstruction. See also **Intrinsic dimensionality**.

Entropy
A measure of the uncertainty based on the probabilities with which events occur. Conditional entropy is a measure of the uncertainty about an event which remains when we know about a related, predictive event. In this way it is a good measure of the predictive power of one set of data for another and may be used for data validation before training a neural network.

Epoch
One presentation of the entire training set to a neural network.

Error function
The function which calculates how close to the desired output any actual network output actually is. It may be the difference between the target and actual values, or it may be based on other criteria.

Eta (η)
A parameter which takes values between zero and one and which dictates the proportion of each error which is used to update weights during back propagation learning. Effectively balances learning speed against stability.

Euclidean distance
The straight line distance between two points calculated using the root of the sum of the differences in each dimension.

Extrapolation
Generalising about a system's behaviour which falls outside the training experience of the network. This is very dangerous as the results will not often be valid.

Eyeballing
Looking at data—usually in a graphical form—as a first, subjective, judgement of its structure.

Fast Fourier transform (FFT)
A fast approximation to the Fourier transform which calculates the constituent frequencies in a complex wave. Requires a signal of size 2^n.

Feature extraction
Deriving general features at a level higher than that of the original data.

Feedforward neural network
A neural network in which the flow of activation is in a single direction.

Gamma (γ)
A network parameter which determines the slope of the activation function. A steeper slope leads to sharper boundaries on categorisation tasks.

Gaussian distribution
Also known as the normal distribution, the Gaussian distribution is symmetrical about its mean and drops exponentially towards zero at infinity on either side.

Generalisation
In the context of neural networks, generalisation is the process of characterising an incomplete set of data with a continuous function. Missing points are interpolated to provide a general model of the data.

Gradient descent
The process of incrementally reducing network error via changes to weights.

Hidden units/Hidden layer
The units in a network which do not receive input or generate output. Hidden units combine and input variables and extract features from the input data.

Ill posed tasks

A task is said to be ill posed if the neural network is required to produce a single output to a given input pattern but the training set contains more than one distinct correct output for any training pattern. A network trained on such a task, without due care, will learn an erroneous average between all the possible correct outputs. One example of an ill posed task is learning the inverse kinematics of a robot arm.

Incomplete data

Training data may be incomplete in one of two ways. The training set may not contain an example from every possible combination of inputs to the network. This is common, will lead to generalisation from the network and requires no extra consideration. In the more extreme case, certain fields may be missing from certain training examples, in which case values must be calculated and substituted for entry to the network.

Independent validation set

A proportion of the collected data (usually around 25%) which is not used to alter the weights' values but to test the network's generalisation ability.

Input units/Input layer

The input layer holds the data values which we will know during the normal operation of the network (i.e. after training has been completed). These input values are used by the network to calculate the output values.

Input variable

A single element from the input vector.

Input vector

A single input example, made up of one or more values.

Input-Output encoding

The process which converts raw data into a form which the neural network may use.

Interpolation

Generalisation by fitting a smooth curve between training points.

Intrinsic dimensionality

The number of variables required to describe a system state. May be less than the actual number of variables used if any of those variables are co-dependent.

K nearest neighbour

A statistical classification method which assigns a new point to the class in which most of its neighbours fall. The method is expensive in terms of both computation time and storage requirement.

Lambda (λ)

The parameter which controls the level of noise or degree of regularisation applied to

a neural network during learning to improve generalisation. **Layer**
A network layer in a feedforward multi-layer preceptron consists of units which are not connected to each other. Each unit in a given layer in connected to units in the layer above and below.

Learning
Learning, in a statistical sense, refers to any process requiring the use of data for tuning a set of parameters which describe a statistical model of that data. It does not imply any human qualities such as understanding, consciousness or intelligence associated with our learning abilities.

Learning rate
See **Eta**.

Local minimum
A combination of weights values which does not lead to the lowest possible error for a training set but which, due to the local shape of the error, appears to be optimal and consequently prevents a gradient descent algorithm from proceeding further.

Metric
A term meaning measurement or calculation of distance.

Momentum term (alpha)
Dictates the proportion of the last weight change to be included in the current weight update. Used to speed up learning and avoid local minima.

Multi-layer perceptron (MLP)
A neural network with distinct input, hidden, and output layers.

Neural network
A term which refers to any neurally inspired method of computation, relying on local calculations and interactions to produce the desired behaviour from the network as a whole.

Novel data
Data which falls outside the training experience of a neural network, leading to an extrapolated result and potentially incorrect generalisation.

Novelty detection
Deciding whether a given input pattern is representative of the single category of data with which the neural network was trained. Useful in condition monitoring applications where the only available data describes the correct operation of the system and any deviation from that behaviour should be detected.

On-line training
The opposite of batch training. The network weights are updated after presentation of each training pattern in turn. This requires the order of the training presentations

to be randomised but is less likely to become trapped in a local minimum.

Output units/Output layer
The units which hold the result of a neural network computational cycle. The representation used on these units should express this result in human understandable form.

Output vector
The set of variables that a neural network is being asked to calculate values for at its output layer.

Overfitting/Overtraining
Overtraining refers to the process of training a network for too many cycles, leading to a loss in generalisation ability as the training set is learned too specifically. Such a generalisation loss is known as overfitting, which may also be caused by use of too many weights in a network, too few training examples, or insufficient network regularisation.

Pattern
Any combination of a set of variables.

Pattern recognition
Mapping a given combination of one set of variables onto a pattern in a second set of variables which make explicit the class membership of the first.

Performance metric
Any measure of how well a neural network performs the task it is required to learn. This may be a simple measure of average error, or some more specific measure based on the task at hand.

Platform
Refers usually to the computer hardware on which a neural network is simulated but is often used to refer to the software simulation or interpretation used.

Post-processing
Any data processing which is carried out on the output values of a neural network. A typical example is that of converting numerical category labels into category names.

Pre-processing
The process of preparing raw data for presentation to a neural network.

Principal components analysis (PCA)
A statistical technique which projects a multi-dimensional set of data onto a new coordinate system in which the principal axis accounts for the majority of the variation in the data. Further, orthogonal, axes account for increasingly smaller amounts of variation in the original data. Allows the least descriptive dimensions to be discarded with a minimal information loss.

Probability density function (PDF)
A function which describes the probability of each possible event in a system actually occurring.

Recall mode
The mode in which no learning takes place. The neural network is simply being used to carry out the task on which it was trained.

Recurrent neural networks
Networks which, due to a short term memory which allows past network states to influence current calculations, are able to process temporally dependent data.

Redundant data
Data or variables which do not carry any information relevant to the task on which a neural network is being trained.

Regularisation
Any device which limits the complexity, and consequently the bias of a statistical model such as a neural network. Often used to limit weight growth.

Sigmoidal activation function
An activation function which squashes its input into the range from zero to one. As the input to the function grows in magnitude, it is squashed into an exponentially smaller part of the extremes of the output range.

Spread encoding
A form of local coding scheme in which a value is represented by activation across a set of units. Each unit represents a certain value is activated by an amount proportional to the inverse distance of the value to be represented from its particular value.

Stopping criteria
Criteria for deciding when to stop training a neural network.

Target vector
The set of output values required from a network during training.

Temporally dependent system
Any system for which the output depends to some extent on previous inputs to the system or on previous system states.

Test set
A set of data which is not used during training so that the network's generalisation abilities may be tested.

Topology
See **Architecture**.

Training
The process of allowing a neural network to learn. See **Learning**.

Transfer function
See **Activation function**.

Unseen data
See **Test set**.

Validation set
A set of data which is used during training, not to alter network weights but to check the progress of the network's generalisation abilities. Used to avoid overfitting. May be the same as the **test set**.

Variables and values
A variable may take one of any number of values. The variable *height* for example, might take numbers from a given range. Variables may be numeric or categorical, values will be numbers in the first case and categories in the second.

Vector
An ordered set of variables which define a point in system space.

Weight elimination/Weight decay
A method for simplifying a neural network model by reducing the size or number of weights.

Weights
Connections of varying strength which carry activation information between network units.

Windowing
A process for building static input vectors from a time varying signal by concatenating the contents of a sliding temporal window.

Bibliography

[1] Measuring the value of IT. *Neural Edge*, 3 (Autumn):4, 1993.

[2] Neural war games. *Neural Edge*, 6 (Summer): page 1, 1994.

[3] Radio Rentals improves customer targeting. *Neural Edge*, 6 (Summer):5, 1994.

[4] A. Abhyankar. Linear and non-linear Granger causality: Evidence from the FT-SE 100 stock index futures and cash markets. *Working paper, Department of Accounting and Finance, Stirling University*, (94/04), 1994.

[5] D. Albesano, R. Gemello, and F. Mana. Connected word recognition with recurrent neural automata. In M. Marinara and G. Morasso, editors, *Proceedings, ICANN*, volume 2, pages 901–904. Springer-Verlag, 1994.

[6] E. Baek and W. Brock. A general test for non-linear Granger causality: Bivariate model. *Working paper, Department of Economics, Iowa State University*, 1992.

[7] B. Le Baron. Non linear diagnostics and simple trading rules for high frequency foreign exchange rates. In A. S. Weigend and N. A. Gershenfeld, editors, *Time Series Prediction. Forecasting the Future and Understanding the Past*, pages 457–474. Addison Wesley, 1993.

[8] B. Le Baron. Chaos and nonlinear forecastability in economics and finance. In H. Tong, editor, *Chaos and Forecasting. Proceedings of the Royal Society Discussion Meeting*. World Scientific, 1995.

[9] B. Le Baron and A. S. Weigend. Evaluating neural network predictors by bootstrapping. *Working paper, Department of Economics, University of Wisconsin, Madison*, 1994.

[10] E. B. Bartlett. Dynamic node architecture learning: An information theoretic approach. *Neural Networks*, 7:129–140, 1994.

[11] G. Barto, R. S. Sutton, and C. J. C. H. Watkins. Learning and sequential decision making. Technical report, COINS, 1989.

[12] R. Battiti. Using mutual information for selecting features in supervised neural network learning. *IEEE Transactions on Neural Networks*, 5(4):537–550, 1995.

[13] E. B. Baum and D. Haussler. What net size gives valid generalisation? *Neural Computation*, 1(1):151–160, 1989.

[14] F. Beaufays, Y. Abdel-Magid, and B. Widrow. Application of neural networks to load-frequency control in power systems. *Neural Networks*, 7(1):183–194, 1994.

[15] C. Bishop. Bayes for beginners. *NCRG 4321 Tutorial Viewgraphs, NCAF, Oxford*, June, 1994.

[16] C. Bishop. Training with noise is equivalent to Tikhonov regularization. *Neural Computation*, 7(1):108–116, 1995.

[17] U. Bodenhausen and A Waibel. The tempo2 algorithm: Adjusting time-delays by supervised learning. In *Advances in Neural Information Processing Systems*, volume 3, pages 155 –161. Morgan Kaufmann, 1991.

[18] R. Brealey. *An Introduction to Risk and Return*. Basil Blackwell, 1983.

[19] J. Bromley and S. Denker. Improving rejection performance on handwritten digits by training with "rubbish". *Neural Computation*, 5(3):270–284, 1993.

[20] N. Burgess. Neural networks and financial asset management. *Talk to NSYN Launch Event*, 29 September, 1994.

[21] N. Burgess. Neuroforcasting. *Talk to Neural Computing Applications Forum*, 12 January, 1995.

[22] P. Le Cerf, W. Ma, and D. Van Compernolle. Multilayer perceptrons as labelers for Hidden Markov Models. *IEEE Transactions on Speech and Audio Processing*, 2(1):185–193, 1994.

[23] B. Cheng and H. Tong. Embedding dimension and sample size requirement. In H. Tong, editor, *Chaos and Forecasting. Proceedings of the Royal Society Discussion Meeting*. World Scientific, 1995.

[24] A. Cleeremans. Finite state automata and simple recurrent networks. *Neural Computation*, 2(1):372–381, 1989.

[25] M. Cook. *Personnel Selection and Productivity*. John Wiley and Sons, 1993.

[26] G.W. Cottrell, P. Munroe, and D. Zipser. Image compression by neural networks: An example of extensional programming. Technical report, ICS report 8702 University of California at San Diego, 1987.

[27] D. C. Cressy, I. T. Nabney, and A. M. Simper. Neural control of a batch distillation. *Neural Computing and Applications*, 1(2):115–123, 1993.

[28] S. Cullen. Economic time series forecasting: A comparison of encoding techniques. Technical report, Department of Computing Science, Stirling University, 1992.

[29] Y. Le Cun, J. S. Denker, and S. A. Sollar. Optimal brain damage. In *Advances in Neural Information Processing Systems*, volume 2, pages 598–605. Morgan Kaufmann, 1990.

[30] N. Dodd. Neural system monitors intensive care. *Neural Edge*, 7 (Autumn):4, 1994.

[31] DTI. *Best Practice Guidelines for Developing Neural Computing Applications*. Touche Ross for the DTI, 1994.

[32] C. Dugast, L. Devillers, and X. Aubert. Combining TDNN and HMM in a hybrid system for improved continuous-speech recognition. *IEEE Transactions on Speech and Audio Processing*, 2(1):217–223, 1994.

[33] J. L. Elman. Finding structure in time. *Cognitive Science*, 14:179–211, 1990.

[34] J. L. Elman. Distributed representations, simple recurrent networks, and gramatical structure. *Machine Learning*, 7:195 – 225, 1991.

[35] S. E. Fahlman and C. Lebiere. The cascade-correlation learning architecture. In D. S. Touretzky, editor, *Advances in Neural Information Processing Systems*, volume 2, pages 524–532. Morgan Kaufmann, 1990.

[36] D. Foster. Regions of unpredictability in neural network classification tasks. Technical report, CCCN, Stirling University, 1994.

[37] M. Frean. The upstart algorithm: A method for constructing and training feedforward neural networks. *Neural Computation*, 2:198–209, 1990.

[38] C. R. Gent, C. P. Sheppard, and G. L. Wray. Time series forecasting with neural networks. Technical report, SD-Scicon UK Limited, 1994.

[39] F. Girossi and T. Poggio. Representation qualities of neural networks: Kolmogrov's theorem is irrelevant. *Neural Computation*, 1(4):465–469, 1989.

[40] M. W. Goudreau and C. L. Giles. Using recurrent neural networks to learn the structure of interconnection networks. Technical Report UMIACS-TR-94-20 and CS-TR-3226, University of Maryland, 1994.

[41] C. Granger. Investigating causal relations by econometric models and crossspectral methods. *Econometrica*, 37:424–438, 1969.

[42] C. De Groot and D. Würtz. Forecasting time series with connectionist nets: Applications in statistics,, signal processing and economics. In F. Belli and F. J Radermacher, editors, *Lecture Notes in Artificial Intelligence*, volume 604, pages 461–470, 1991.

[43] J. B. Hampshire and B. A. Pearlmutter. Equivalance proofs for multi-layer perceptron classifiers and the Bayseian discrimination function. In *Proceedings of the 1990 Connectionist Models Summer School*. Morgan Kaufmann, 1990.

[44] L.K. Hansen, C. Liisberg, and P. Salamon. The error-reject tradeoff. Technical report, Technical University of Denmark, 1994.

[45] R. Hecht-Neilson. *Neurocomputing*. Addison Wesley, 1990.

[46] J. Hertz, A. Krogh, and R. G. Palmer. *Introduction to the Theory of Neural Computation.* Addison Wesley, 1991.

[47] C. Hiemstra and J. Jones. Testing for non-linear Granger causality in the stock price volume relationship. *Journal of Finance*, 49(5):1639–1664, 1994.

[48] G. E. Hinton. Shape representation in parallel systems. In *7th Joint International Conference on Artificial Intelligence*, volume Vancouver, BC, Canada, pages 1088–1096, 1981.

[49] R. G. Hoptroff. The principles and practice of time series forecasting and business modelling using neural nets. *Neural Computing and Applications*, 1:59–67, 1992.

[50] G Jang, F. Lai, B. Jiang, and C. Pan. An intelligent stock portfolio management system based on short-term trend prediction using dual-module neural networks. In T. Kohonen, K. Makisara, O. Simula, and J. Kangas, editors, *Artificial Neural Networks*. Elsevier Science Publishers B.V North-Holland, 1991.

[51] B. Jepson, A. Collins, and A. Evans. Post-neural network procedure to determine expected prediction values and their confidence limits. *Neural Computing and Applications*, 1(3):224–228, 1993.

[52] M. I. Jordan. Supervised learning and systems with excess degrees of freedom. Technical report, COINS 88-27, MIT, 1988.

[53] W. Karjala, D. M. Himmelblau, and R. Miikkulainen. Data rectification using recurrent (Elman) neural networks. In *Proceedings of the International Joint Conference on Neural Networks*, volume 2, pages 901–906, 1992.

[54] G. Kechriotis, E. Zervas, and E. S. Manalakos. Using recurrent neural networks for adaptive communication channel equalization. *IEEE Transactions on Neural Networks*, 5(2):267–278, 1994.

[55] T. Kohonen. Self organising formation of topologically correct feature maps. *Biological Cybernetics*, 43:59–69, 1982.

[56] V. Kúrková. Kolmogrov's theorem is relevant. *Neural Computation*, 3(4):617–622, 1991.

[57] L. Lin and T. M. Mitchell. Memory approaches to reinforcement learning in non-Markovian domains. Technical report, CMU-CS-92-138, CMU, 1992.

[58] R. P. Lippmann. Review of neural networks for speech recognition. *Neural Computation*, 1(1):1–38, 1989.

[59] D. Lowe and A. R. Webb. Time series prediction by adaptive networks: A dynamical systems perspective. In *IEEE, Artificial Neural Networks. Forecasting Time Series*, pages 17–24. IEEE Computer Society Press, 1991.

[60] G. R. Madey, J. Weinroth, and V. Shah. Integration of neurocomputing and system simulation for modeling continuous improvement systems in manufacturing. *Journal of Intelligent Manufacturing*, 3:193–204, 1992.

[61] P. Manolios and R. Fanelli. First-order recurrent neural networks and deterministic finite state automata. *Neural Computation*, 6(6):1155–1173, 1994.

[62] A. Maren, C. Harston, and R. Pap. *Handbook of Neural Applications*. Academic Press, 1990.

[63] M. P. Maund, D. Boussalis, and S. J. Wang. Direct adaptive control of flexible space structures using neural networks. In *Proceedings of the International Joint Conference on Neural Networks*, volume 2, pages 844–849, 1992.

[64] J. L. Mclelland and D. E. Rummelhart. An interactive activation model of context effects in letter perception: Part 1. an account of basic findings. *Psychological Review*, 88:380, 1981.

[65] P. Millar. Personal communication. 1994.

[66] S. Mitra, S. K. Pal, and M. K. Kundu. Fingerprint classification usaing a fuzzy multilayer perceptron. *Neural Computing and Applications*, 1:59–67, 1994.

[67] A. J. Morris. Neural networks for process control. *Talk to NSYN Launch Event*, 29 September, 1994.

[68] M. C. Mozer. A focused back-propagation algorithm for temporal pattern recognition. *Complex Systems*, 3:349–381, 1989.

[69] M. C. Mozer. Neural net architectures for temporal sequence processing. In A. S. Weigend and N. A. Gershenfeld, editors, *Time Series Prediction. Forecasting the Future and Understanding the Past*, pages 243–264. Addison Wesley, 1993.

[70] T. Mulhall. How much data is needed to train a neural network. *Neural Edge*, 8 (Winter):4–5, 1995.

[71] D. Nguyen and B. Widrow. The truck backer-upper: An example of self learning in neural networks. In *Proceedings of the IEEE Second International Conference on Neural Networks*, volume 1, pages 357–363, 1989.

[72] B. Pearlmutter. Learning state space trajectories in recurrent neural networks. *Neural Computation*, 1(2):263–269, 1989.

[73] R. R. Petit. Dividend announcements, security performance and capital market efficiency. *Journal of Finance*, (December):993–1007, 1972.

[74] S. W. Piché. Steepest descent algorithms for neural network controllers and filters. *IEEE Transactions on Neural Networks*, 5(2):198–212, 1994.

[75] J. Pilkington. Two ways of extracting meaning from neural networks. In *Proceedings, NSYN Conference on Intelligent Techniques for Data Mining*, volume 30 November, 1994.

[76] T. Poggio, V. Torre, and C. Koch. Computation vision and regularization theory. *Nature*, 317(September):314–319, 1985.

[77] W. H. Press, S. A. Teukolsky, W. T. Vetterling, and B. P. Flannery. *Numerical Recipes*. Cambridge University Press, 1992.

[78] A. Psarrou and H. Buxton. Motion analysis with recurrent neural nets. In M. Marinara and G. Morasso, editors, *Proceedings ICANN*, volume 1, pages 54–57. Springer-Verlag, 1994.

[79] A. N. Refenes. Constructive learning and its application to currency exchange rate forecasting. In E. Turban and R. Trippi, editors, *Neural Network Applications in Investment and Finance Services*. Probus Publishing, USA, 1991.

[80] A. N. Refenes. Neural networks in investment and management: Testing strategies and performance metrics. *Proceedings, Adaptive Computing and Information Processing*, Unicom Seminars, Brunel Conference Centre, 1994.

[81] A. N. Refenes and M. Azema-Barac. Neural network applications in financial asset management. *Journal of Neurocomputing and Applications*, 2(1):13–39, 1994.

[82] S. Renals, N. Morgan, H. Bourlard, M. Cohen, and H. Franco. Connectionist probability estimators in hmm speech recognition. *IEEE Transactions on Speech and Audio Processing*, 2(1):161–174, 1994.

[83] B. D. Ripley. Statistical aspects of neural networks. *Invited lecture, NCAF*, Oxford, 1994.

[84] S. Roberts and L. Tarassenko. A probabilistic resource allocating network for novelty detection. *Neural Computation*, 6(2):270–284, 1994.

[85] D. Ruelle. *Chaotic Evolution and Strange Attractors*. New York: Cambridge University Press, 1989.

[86] D. E. Rummelhart and J. L. McClelland. *Parallel Distributed Processing. Explorations in the Microstructure of Cognition*, volume 1. MIT Press, 1988.

[87] C. J. Satchwell. Finding error bars (the easy way). *Networks: NCAF News Letter*, 5(November): page 2, 1994.

[88] C. E. Shannon. *The Mathematical Theory of Communication*. Urbana, IL: University of Illinois Press, 1948.

[89] C. P. Sheppard, C. R. Gent, and R. M. Ward. A neural network based furnace control system. *SD Scicon internal report for British Gas plc*, 1994.

[90] J. A. Sigüenza, C. Santa Cruz, R. Huerta, V. López, and J. R. Dorronsoro. Neural forecasting in real time industrial control. In M. Marinara and G. Morasso, editors, *Proceedings, ICANN*, volume 2, pages 1193–1198. Springer-Verlag, 1994.

[91] L. A. Smith. Nonlinear predictions and local optimal forecasting from time series. In H. Tong, editor, *Chaos and Forecasting. Proceedings of the Royal Society Discussion Meeting*. World Scientific, 1995.

[92] L. S. Smith and C. Tang. Speaker independent vowel recognition. In R. Linggard, D. J. Myers, and C. Nightingale, editors, *Neural Networks for Vision, Speech and Natural Language*, pages 149–159. Chapman and Hall, 1992.

[93] H. P. Snippe and J. J. Koenderink. Discrimination thresholds for channel-coded systems. *Biological Cybernetics*, 66:543–551, 1992.

[94] S. Snowden. Neural computing saves lives at Jimmy's hospital. *Neural Edge*, 3 (Autumn):4, 1993.

[95] A. N. Srivastava and A. S. Weigend. Computing the probability density in connectionist regression. In M. Marinara and G. Morasso, editors, *Proceedings, ICANN*, volume 1, pages 685–688. Springer-Verlag, 1994.

[96] A. Stévenin and P. Gallinari. Use of contextual information to improve conceptual clustering. In M. Marinara and G. Morasso, editors, *Proceedings, ICANN*, volume 1, pages 905–908. Springer-Verlag, 1994.

[97] T. A. Sudkamp. *Languages and Machines*. Addison Wesley, 1988.

[98] C. Svarer. Neural networks for signal processing. Ph.D. thesis. CONNECT Electronics Institute, Technical University of Denmark, 1995.

[99] K. Swingler. Financial prediction: Some pointers, pitfalls, and common errors. *Neural Computing and Applications*, 4(4), 1996.

[100] K. Swingler and L. S. Smith. Predicting driver alertness from steering actions. Technical report, The Ford Motor Company, 1995.

[101] K. Swingler and L. S. Smith. Producing a neural network for monitoring driver alertness from steering actions. *Neural Computing and Applications*, 4(2), 1996.

[102] K. M. Swingler. Sequence categorisation using multiple recurrent layers to create many trajectories through network state space. In M. Marinara and G. Morasso, editors, *Proceedings, ICANN*, volume 2, pages 1025–1028. Springer-Verlag, 1994.

[103] F. Takens. Detecting strange attractors in fluid turbulence. In D. Rand and L. S. Young, editors, *Dynamical Systems and Turbulence*. Springer-Verlag, 1981.

[104] K. Y. Tam and M. Y. Kiang. Manegerial applications of neural networks: The case of bank failure predictions. *Management Science*, 38(7), 1992.

[105] C. Tarriere, D. Chaput, and C. Petit-Poilvert. Research to prevent the driver from falling asleep behind the wheel. Technical Report 88055, Peugeot SA/Renault France, 1993.

[106] G. Tesauro. Practical issues in temporal difference learning. *Machine Learning*, (8):257–277, 1992.

[107] M. Tomita. Dynamic construction of finite state automata from examples using hill-climbing. In *Proceedings of the Fourth International Cognitive Science Conference*, pages 105–108, 1982.

[108] Thomas Cook Travel. Neural computer identifies holiday "personalities". *Neural Edge*, 2 (summer): page 1, 1994.

[109] E. Tyree. Forecasting currency exchange rates: Neural networks and the random walk model. M.Sc. dissertation, Department of Computing Science, Stirling University, 1994.

[110] B. R. Upadhyaya and E. Eryurek. Application of neural networks for sensor validation and plant monitoring. *Neural Technology*, (97):170–176, 1992.

[111] B. De Vries and J. C. Principe. The gamma model - A new neural model for temporal processing. *Neural Networks*, 5:565–576, 1992.

[112] A. Waibel. Modular construction of time delay neural networks for speech recognition. *Neural Computation*, 1(1):39–46, 1989.

[113] A. Waibel, T. Hanazawa, G. Hinton, K. Shikano, and K. Lang. Phoneme recognition using time delay neural networks. *IEEE Transactions on Accoustics, Speech and Signal Processing*, March, 1989.

[114] R. Watt. *Understanding Vision*. Academic Press, 1991.

[115] A. S. Weigend and N. A. Gershenfeld. *Time Series Prediction. Forecasting the Future and Understanding the Past*. Addison Wesley, 1993.

[116] A. S. Weigend, B. A. Huberman, and D. E. Rummelhart. Predicting sunspots and exchange rates with connectionist networks. In M. Casdagli and S. Eubank, editors, *Nonlinear Modeling and Forecasting, SFI Studies in the Sciences of Complexity*, volume XII, 1992.

[117] H. White. Economic prediction using neural networks: the case of IBM daily stock returns. In *Proceedings, IEEE International Conference on Neural Networks, San Diego*, pages II.451–459, 1988.

[118] B. Widrow and M. Lehr. 30 years of adaptive neural networks: Perceptron, madaline and backpropagation. *Proceedings of the IEEE*, (78):1415–1451, 1990.

[119] R. J. Williams and D. Zipser. A learning algorithm for continually running fully recurrent neural networks. *Neural Computation*, 1:270–280, 1989.

[120] P. C. Woodland. Spoken alphabet recognition using multilayer perceptrons. In R. Linggard, D. J. Myers, and C. Nightingale, editors, *Neural Networks for Vision, Speech and Natural Language*, pages 135–147. Chapman and Hall, 1992.

[121] W. A. Wright. Contextual road finding with a neural network. Technical report, Sowerby Research Centre, British Aerospace, 1988.

[122] Q. Yao and H. Tong. On prediction and chaos in stochastic systems. In H. Tong, editor, *Chaos and Forecasting. Proceedings of the Royal Society Discussion Meeting*. World Scientific, 1995.

[123] X. Zhang and J Hutchison. Simple architectures on fast machines: Practical issues in nonlinear time series prediction. In A. S. Weigend and N. A. Gershenfeld, editors, *Time Series Prediction. Forecasting the Future and Understanding the Past*, pages 219–241. Addison Wesley, 1993.

Index

Professional Neural Network Software

All of the methods and techniques described within this book have been incorporated into a Windows program. This program will help you to build successful neural network solutions without needing any expertise in that field. It will take your raw data, check its quality and quantity, choose a coding scheme, build, train and test a number of neural networks, find an optimal trade-off between accuracy and generalisation, and create a Windows program which runs your neural network. You will be able to use your neural program on new data to generate answers with explanations, optimise the real world system the network was trained on, and derive required input settings for desired outputs.

The program is also capable of building novelty detection networks and incorporating temporal dependencies. It is able to optimise input data using principle components analysis, spot ill posed problems and offer a number of possible methods for their solution, and even help with project management.

This software, which has already won two Government innovation awards, is ready to run on any PC running Windows. You do not need to know about programming or about neural networks in order to use it.

If you would like more information about this software, please write to Kevin Swingler at the address below.

Neural Innovation Ltd
Unit 3, Alpha Centre
Stirling University Innovation Park
Stirling. FK8 4NF
Scotland.

Tel: (44) 01786 466920
Fax: (44) 01786 466921
http://www.neural.co.uk/